RE-VISIONING
EDUCATIONAL LEADERSHIP

STUDIES IN EDUCATION AND CULTURE
(VOL. 1)

GARLAND REFERENCE LIBRARY
OF SOCIAL SCIENCE
(VOL. 614)

Studies in Education and Culture
David M. Fetterman, General Editor

1. Re-visioning Educational Leadership:
   A Phenomenological Approach
   by John G. Mitchell

2. Schooling, Jobs, and Cultural Identity:
   Educational Reform in Quebec
   by Linda Kahn

RE-VISIONING
EDUCATIONAL LEADERSHIP
A Phenomenological Approach

John G. Mitchell

GARLAND PUBLISHING, INC. • NEW YORK & LONDON
1990

Library of Congress Cataloging-in-Publication Data

Mitchell, John G., 1936–
    Re-visioning educational leadership : a phenomenological approach
/ John G. Mitchell
        p.   cm. — (Studies in education and culture ; vol. 1)
    (Garland reference library of social science ; vol. 614)
    Includes bibliographical references and index.
    ISBN 0-8240-7207-3 (alk. paper)
    1. School management and organization—United States.
2. Leadership. 3. Phenomenology. 4. Education—Philosophy.
I. Title. II. Series. III. Series: Garland reference library of
social science ; vol. 614.
    LB2805.M555   1990
    371.2'07—dc20   90–41109
                                                                 CIP

Printed on acid-free, 250-year-life paper
Manufactured in the United States of America

Dedication

To Barbara, a wife who always encouraged and supported me and
who was with-me in every stage of the birth of this project
and
to David and Angela who anchored me in a lived-world
as they grew into adulthood during the
research and writing of this book.

SERIES EDITOR'S FOREWORD

This series of scholarly texts, monographs, and reference works is designed to illuminate and expand our understanding of education. The educational activity each volume examines may be formal or informal. It may function in an exotic and distant culture or right here in our own backyard. In each book, education is at once a reflection and a creator of culture.

One of the most important motifs sounding through the series is the authors' efforts to shed light on educational systems from the insider's viewpoint. The various works are typically grounded in a phenomenological conceptual framework. However, they will vary in their manifestation of this common bond. Some authors explicitly adopt anthropological methods and a cultural interpretation of events and circumstances observed in the field. Others adopt a more generic qualitative approach—mixing methods and methodologies. A few adhere to a traditional phenomenological philosophical orientation.

These books are windows into other lives and other cultures. As we view another culture, we see ourselves more clearly. As we view ourselves, we make the familiar strange and see our own distorted images all the more clearly. We hope this immersion and self-reflection will enhance compassion and understanding at home and abroad. An expression of a common human spirit, this series celebrates our diversity.

David M. Fetterman
Stanford University and Sierra Nevada College

Contents

Foreword

The concepts of leadership practiced within any culture constitute the qualities of all present human relationships and the future prospects of that culture. This inescapable expectation is especially true of educational leadership in families, schools, and communities in which contemporary humanity struggles for meaning, identity, liberation, and destiny. From this perspective, leadership and the preparation of leaders are too crucial to be left exclusively to leaders themselves since leaders are forged within the cauldron of tacit, taken-for-granted social values and shared perspectives of the whole culture. Apart from merely performing leadership tasks, even effectively, *being* a leader requires philosophy-in-action, and the *art* of leadership encounters its primary grounds in the critical inquiries of the humanities.

Without uncovering and interpreting the sedimented values of the culture and of its leaders and followers, leadership shrivels into manipulation, exploitation, intimidation, and behavioral adaptation, even if prudent or expedient. The normative strands connecting educational aims, values, and policies must weave meaningful aspirations and values into the total life experiences of both the leaders and the learners. If these life experiences are to avoid dehumanizing practices and become characterized by democratic processes, leaders will have to learn and teach their followers how to critically interpret, understand, and apply the tacit meanings of ideals, symbols, rituals, legends, myths, history, and heroic images of their cultural context. These are the tasks and aims of the humanities in general, and of philosophy in particular, and cannot be reduced to some automated technology.

On these terms which are clearly amplified by John Mitchell's *Re-Visioning Educational Leadership*, we can hardly afford to conceptualize and practice leadership as a particular set of innate, natural traits. Nor is humanizing leadership possible simply as a happy, circumstantial conglomeration of otherwise discrete, independent, behavioral skills which can be causally explained and taught by technical training. Rather, the meaning and the practice of leadership are written into, lived through, and read out of teaching and learning by administrators, teachers, students, and their parents through the philosophical examination of the reemergent ideals and exemplars of everyday life experiences.

John Mitchell reminds us where and how to look for our unspoken, unarticulated, and uncriticized beliefs and perspectives on the aims, theories, and philosophical grounds of education, schooling, and leadership. He is convinced that such basic ideas and values are legitimate sources of leadership in the world of learning and human development. This humanistic, phenomenological approach to leadership refuses to acquiesce to a meaningless, heartless, "value-neutral" world of un-lived experiences. In the last analysis, even the classroom methods, the teaching and learning techniques, the criteria of evaluation, the means of discipline, dialogue, and decision making emerge within the landscape of our perceptions. They are lived and modified, learned, and shared, not as "objective" rules or regulations, not as competencies or performance skills, but as the constituting intentionalities of the larger cultural context of the learning environment.

At the very least, therefore, *becoming* a leader, growing into leadership, preparation for the rigors and responsibilities of leadership, and above all, the reflective actions of leadership require the Socratic self-knowledge and self-criticism of the leader's own values and beliefs. The leader's intentionalities involve the entire process of motives, meanings, actions, and results as a synergistic network of ideals and principals. Far from being value-free standard operating procedures, educational policies reflect the values and aims of educational leaders which must respond meaningfully to the intentions within the lives of the followers.

Thus, a critical analysis and judicious appreciation of the values and beliefs of others are equally as important as are the motives, purposes, intentions, and good reasons for holding such perspectives. Through these comprehensions, interpretations, criticism, and insights, leadership consists of *being* a leader and expressing that being through reflective and dialogic *action,* rather than coercive, self-protective *behaviors,* pressures, or threats.

Being a leader simply draws followers into the openness of critical dialogue. Through philosophical reflection and even contention and controversy, the inherent power of goals, values, and ideals enables leaders and followers alike to experience the other side, to envision novel horizons, and to build community. Within the community of dialogic leadership the leader knows and regards the followers as Subjects and persons, not as objects belonging to the world or to the leader. Through participation in decision making and policy formulation within the dialogic community followers encounter their own inherent abilities to constitute the meaning of being human and become leaders themselves, which is the ultimate goal of both leadership and the humanities.

Jack Conrad Willers
George Peabody College
Vanderbilt University
Nashville, Tennessee
1990

Preface

This book began while I was taking doctoral seminars at George Peabody College for Teachers of Vanderbilt University. During one particular semester I happened to be taking courses both in philosophy of education and in educational administration. Two things struck me. First, almost all the textbooks and readings I did in the educational administration courses were the same texts which the Vanderbilt's Owen Graduate School of Management required in business management courses. I began to wonder if the nature of educational administration and business administration should be equated. Second, the only two paradigms of educational leadership which were considered in the textbooks which I was required to read were "leaders are born" or "leaders are made." Some of the world's leaders could not be placed within either of these paradigms, e.g., Martin Luther, Abraham Lincoln, Winston Churchill, and Mohandas Ghandi. How then shall we explain the worldwide impact of the leadership of the Polish electrician, Lech Walesa, who has neither the personal traits nor the formal training required for such leadership? The third thing that struck me was the holistic perspective which the phenomenological philosophy of Edmund Husserl and other continental philosophers could bring to an examination of the nature and meaning of educational leadership. Husserl's phenomenology, to be distinguished from descriptive phenomenology and phenomenalism, seems to bridge the gap between the idealism of the Great Man ("leaders are born") theories and the positivism of the behavioristic and human relations ("leaders are made") theories; considering both objective and subjective evidence results in a more comprehensive and more meaningful explanation of educational leadership. This book is an attempt to apply the phenomenological method of Husserl to the theory and practice of educational leadership.

The following study is not intended as a practioners guide for educational leaders, although many suggestions and illustrations are included to make the examination of educational leadership clearer and more concrete. My purpose is to raise questions, provoke discussion, and to point out some areas which need additional study. Because I feel strongly about certain issues, I was not able to separate my values and attitudes from the vision which I attempted to present of educational leadership.

Admittedly, some areas of this book lack continuity and even consistency; at other points I reveal an inadequate background in philosophy and organizational dynamics. After reading in these areas for years, I concluded that one cannot be an expert in all fields. Therefore, I chose to draw on my years of experiences in education, business, and consulting and to present my study in its present form, asking my readers to help me clarify and develop my positions. Or better still, perhaps my readers will go far beyond what I have tried to accomplish here. Maybe your visions of educational leadership will be clearer and more helpful than mine. I only hope that what you read in the following pages will cause you to re-vision, re-think, re-conceptualize, re-form the nature and meaning of educational leadership in the coming decades.

I could not begin to list all the people who have participated in the development of this book. However, let me hasten to add that I am fully responsible for the presentation of the materials and for the conclusions which follow. I am particularly endebted to Jack C. Willers of Vanderbilt who challenged, counseled, and encouraged me in this project. The two of us consumed many gallons of coffee in the Cumberland Room cafeteria on the Peabody campus while philosophizing on the nature of education and criticizing the present educational system in America. These discussions improved the quality of my work immensely and lessened the impact of some of my weaknesses.

I am grateful for the support which my wife, Barbara, my son, David, and my daughter, Angela, provided during the years which were given to the research and writing of this book. Their lives are indelibly etched on each page. Their souls are woven into every thread of ideas which are herein presented.

Various other people have typed and proofed numerous drafts of the seven chapters of this book. Linda Cartlidge typed a draft of several chapters. A host of students helped in the preparation of the manuscript; among them were Sonja Johnson, Angela Clements, Dawn Jones, Jana Arrington, Patti Ayers, Gina Wolf, Lawna Greene, Laura Ralston, and

Michelle Johnson. Barbara Lambert has provided most able secretarial assistance.

Chapter 1

Foundations of Educational Leadership

Recent studies on leadership theory unapologetically admit that research on leadership is ambiguous, unclear, inconclusive, and desperately in need of a new beginning. This impasse in knowledge has spawned a number of "new" theories of leadership. However, the "new" theories are more concerned with what leaders do than with what leadership is.

If research in leadership theories is in such a state of chaos, what can we possibly expect to gain from studying educational leadership? Quite simply, this study does not pretend to be a new theory of leadership. This study is about *being* an educational leader. What does *being* an educational leader mean in America in the last part of the twentieth century, what can *being* an educational leader mean, and what should *being* an educational leader mean? The purpose of the following study is to look at educational leadership from a different perspective. The anticipated result will be a better understanding of what the nature of educational leadership is, what it means to be an educational leader, what it means to become a better educational leader, and what it means to train educational leaders.

SEEING WITH NEW EYES

What is needed is a basic tool to see and interpret educational leadership from a new perspective. The phenomenological method developed by the German philosopher Edmund Husserl provides a new way to view educational leadership. The phenomenological method is a way to get beyond the assumptions and biases of empirical and metaphysical studies which dominate leadership studies. An appendix which outlines Husserl's method is provided for readers who are unfamiliar with it. However, Husserl's phenomenology is not to be equated with an objective description of phenomena which is practiced by some positivists. All who call themselves phenomenologists are not using the same method, while others who do not refer to their method as phenomenological are included in this study under phenomenology. Husserl's method focuses on two major concerns: first is a search for certainty in all knowledge, including science; second is a critique of an excessive dependence on positivism and what he called psychologism. The attractive thing about Husserl's method is that it attempts to keep the objective and subjective world together, considering evidence from any source of knowledge: empirical data, subjective feelings and attitudes, dreams, illusions, irrational views, and logic. Phenomenology as herein used is a subjective, intuitive, reflective method to analyze and interpret the things which are given to our consciousness; it is a way of getting at the nature and meaning of the phenomena which are being experienced and examined.

Reduction (Bracketing)

Some phenomenologists consider reduction (not to be confused with "reductionism," i.e., "selecting a representative sample to stand for a complex category or group") as the basic tool of Husserl's phenomenology. Reduction might be viewed as taking a snapshot of one's consciousness, exposing and labeling the contents which are pictured; nothing is excluded. The purpose of reduction is to reduce or nullify the prejudicial impact of the wealth of presuppositions and biases which a researcher brings to a thing to be studied, like educational leadership. The first step in reduction is to apply Cartesian doubt to the phenomena to be examined. This reduction is sometimes called "bracketing," as in mathematics, a setting aside of conclusions temporarily, a holding in abeyance and suspending of judgment until all available evidence is considered. The purpose of reduction is to get back to the way the phenomena are structured and interpreted in our consciousness (as Husserl would say, "to the things themselves").

What are the frames of reference, the world views, the metaphysical assumptions which are reflected in our consciousness of the phenomena which are presented? The question of the reality of a thing is not raised; rather, questions about the nature, structures, and meanings of consciousness are raised. For instance, what are the frames or reference, the world views, and biases which the paradigms of "born" and "made" leaders assume?

The success of reduction depends on the accuracy of the description of the phenomena which are presented to the consciousness. Over and over again they are examined from all perspectives possible in order to see clearly and to grasp fully the meaning of the phenomena. The data which are presented directly and immediately to our consciousness are tagged and put aside until a holistic interpretation is attempted. This kind of description requires a high sensitivity to both empirical and subjective data. Returning again and again to the phenomena an attempt is made to describe both the contents and their structure in the consciousness of the one experiencing, in this case, educational leadership. Thus, a phenomenology of educational leadership examines the acts, beliefs, goals, feelings, dreams, illusions, and frames of reference of the total experience of one who is involved in the process of educational leadership.

One of the results of this descriptive exercise is what Husserl called the "natural attitude," the unreflective, naive, common sense, everyday, natural frame of reference of the world. The natural attitude is that complex group of attitudes and assumptions which ordinary people share, but do not question, about the everyday world in which they live. All those images and conceptions of the world which are so familiar that they are natural to the individual are the "natural attitude." A person slips into the natural attitude "naturally," without being aware of it because the assumed frame of reference is so much a part of everyday life. An unbiased study of educational leadership must take seriously the Western mind set, the language bias, the business management bias, myths and symbols, and other cultural perspectives which researchers bring to their study of educational leadership.

Intentionality

A second major concern of Husserl is to examine the way in which phenomena of consciousness are structured and constituted into meanings; this process of meaning-intending is referred to as "intentionality" of consciousness. Intentionality is the distinctive characteristic of the experience of the consciousness *of* something. The object of intentionality is to demonstrate that one datum of consciousness cannot be established without considering the wider context, horizon, lived-world of consciousness itself. Every perception of something has a zone of tacit assumptions attached to it. Intentionality of consciousness denies the separation of subject and object, mind and body, thinking and object of thought, consciousness and content of consciousness. The interrelatedness of the various dimensions of any experience is highlighted by the intentionality of the consciousness of that experience. The sedimented meanings in the contexts and horizons of education itself are the points to begin a study of educational leadership.

One of the vantage points of constituting the meanings of consciousness in an everyday world is referred to as the "life-world" by Husserl. The life-world is a cluster of meanings which gravitate around a person's total involvement in the everyday affairs of life; it includes the totality of one's consciousness of a given experience. The goal is to recover the life-world as a constitution of the meaning of the consciousness of one who is involved in a particular experience. All knowledge is personal since all meaning is constituted out of individual consciousness. One of the tasks facing theorists is to find the basic modalities of being-in-the-world and to affirm an authentic mode of being a human in the everyday affairs of life. An analysis of the situatedness of a given consciousness brings to light interrelatedness of consciousness and world. All the knowledge, experiences, and interpretations of an educational situation comprise the lived-world of an educational leader. Such a study will explore the horizons, landscapes, and sedimented meanings of an educational leader as the meanings of educational leadership are constituted in the consciousness of that particular educational leader.

The beginning point of an analysis of the lived-world is the description and clarification of that meaning-cluster as it is available to the common sense perspective of the ordinary members of society. All interpretations of this world are based on a stock of knowledge of previous experiences and of knowledge handed down by parents, teachers, and significant others. All interpretations of the social world are personal constructions of the stock of knowledge which is presented to consciousness. Thus, the foundation of knowledge of the lived-world is constructed out of one's perceptions of the phenomena which are presented to the interpreter's consciousness. In fact, the social world of the educational leader is intersubjective, and the stock of knowledge which is involved in the landscape or horizon of educational leadership is of great concern to an interpretation of educational leadership. Knowledge of educational leadership cannot be separated from those who have constructed the meanings of educational leadership out of their own consciousness of educational leadership.

Hermeneutics

Hermeneutics is a method of phenomenology which analyzes the basic assumptions, presuppositions, prejudices, and precritical understandings of any body of knowledge or of any concept. As a "science" of interpretation, hermeneutics is an extension of phenomenology. In a broad sense it refers to any activity of clarifying the unclear, hidden, mysterious, obscure meanings of life expressions which have become fixed in writings or have become sedimented in meaning clusters. The method of hermeneutics requires that the interpreter engage texts and concepts in a deeply felt experience, recreating the original situation, experiences, and consciousness which produce the meanings. Thus, hermeneutics is an interpretation of the residue or sedimented meanings of human existence contained in writings and other objectifications of meanings of human existence. Depth psychologists use hermeneutical exercises to identify the meanings of motives, feelings, and behaviors which are eclipsed or hidden in the consciousness of subjects. Since language is a reservoir of culture and a medium of experiencing and interpreting the world, analysis of linguistic structures, modes, and styles opens up all sorts of interpersonal data for deeper understanding. All hermeneutics is self understanding and must overcome the distance between consciousness of self and consciousness of the world. Hermeneutics is an important tool for probing the pre-theoretical interpretations of educational leadership. All theories of educational leadership assume data and concepts which need clarification and interpretation, and hermeneutics inquires about the nature and interpretation of that knowledge which is accepted as the "theory of educational leadership."

Popular Paradigms of Leadership

In contrast to most of the studies of educational leadership which have used the scientific method to analyze the behaviors, situations, and traits of leaders, this study will utilize philosophical tools to develop the foundations and meanings of being an educational leader. Do not let the word "philosophy" scare you, though. Philosophy as herein used is not an exercise in academic gymnastics within the ivy-draped halls of learned societies. Neither is this study an attempt to build a system of ideas about educational leadership out of existing theories of leadership in business, politics, or religion. Further, philosophical tools are not intended to be substitutes for scientific or logical methods of research. Rather, philosophical questioning and analysis focus on the "is-ness" of educational leadership, i.e., what it means to be an educational leader.

The meanings of leadership are overlaid with the individual perspectives of researchers since they bring to the study of educational leadership a tacit reservoir of "cultural baggage," i.e., presuppositions, biases, myths, and meanings of leadership which need to be set aside if new understandings of educational leadership are expected.

For example, certain biases are prominent in most studies of leadership. First, most of the definitions of leadership deal with facts about leaders instead of meanings of leadership. Second, leadership is described in terms of observable behaviors instead of in terms of states of existence of persons who are leading followers. Third, leadership is identified with the power to cause followers to change or to perform what leaders want them to do instead of with a voluntary choice of a person to follow a leader.

Conceptually, positivistic science and platonic idealism are the philosophical roots of modern theories of educational leadership. Although leadership theorists are not always explicit about the basic assumptions which inform their point of view, they bring to their studies of leadership a frame of reference which reflects their views of the world, humanity, the nature of knowledge, and values. A convenient way to conceptualize the philosophical assumptions of studies of educational leadership is to examine the assumptions of the major models of educational leadership.

All theories of leadership are based upon presuppositions about the nature of human beings and their views of their world. First, researchers approach the study of leadership with assumptions about the nature of the phenomena which they are studying. Is the reality of leadership an external, objective, empirically verifiable reality "out there" which can be observed, quantified, tested, and evaluated? Or is leadership a product of individual consciousness, subjective, internal, a construction of the mind? Closely related to these questions are questions about the human nature of leaders. Are leaders born with certain genetic characteristics which need to be discovered and cultivated, or are all people capable of being trained to become leaders? In other words, is the nature of human beings determined and fixed by the laws of nature and thereby determined by their environment ("beyond freedom and dignity"), or do humans possess free will to choose and to determine the shape of their nature? Are these the only alternatives about our world-views which shape how we see educational leadership or what we believe educational leadership is?

In 1980, the editors of *Harvard Business Review* brought out a collection of "classic" articles under the subtitle: "Leaders Are Made, Not Born."[1] These editors reflect a popular view of the countless theories of leadership under two rubrics: "leaders are made" or "leaders are born." This over-simplification of the various leadership theories is significant philosophically because it reveals two major ways of viewing leadership, or two "philosophies" of leadership. What are the assumptions behind these two philosophies of leadership? Is there a philosophical alternative to "born leaders" and "made leaders?"

BEING BORN A LEADER

In the Western world a consistent tradition exists which attributes leadership to hereditary traits of certain individuals. Leaders possess certain extra-ordinary personal traits which predispose them for leadership roles. Leaders are born with unique, superior traits which allow them to influence and control the followers. Thus, the personal attributes of great leaders seem to have determined the course of history. Until the beginning of the twentieth century leaders were generally thought to be superior individuals who as a result of a fortunate heredity of social adventure were endowed with qualities and abilities that set them apart from people in general. 1948 marks a turning point in the study of leadership; before 1948, leadership was generally attributed to a universal set of traits.

What do Moses, Alexander the Great, Paul of Tarsus, Martin Luther, Napoleon, Abraham Lincoln, Winston Churchill, Franklin Roosevelt, Mohandas Gandhi, and Martin Luther King, Jr. have in common? The earliest leadership studies compiled lists of physical, personality, and intellectual traits which were common in great leaders of history. These lists included such things as high intelligence, physical prowess and attractiveness, sense of humor, pleasant voice, enthusiasm, extraversion, self confidence, sensitivity, and a sense of purpose. Some time ago Mort Walker in the comic strip "Beetle Bailey" presented Beetle asking Sarge why someone else made corporal, and Beetle did not. Sarge says that the other person had "leadership potential." Beetle then enumerates all the things he knew how to do better than the person who was made corporal. To which Sarge replies, "Let me put it *this* way. . . . Do you know how to be *tall*?" Sarge gestured toward the obviously taller person who was made corporal.

Several of the early leadership theorists studied the families of great leaders and found that the families of leaders tended to become leaders also. Thus, theorists concluded that the families of leaders formed an aristocratic class that differed biologically from the followers. The "born leader" would become a leader, no matter where he or she was found, and regardless of what the circumstances were. The masses are always led by the superior few.

If leaders are born with superior traits which differentiate them from the followers, theorists concluded that it would be possible to identify these traits. Shortly after World War I psychologists were commissioned to devise tests which would identify personalities likely to become leaders. Theorists developed long lists of traits of personality and character which were identified with leaders. However, by 1948, Stogdill found 124 different traits identified in the literature of the theorists.[2] The question arose as to just which traits were true leader traits. Some theorists began to look at situational factors and discounted the trait theory, but most recently the personal factor in leadership is being restudied.

What are the philosophical assumptions of the view which holds that leaders are born? Being born with special traits which give one the potential to be a leader can be traced back to the Greeks. In Homer and other ancient Greek writers the gods played a direct role in the lives of humans and determined whether individuals would become leaders. Plato believed that individuals were predestined to become philosophers, rulers, or slaves. Aristotle said, "for that some should rule and others be ruled is a thing not only necessary, but expedient; from the hour of their birth, some are marked out for subjection, others for rule."[3]

The Judeo-Christian heritage also preserves a strong emphasis on leaders being born. The Lord God of Israel said to Abraham, "Go from your country and your kindred and your father's house to the land that I will show you. And I will make of you a great nation, and I will bless you, and make your name great, so that you will be a blessing (Gen. 12:1-2). In the seventh century B.C., God told the prophet Jeremiah, "Before I formed you in the womb I knew you, and before you were born I consecrated you; I appointed you a prophet to the nations" (Jer. 1:5). Paul of Tarsus wrote to the Church at Corinth, "And God has appointed in the church first apostles, second prophets, third teachers, then workers of miracles, then healers, helpers, administrators, speakers in various kinds of tongues" (I Cor. 12:28). The Hebrew–Christian faith has preserved the belief that God chooses who will be leaders before they are born.

The philosophical basis of the "leaders are born" view is that the leader traits exist as a part of a nonmaterial world which is the final reality. Philosophers refer to this view of reality as Idealism. The idealist holds that back of the physical, visible world is the real world of form, spirit, idea. Thus, a human being is not the measure of all things; rather, humans are part of a larger system which exists beyond the physical realm. This reality is final, absolute, and unchanging, and the individual person's purpose and goal in life is to find harmony with the world form or infinite spirit. The true world is the changeless, absolute, eternal world of ideas, forms, essences, universal, and absolute truths which have a real existence independent of human beings. Since these truths, unities, and values exist prior to and beyond the physical reality, leaders discover the principles and laws which govern the idealistic world. If a leader is essentially a spiritual, rational, synthesizing being, he or she is related to ultimate reality through logical reasoning and self reflection, uncovering the ideas, principles, and laws which have been present in him since birth. Having arrived at the absolute ideas, the idealist does not hesitate to insist that other recognize the infinite authority through faith, obedience, and discipline.

What does it mean to be born an educational leader? First, the leader must discover his destiny or calling which has been determined in a spiritual, infinite, transcendental realm. Leaders become aware of their calling by self reflection, reason, and revelation. Somehow contact must be made with the abstract, rational, spiritual world where leaders are really determined. Those who are born to be leaders must realize their true selves because they are marked out to become leaders. Thus, an individual recognizes his or her calling to be an educational leader through clarifying his or her identity, or by differentiating oneself from those who are not born to become leaders in education. Those who spend time thinking about education and abstract reality are likely to hear the call to be an educational leader. Yet, the educational leader is just waiting for the circumstances or the right moment to be recognized for what he or she really is.

Leadership is delegated to born leaders by an infinite, absolute, eternal source. Consequently, born educational leaders tend to be authoritarian, structured, detached from followers, directive, task oriented, closed, and self centered. If you feel you have received a calling from an absolute and eternal source and that you know what the essentials of education are, why would you not think that your authority is absolute? One of the earliest authorities on American education states the authoritarian position well:

> The authority of the teacher as sovereign in the school is in no way derived from, or dependent on the will of the pupil as subject; nor is this teacher in any way amenable to the pupil for his mode of exercising it. So far as the pupil–subject is concerned, the teacher is, in the better sense of the term, a *true autocrat*, and may both take his stand and carry himself as such. . . .
> The teacher's authority as absolute, must be imperative, rather than deliberate or demonstrative. His requirement and decisions, in whatever form presented, whether that of request, demand, or mandate, must be unargued. *What he resolves upon and pronounces law should be simply and steadily insisted upon as right,* per se and should be promptly and fully accepted by the pupil as right, on the one ground that the teacher, as such, is governor.[4]

Since "born leaders" are idealists at heart, one would expect them to embrace an idealistic theory of knowledge, as well as a idealistic metaphysical view. And since ultimate reality for the idealist is the purely spiritual forms (ideas) of things, knowledge of reality is true to the extent it comprehends the essence or true forms of things. Knowledge becomes the product of reason which is the faculty that discerns essence, systematic structure, and meaning and order of information gathered by the senses, but since the material world is a distorted copy of the real world of spiritual forms and ideas, knowledge acquired through the senses is always uncertain, incomplete, and distorted.

The "born leader" in education exhibits acceptance of an epistemology based on idealism. Schools of "born leaders" favor a hierarchical structure with power and authority focused in the leader. Communication from the "born leader" is one–way (from top to bottom, from leader to the led) because the leader has possession of absolute truths and knowledge which are to be transmitted to the followers. Memorization, drill, and discipline are ways to train the mind to comprehend the fixed truths which have been handed down through history. Discipline is the key word in the "born leader's" school. Students are evaluated according to the fixed, unchanging standards which the leader has learned from an infinite, unchanging, absolute source. "Born leaders" require that all followers, who are truly subordinates, accept the transcendental truths which bind all things together. Opposing social, psychological, recreational, and vocational concerns because they are hindrances to the educational enterprise (our Colonial forefathers called these "carnal," "evil," and "worldly"), "born leaders" emphasize the priority of ideas over matter.

The foregoing discussion of "born leaders" is presented with full knowledge that idealism is a term which cannot be defined explicitly and is totally disdained by some contemporary philosophers. However, some of the leaders of the educational reform of the 1980's (e.g., Bloom and Hirsh) resemble the "born leader" paradigm of leadership. "Back-to-the-Basics," "Literacy," "Competency Testing," "Accountability," etc. are cries which sound very much like concerns of the "born leader." In fact, some clearly religious concerns are mixed in with the calls of some reformers. The absolute truths of God are not uncommon aims of many of the "born leaders."

Criticism of the "born leader" model in education is essentially a criticism of the philosophical approach of idealism. The "born leader" assumes that the aims of education come from some infinite source outside the educational setting. Further, the standards and content of education are distilled into textbooks and policies which should be imposed upon all subordinates. Thus, the attitude of followers of a "born leader" must be submission, receptivity, and obedience. The consequence of a "born leader" model of leadership in education are concern with ideals and rules at the expense of individual students, concern with power and control of people instead of leading, concern with bodies of information instead of with the process of learning, and concern with formal structure instead of life within the organization.

Historically two reasons can be cited for the fact that the "born leader" model dominated education until well into the twentieth century. First, traditional theories of education leaned heavily on the philosophical tenets of idealism. Both the aims and content of education were based on acquisition of a body of information which needed to be transmitted to future generations, and the "born leader's" dominance in education has to do with the religious support of education in American history. Historically the great leaders in American education came out of religiously supported schools. The aims and ideals of both public and private schools were based upon the truths of the Judeo-Christian religious heritage. Many of these leaders interpreted their careers in terms of a calling of God. Their goal, or "mission," was to pass on to students ideals and truths which had been revealed to them from God. Again, the "born leader" is the agent of God to promote the Kingdom of God on earth, and education is the means of transmitting these eternal truths.

Max Weber made a serious error when he identified "charismatic" authority almost exclusively with radical, religious, insane, immoral, demagogic types of leaders. In reality, much of what Weber refers to as "rational" and "traditional," as well as "charismatic," authority can be attributed to a philosophical dependence on idealism. All three of Weber's types of authority look to legal rules, personal status, and revealed ideals and could very easily be classified under "born leaders."

Although "born leaders" were found mostly in religious groups by the mid-point of the twentieth century, the "born leader" model is reappearing in educational circles in the 1980's. The resurgence of the "born leader" model parallels the rise in popularity of authoritarianism throughout American society. If religious and political conservatism continues to thrive, the likelihood of "born leaders" rising to prominence in education is quite probable.

BECOMING A LEADER

If a person is not "born a leader," then almost anyone can learn to "become a leader" through training and development of leadership skills, or so goes a lot of shop talk in business schools and among management practitioners. Some business schools advertise that they can make a leader out of anyone. The clear assumption of this view is that a set of behaviors, facts, skills, and appropriate experiences can make a person a leader no matter what their physical, emotional, cultural, and intellectual heritage happen to be. The mail which was placed on my desk while writing the above sentence included a management seminar brochure which contained the following words: "Effective leaders are made, not born. . . . It's the skills and style of leadership they learn that makes the difference." A recent study of leadership states that leadership can be learned by anyone.[5]

"Becoming a leader" is a model of educational leadership which assumes that leaders are made, not born. Although countless variations exist within this broad category of "becoming a leader," those who hold this view agree that leadership is influencing the "behaviors" of the leader and followers in efforts to achieve goals in given situations. Whether the concern is focused on the behavior of the leader and follower to accomplish a task (Taylor's "scientific management") or on the behavior of the individuals relating to each other in groups and organizations ("human relations" and "organizational development") or on the style of behavior appropriate for a leader in a given situation ("leadership contingency" and "situational leadership"), the common assumption is that becoming a leader is primarily what a person *does* in a relationship with followers. The "becoming a leader" model is not to be equated with classical behaviorism, but the one thing which clearly distinguishes "being born a leader" from "becoming a leader" is that the latter view has to do with behavior while the former view focuses on personal traits.

A review of the educational leadership theories of the past fifty years shows that "becoming a leader" is the prevailing model of educational leadership in American schools of education today. In 1950–51 the W. K. Kellogg Foundation funded the Cooperative Program in Educational Administration (CPEA) which involved grants to the University of Chicago, George Peabody College for Teachers, Harvard University, Teachers College of Columbia University, University of Texas, Ohio State University, University of Oregon, and Stanford University. The stated purpose of this effort was to implement the administrative theory of Herbert Simon who had acknowledged his major debt to a philosophical position called logical positivism. Simon's own words are: "Hence, the conclusions reached by a particular school of modern philosophy--logical positivism--will be accepted as a starting point, and their implications for the theory of decisions examined."[6] The success of the CPEA project is demonstrated by the fact that after 1950 administration in education is referred to in the literature as a "science." Thus, logical positivism has had a profound impact on educational leadership theory through the work of Simon and others and is the basic philosophical position which is behind the model of leadership which claims that leaders are "made" or that one "becomes" a leader. However, hardly any theorists in educational leadership have acknowledged this monumental debt to logical positivism--let alone attempt to interpret its significance for educational leadership.

The only kind of knowledge recognized by the "becoming a leader" model is empirical. Both leaders and followers exist over against the body of knowledge about leadership. Leadership is studied in the same way as any other natural phenomenon in nature since leaders are finally physical realities. The essence of leadership is a very high degree of conformity to the laws and principles of the natural phenomena of the world. Thus, the dynamics of leadership involve the leader's possession and use of knowledge, rewards and punishment, and awareness of the basic needs of the followers in order to influence and control their behavior.

Therefore, much of the research on leadership during this century has focused on acquiring facts about what leaders do or what leaders should know in order to control the behavior of the followers.

Logical positivists have stigmatized metaphysical, theological, and ethical pronouncements as devoid of cognitive meaning and have advocated a radical reconstruction of philosophical thinking after the patterns set forth in physical science and mathematical logic.[7] They want to treat philosophy with the same degree of logical rigor, cogent argument, and precise clarity which is found in mathematics and science. Concepts and propositions are stated in a purely formal manner without regard to content. Moritz Schlick maintains that the truth of factual statements consists in "a none-to-one (or at least many-to-one) correspondence" of the words of a sentence to the objects, properties, or relations denoted by the words.[8] Thus, logical positivism provides a means of settling all so-called philosophical disputes in an absolutely final and ultimate manner through the use of the hypothetico-deductive method.[9] Knowledge about natural phenomena is the same as knowledge about human phenomena.

The "becoming a leader" model assumes that an individual human being is a collection of behaviors, a concrete, objective, external, factual, physical reality which can be observed, described, and evaluated as any other physical object. This position includes philosophical views of positivists and empiricists. Although neither of these terms fully describes the philosophical views of those who advocate that leader are "made," they do hold to many of the same assumptions: that the world consists of a physical reality which exists apart from the mind of human beings; that the real world can be known objectively as it is; that every thing and every action in the universe is matter in motion and can be explained in terms of cause and effect; that human behavior can be explained in terms of physico-chemical properties and actions of the nervous system; and that the aim of humans is to behave in conformity to the principles of the physical reality. Everything subjective, personal, emotional, religious, or axiological (pertaining to values) is carefully kept out of the picture of the "leaders are made" paradigm.

In contrast to "being born a leader," "becoming a leader" involves conforming to the principles or laws of the natural order as these laws operate in a human being. Through the use of the scientific method, the behavior of the leader and the followers is studied carefully to discover the specific causes and effects of each action of the leader and the followers. Frederick Taylor's "scientific management" is a classic example of this position; he studied the time and motion required to accomplish desired results in workers. No less is this true when individual leaders are observed in groups in order to learn how to produce desired behaviors in group members. Behaviors of leaders and followers are observed, described, and evaluated as if they are an external reality which includes all that a human being is.

If the "becoming a leader" model assumes that leaders and followers are ultimately physical realities, then leaders and followers can be observed, described, and modified in order to achieve the desired outcomes which the leaders desire. Thus, leaders can be "made" by applying the appropriate techniques to any given subject. The obvious question arises then as to precisely what a person must do to become a leader. What must a leader know about himself or herself and about others to influence the behavior of the followers? What particular behavior in the leader will cause the desired behavior in the followers? Should the leader use the "carrot" or the "stick" to get the followers to do what the leader desires? How are mathematical models utilized in the selection of potential leaders and in the decision processes of leaders? What communication techniques will convince followers and cause them to behave according to the wishes of the leader?

Consequently a set of leadership principles, theories, and practices are developed using the scientific method. This systematic body of knowledge becomes a theory of leadership and can be applied to any person in a leadership situation. According to this theory of leadership, the same principles can be applied with equal force to any leadership ("social activities") situation.[10]

Positivism treats ethical questions as if they are scientific problems. If ethical questions have any meaning or are capable of being answered, positivists consider ethics to be "a science."[11] Positivistic researchers claim to be neutral toward the subjects which they study, including human subjects; thus, science can take a "value-free" position toward any subject.

Clearly, logical positivism is the foundation of the majority of the contemporary theories of educational leadership. Hoy and Miskel in one of the standard texts on educational leadership acknowledge their debt to logical positivism in the following quote:

> Halpin and Griffiths agree that the definition of theory
> proposed by Herbert Feigl is an adequate starting point for
> students of educational administration. Feigl defined theory as
> a set of assumptions from which a larger set of empirical laws
> can be derived by purely logicomathematical procedures. . . .

We will use the following definition of theory in our study
of educational administration: Theory is a set of interrelated
concepts, assumptions, and generalizations that systematically
describes and explains behavior in educational organizations.
. . . This definition suggests three things. First, theory is
logically   comprised   of   concepts,   assumptions,   and
generalizations. Second, the major function is to describe,
explain, and predict behavior. Third, theory is heuristic; that
is,   it   stimulates   and   guides   further   knowledge   and
development. [12]

Thus, for logical positivists the ultimate purpose of theories of
educational leadership is to provide general explanations for observable
leadership phenomena in educational leaders, which in turn has a more
specific function: to guide further empirical research concerning the
attributes of the office and position of leaders, the characteristics of
leaders, and the categories of actual behavior of leaders.

Consequently, the data and generalizations about what effective
educational leaders know and do become the "science" of educational
leadership according to logical positivism. One learns to become a
leader in education exactly the way one learns to become a business
leader, military leader, religious leader, or political leader. In fact, the
textbooks used in typical graduate courses to teach students to become
educational leaders are the same ones the business schools use to teach
business   management.   The   curriculum   includes   courses   on
administrative theory, organizational behavior, power in organizations,
human processes, negotiating, personnel administration, assessing
effectiveness, organizational development and renewal, and other
courses which are designed to give the student the technology necessary
to become an educational leader. Educational leaders are made the
same way business students learn to become a manager of people in
organizations.

The "becoming a leader" (or "leaders are made") model is not an
adequate basis for developing a theory of educational leadership. First,
the human phenomena of educational leadership do not operate the same
way as natural phenomena, nor can leadership phenomena be learned
the same way one learns biology or chemistry. Human affairs are much
easier to change than are natural phenomena. Thus, the ability to collect
enough data to develop a science of leadership is quite dubious.
Leadership does not operate in a fixed pattern or according to
unchanging phenomena as many natural phenomena seem to behave. No
set of principles has been developed which will explain the phenomena

of leadership or predict which particular leadership behaviors will be effective. Many researchers have tried unsuccessfully to identify the leadership behaviors of Plato, Alexander the Great, Jesus of Nazareth, Luther, Napoleon, Washington, Lincoln, Churchill, Martin Luther King, Jr., and John F. Kennedy. These leaders did not try to control and manipulate the behaviors of their followers; they did not have training in group dynamics; and they did not follow a science of leadership. Similarly, some educational leaders have not received training in schools which "make" leaders while other people who have been trained to be leaders will never become leaders.

Second, ethics and values are totally disregarded by the "leaders are made" model. However, every facet of educational leadership involves ethical choices and moral judgments. Educational leaders constantly make decisions concerning what education ought to be, what the aims and purposes of education programs should be, what the content and curriculum should be, how students, faculty, administration, and the constituency should relate to each other, and what the best and fairest methods of evaluation are. Every "ought" and "should" involves values and moral judgments. Although few would deny that values are inherent in the leadership phenomena, those who follow the logical positivistic philosophy do not seem to know how to incorporate values in their value–free science of educational leadership. Decision making, interrelating, and communicating as an educational leader cannot be confined to describing, explaining, and predicting the natural phenomena, or leadership behaviors.

Third, the "leaders are made" model excludes human consciousness from the phenomena of leadership, but the very heart of what leaders do (decision making, interrelating, and communication) is based on mental perceptions, thought processes, and language symbols. What educational leadership is, how leaders relate to followers, how policy is developed and interpreted, and what leader behaviors mean to leaders and followers are dependent on prior experiences and cultural consciousness. Thus, the subjective dimensions of educational leadership are very pervasive and should not be dismissed through attempts to achieve objectivity. Mental perceptions of educational leadership are never totally objective; bias is always at work in human affairs. Therefore, the goal ought to be to identify biases and presuppositions through reasoned thought rather than attempting to be value–free and totally objective.

BEING AN EDUCATIONAL LEADER

Is there an alternative to the "born" and "becoming" models of educational leadership? Neither the "born" nor "becoming" model explains what leadership is or is able to predict leadership effectiveness with any degree of consistency. Further, neither model considers the part which beliefs, values, moral judgments, feelings, motives, intentions, dreams, hopes, illusions, and imaginations play in what leaders actually do. Research in educational leadership needs a conceptual tool which can deal with the whole subjective dimension of leadership. What a leader *is* has more to do with how followers respond to leaders than do physical phenomena, training, knowledge, experiences, or genetic inheritance.

A new conceptual approach to educational leadership is needed to deal with the phenomena of communication between leaders and their followers. McLuhan has reminded us that the message cannot be separated from the medium. Non-verbal phenomena of communication play a very important role in what a leader does. The field of hermeneutics also must be considered in the analysis of language and meanings of communication between leaders and followers. The whole process of communication between leaders and followers goes far beyond inherited abilities ("born" leader model) or learned behaviors ("made" leader model).

The need for a new conceptual model of educational leadership is seen in the confusion about the meaning of interpersonal relationships between leaders and followers. Questions remain about the role of power and authority in leadership, when and if leaders should employ direction and coaching of followers, and how followers and leaders view each other. The phenomena of leadership surely involve that illusive field of interpersonal relationships as these leadership phenomena relate to self concept and group dynamics. Interrelating is fundamental to being a leader, but interrelating cannot be considered apart from the other essentials of leadership. The "born" leader model focuses on the inherited abilities in human relationships, and the "made" leader model views interrelating in terms of behavior. Educational leadership is a process of interrelating within a larger framework.

The philosophical method of phenomenology is a way to deal with certain phenomena of educational leadership with which the "born" and "made" models of leadership do not deal. The phenomenological method, which was developed by the German philosopher Edmund Husserl (1859-1938), allows for the consideration of research evidence and knowledge from empirical and rational sources, as well as evidence from subjective and irrational sources. Thus, the human consciousness of educational leadership, or the experience of being a leader in education, includes beliefs, values, moral judgments, feelings, motives, intentions, dreams, hopes, illusions, and imaginations as a part of the leadership phenomena.

A phenomenology of educational leadership is the analysis of the subjective experience, or consciousness, of leadership in education. In contrast to the theories of educational leadership which focus on the personality traits and genetic inheritance of successful leaders, on the behaviors and knowledge of effective leaders, or on an appropriate style of behavior for a particular situation, a phenomenology of educational leadership focuses on the "is–ness," the nature and meaning of educational leadership. The phenomenological method can be used to analyze the subjective and interpersonal dimensions of educational leadership and to reflect on what educational leadership means in itself as a state of existence for leaders and followers. Phenomenology is the philosophical foundation for this study of educational leadership. However, the phenomenological method employed herein is not to be confused with the "phenomenalism" of Kant, the rational phenomenology of Hegel, the analysis of language phenomena by logical positivists, or the analysis of psychic phenomena by psychologists.

The subject matter of a phenomenology of educational leadership is the description and interpretation of the consciousness of educational leadership as it is experienced by leaders and their followers. In order to get all this "pure" consciousness of educational leadership, all prior theories, presuppositions, preconceptions, and biases of research about educational leadership must be "bracketed," or set aside temporarily, until the phenomenological description and interpretation can be performed. Thus, educational leadership is not an object about which empirical data can be gathered and evaluated. Phenomenology views educational leadership as a unified experience, a state of being, which can be known by direct awareness, intuition, reflection, imagination, valuing, judging, hoping, and intending. John Gardner has identified nine functions of leadership (envisioning goals, affirming values, motivating, managing, achieving workable unity, explaining, serving as a symbol, representing the group, and renewing) which really describe a "state of existence" more than inherited traits or learned behaviors.[13]

The "being" model of educational leadership is not to be understood as totally subjective, abstract, transcendental, and always existential, as phenomenology is often mistakenly described. "Being" is here understood as a parallel to "phenomenological," and "phenomenological" is to be taken in the Husserl mode, not as subjective idealism or the "touchy–feely" existentialism of the nineteen–sixties. [14] "Being" begins with educational leadership itself, analyzes the "lived–world" of leadership, examines the structure of the consciousness of leadership within the individual, and attempts to interpret the meaning of the experience of leadership to the leader and the follower.

Thus, an understanding of Husserl's phenomenology is imperative for a proper understanding of the following study of "being" an educational leader. Further, practicing the phenomenological method is the best way to understand it; some would even say that practicing it is the only way to understand it.

CONCLUSION

Current studies on educational leadership seem to be going nowhere; the same two paradigms of leadership are employed over and over again with very similar results, only dressed in new words and new prescriptions. Although the phenomenological method of Edmund Husserl does not promise to answer all our questions about educational leadership nor provide a quick–fix or "one–minute" plan for leaders, it does provide a tool to look at educational leadership from a different perspective. The phenomenological method encourages the researcher to identify biases and prejudices which color definitions of educational leadership and to focus on the meanings of leadership for those who are experiencing leadership in an educational situation. Husserl's method also insists on the "intentional" nature of human consciousness, i.e., the way the meanings of educational leadership are structured in consciousness. Thus, the landscapes of educational leadership are set in the "lived–world" of those experiencing the leadership as a leader or as a follower. A science of interpretation, or hermeneutics, emerges during the analysis of educational leadership. If the reader understands phenomenology as simply a description of appearances or is not familiar with Husserl, a brief introduction to the method herein used is provided in the Appendix.

A survey of contemporary studies of educational leadership reveals a striking division of theories in one of two camps: the "leaders are born" or "leaders are made" theory. Those who lean toward the "leaders are born" paradigm are concerned with I.Q.'s and other personal traits which need to be nurtured so that the "cream rises to the top," and the true leaders can discover their destinies. On the other hand, the "leaders are made" theorists are concerned with managing the behaviors, the interpersonal relationships, and the situations in which the leader chooses what he or she wants the followers to do. Neither of these paradigms explain the nature and meanings of educational leadership. The subjective dimensions of educational are proposed as a third paradigm for educational leadership. What are the meanings of leadership which the leader and the followers experience in the context of an educational situation? The following chapters will analyze educational leadership by using the phenomenological method and will offer explanations and comments on the nature and meanings of educational leadership in the "lived-world" of educational leaders.

NOTES

1. The Editors, "Paths Toward Personal Progress: Leaders Are Made Not Born," reprint from *Harvard Business Review*, Copyright 1980, by the President and Fellows of Harvard College.

2. Bernard M. Bass, *Stogdill's Handbook of Leadership*, rev. and expanded ed. (New York: The Free Press, 1981), 73.

3. Aristotle, *Politics*, 1254a, 12.

4. Frederick S. Jewell, *School Government* (New York: A.S. Barnes & Co., 1866), 50–54.

5. Warren Bennis, *Leaders: The Strategies for Taking Charge* (New York: Harper & Row, Publishers,f 1985), 27.

6. Herbert A. Simon, *Administrative Behavior: A Study of Decision Making Processes in Administrative Organizations*, 3rd ed. (New York: The Free Press, 1945, 1947, 1957, 1976), 45.

7. P. Achinstein and S.F. Barker, eds., *The Legacy of Logical Positivism* (Baltimore: The John Hopkins Press, 1969), v.

8. H. Feigl, "The Origin and Spirit of Logical Positivism," in achinstein and Barker, *Legacy of Logical Positivism*, 13.

9. Moritz Schlick, "The Turning Point in Philosophy," in A.J. Ayer, ed., *Logical Positivism* (Glencoe, Ill.: The Free Press, 1959), 53–59.

10. Frederick W. Taylor, *The Principles of Scientific Management* (New York: W.W. Norton and Co., Inc., 1911, 1967), 8.

11. Schlick, "What Is the Aim of Ethics?" in Ayer, *Logical Positivism*, 247.

12. Wayne K. Hoy and Cecil G. Miskel, *Educational Administration: Theory, Research, and Practice* (New York: Random House, Inc., 1978), 20–21.

13. John W. Gardner, *The Tasks of Leadership*. Leadership Paper/2. Washington, D.C.: Independent Sector, 1986.

14.   Cf. Howard A. Ozmon and Samuel M. Craver, *Philosophical Foundations of Education*, 4th ed. (Columbus: Merrill Publishing Company, 1990): 232–69, who lump together existentialism and phenomenology and fail to explain that existentialism is a result of the application of the phenomenological method. However, to their credit, they identify Maxine Green as a phenomenologist. The best example of phenomenology as applied herein is the work of Paulo Freire, the Brazilian who attempted to educate illiterate peasants.

Chapter 2

Bracketing Leadership Biases

Rather than survey what we know about educational leadership as Bernard Bass and Ralph Stogdill have done for leadership in general, someone needs to study what we do not know. For example, some people are definitely leaders in an area like business, but are miserable failures in education, even after the very best training experiences. Others seem to emerge as leaders in education without any kind of formal training in education or leadership. H. Ross Perot, a Texas billionaire and computer magnate, has become a formidable educational leader in Texas and on the national scene. Further, to say someone is an educational leader does not mean that the person is necessarily making a positive contribution. In fact, Perot's leadership in Texas' education disturbs many professional educators. Traditional notions of educational research seem to be leading us nowhere. Thus, a better understanding of educational leadership does not reside in present research trends or in attempting to integrate existing research. What an educational leader is is so complex that a radical shift in the focus of educational leadership studies is needed badly.

What is required is a new beginning in a new direction. In order to make a radical change in the direction of research on educational leadership, the overpowering influence of existing theories must be restricted and neutralized if possible. The following study is an attempt to bracket some of the standard biases and assumptions about educational leadership in order to focus on the nature of educational leadership itself.

BRACKETING THE LANGUAGE BIAS

Although the phenomenologist is not content merely to analyze the linguistic structure of statements about leadership, the phenomenological method acknowledges that language is a given in a situation of educational leadership. However, the language of educational leadership is quite confusing and ambiguous.

James MacGregor Burns found at least 130 definitions of leadership in general.[1] Almost as many different definitions of leadership exist as there are studies of leadership. Nevertheless, certain biases are common to most of these definitions. Facts about leaders far outnumber theories about leadership. A dominant perspective of these definitions is the description of leadership in terms of behaviors which are appropriate to a given leadership situation: whether democratic or autocratic, task oriented or relationship oriented, carrot or stick, etc. Another pervasive view in these definitions is that leadership is an aspect of power by which leaders cause others to change or to do what the leaders want them to do; thus, the elements of force, coercion, manipulation, and inducement are considered be to integral to what leadership is. Current definitions of leadership are empirically based and do not necessarily reflect the historical meaning of the word "leader." The phenomenological approach attempts to bracket, to set aside, to nullify the accepted definitions of leadership in order to identify the biases and prejudices in the current usage of the word leadership.

An etymological study of the word "leadership" directs attention away from current definitions of leadership and toward a common, historical core of meaning for the concept of leadership. The term "leadership" has a long history of usage in English and cognate languages which antedates psychological and organizational presuppositions about its meanings. The modern English word "lead" comes from the Middle English word. *leden*, which in turn is derived from the Old English word. *laedan*: both words mean "lead." "Lead" is akin to the Old High German word *leiten*, "to lead," as well as to the Old English word. *lithan*, "to go." Thus, "lead" meant for one person to "go ahead of, guide, or direct" other persons. The suffix, "-ship," refers to a "state, condition, or quality" and is akin to the German suffix, "-*schaft*," "nature, condition, or quality."[2]

Two important considerations may be drawn from the etymology of the word "leadership." First, leadership is a state, condition, or quality of being a person. Thus, leadership encompasses all that is involved in being one whom others desire to follow: desiring, willing, feeling, judging, knowing, and acting.

The second point is not as clear as the first, but the etymology of "leadership" does imply that the follower voluntarily chooses to follow the person who is "being" the leader. The children's game "Follow–the–Leader," assumes that a leader is someone to follow freely and happily. The old proverb, "You can lead a horse to water, but you cannot make him drink," implies that leading does not entail force. To resort to force, manipulation, coercion, threat, or power deviates from the historical meaning of the term "leadership."

An equally interesting point can be made about the etymology of the word "education." The English term "education" is derived directly from the Latin "*educatus*," a past participle of "*educare*," "to rear, bring up, educate." "*Educare*" is built on the root "*ducere*," "to draw, lead," plus the prefix "*ex-*," "out of, forth, away from."[3] Thus, etymologically "educational" means that which pertains to the state or condition of leading out or drawing out. The implication of "educational" is that someone is in the process of "drawing out" something from someone. What the "something" is can be debated, but the state of leading out is basic to what education is. "Leading out" is in sharp contrast to the meanings which have attached themselves to the word "education." For instance, the root idea of education does not imply "modifying the behavior of others," nor "causing others to learn a skill or body of knowledge." Rather, "educational" pertains to the process of drawing out from a "student" a way of living, a perspective of living, an assumed consciousness of what living is, and an evaluation of what the good life is.

Therefore, "educational leadership" is the state of being a person whom others choose to follow which pertains to the process of drawing out of a student's will, desire, and capacity to learn about oneself, the world, and others. Historically, the meanings of educational leadership have focused on the ontological foundations of being the kind of person others want to follow in the process of teaching and learning about a successful and meaningful life in this world.

An etymological study of the term "educational leadership " is one way to bracket the biases which the language of educational leadership has acquired over a very long period of time. However, bracketing the modern meanings of educational leadership should not lead to the conclusion that the classical Latin and Greek meanings of these terms are "correct" while the modern usage is "wrong." Bracketing simply helps us to identify the various biases in the contemporary usage of the terms which admittedly are quite ambiguous. An etymological study does reveal a positivistic bias in the current definitions of educational leadership which focus on causing others to do what the leader desires. On the other hand, since the days of the ancient Greeks, the concept of leadership has been associated with an idealistic bias, which assumes that leaders are born with characteristics and traits which are gifts from a transcendental source.

The exercise of bracketing encourages us to redefine the language of educational leadership within a world view which allows us to live day-by-day. Consequently, insisting that the definition of educational leadership be restricted to behaviors, skills, and styles totally changes the meanings which these language characters have had in our culture for centuries. Perhaps this explains why the terms "management" and "administration" often are used as synonyms of "leadership." A good case can be made for considering the subjective dimensions of the experience of leadership, as well as the behavioral aspects. Also, the definitions of educational leadership should come from the experiences and meanings of education itself and not from other disciplines or areas of life. The one thing which makes educational leadership distinctive is that educational leadership has its nature rooted in education, not in business, politics, religion, or the military. Further, unless we make a mockery of the common usage of our language characters, the suffix "-ship" refers to a state or condition of being of a person whom others regard as a leader. Thus, educational leadership is a state of being instead of a particular set of behaviors, skills, styles, and knowledge which is used a certain way in a particular situation in order to control or influence the behaviors and attitudes of followers.

MYTH AND RITUAL OF LEADERSHIP

Western culture assumes a host of myths, rituals, and symbols of leadership in its understanding of educational leadership. A general survey of these leadership myths, rituals, and symbols indicates how the meanings of educational leadership include all sorts of biases and presuppositions. A need exists to identify, bracket, and analyze these myths, rituals, and symbols which are assumed in the interpretation of leadership.

Many contemporary concepts of leadership have roots in myths and rituals of the ancient past. Ancient kings and priests received certain powers from supernatural sources. The ancient world believed that security, peace, and justice resided in the domain of the gods. Kings and priests were the representatives of the gods on earth and were responsible for the health, stability, and general welfare of nature and society. Since the gods were thought to live on the tops of mountains and in the heavens, humans who were located physically higher were considered to be closer to the supernatural powers and could use supernatural powers more effectively. Temples where priests officiated and palaces of kings were situated on the highest geographical point on which it was feasible to construct buildings in order to be closer to the source of authority and power. The movie *The King and I* illustrates how in ancient cultures citizens were careful not to take physical positions which were higher than that of the king.

Interestingly, Western culture still considers the physically higher position as dominant, especially when leaders are involved in social transactions. The teacher's area of the classroom is often a few inches higher than the area occupied by the students. The minister of a church is almost always higher than the congregation. Some churches have two different positions from which the minister addresses the congregation; each position which is higher than the audience has individual significance. The chief executive officer of a corporation often occupies the top floor of the office complex, and the employees are frowned on if they occupy a hotel room higher than the room of their supervisor. In the workplace a supervisor can put a subordinate at a disadvantage by leaning over the latter's desk. In collective bargaining tremendous significance is attributed to the higher position in the room. Also, in modern courts of law the ruling judge often occupies a seat high above the court, clearly signifying the authority which resides in the judge's bench.

In corporate structures housing tends to follow the bureaucratic hierarchy of the organization. In company neighborhoods like General Electric's Schnectady, New York and Dupont's Wilmington, Delaware, company leaders literally live on the tops of the hills. Can it be doubted that the practice of seeking the highest position to live is related to the ancient idea that physical height brings one closer to the source of power and authority? The phenomenon of the prestige of penthouses and the preference for the top floors of an office buildings by the highest echelon of organizational leaders also are carry-overs from these ancient myths of power and prestige.

Once I went to an educational conference in Birmingham, Alabama to interview for an administrative position in higher education. I was reminded by a colleague that I had been assigned a hotel room which was on a higher floor than the institution's president with whom I was to interview. This situation was supposed to be a threat to the authority of the president. The common sense attitude, or natural attitude, of today's educational leadership assumes the myth that power and influence reside in the highest physical position.

In ancient times crowns were thought to bring blessings, power, illumination, and protection to their wearers. Thrones were assigned mysterious powers capable of making men into kings.[4] Seals, robes of royalty, rings, military insignia, houses (cf. the power associated with the White House or the Kremlin), and titles symbolized some ancient concepts of leadership and influence. Also, primitive rites of passage, such as inauguration, initiation, ordination, and installation reveal how certain personal and physical traits were regarded as signs of a leader.

A few years ago a religious educational organization, the Baptist Sunday School Board in Nashville, Tennessee, had a policy that prohibited certain levels of employees from having desks which had an overhang which exceeded about twelve inches; a twelve-inch overhang signified departmental managers and higher. The larger the top of the desk, the more authority a person seemed to have.

Are not educational leaders today identified with academic regalia, diplomas, faculty rank, graduation ceremonies, graduation rings, brief cases, and endowed chairs? Not one of these symbols has the least power to make a person into an educational leader, yet individuals who possess these paraphernalia and symbols often are recognized as educational leaders with hardly any other considerations.

Myths also have grown up around hero-types who have been able to overcome human weaknesses and enemies. In ancient times a successful warrior, a wise magician, a fortune-teller, or a lucky witch doctor acquired a position of leadership by doing something others were not able to do. Sometimes favorable circumstances turned ordinary individuals into heroes and leaders. Performance of certain deeds which were considered to be impossible for ordinary people elevated these miracle-workers to positions of leadership because the populace thought these heroes had been helped by supernatural powers.

Likewise, in the modern world the inventor of light bulbs, the first person on the moon, the coach of the national championship football team, and the doctor who performs the first heart transplant are elevated to positions of influence, power, respect, prestige, and leadership. The heroic deed has the power to change an ordinary citizen into a national or world "leader."

Consider the educational gurus who develop new teaching techniques or business leaders who create new approaches to management. Educators tend to elevate these persons to positions of leadership without considering other factors which are involved in what an educational leader is.

A phenomenological study brackets, holds in abeyance, these biases and presuppositions of educational leadership which are brought to the leadership situation because some of the myths and rituals often associated with leadership are quite foreign to what educational leadership actually is. In fact, much of that which goes under the name of educational leadership is encrusted with myths and symbols which have roots and meanings which are derived from other fields and which often have nothing to do with the nature of educational leadership. Thus, bracketing myths and symbols of educational leadership helps to reveal that which is not indigenous to the experiences and consciousness of educational leadership.

"CULTURAL BAGGAGE" OF LEADERSHIP

Educational leadership and its organizational culture are inseparable, and understanding the "cultural baggage" which is brought to the educational situation is necessary if one is to understand the nature and meaning of educational leadership. The organizational culture of educational leadership is the deeper level of the basic assumptions, beliefs, and values that are shared by members of the educational organization, that operate unconsciously, and that define in a basic, "taken-for-granted" fashion an organization's view of itself and its larger context.

A bombshell was dropped on the educational world when Thomas Barr Greenfield read a paper before the 1974 International Intervisitation Program in Britain in which he questioned the scientific basis of organizational theory. In that speech he said that the crux of the issue of organizational theory is whether social reality is based upon naturally existing systems or upon human perceptions of social forms. Greenfield held that social reality is usually construed as a natural and necessary order which allows human society to develop and people within it to meet their basic needs by conforming to the principles inherent in the natural order. But Greenfield believes that social reality may be construed as images in the mind of man having no necessary or inevitable forms except authority. Thus, he concluded that organizations are either natural objects, systems of the natural order which man discovers, or organizations are social constructions which are shaped within limits given by one's perception and the boundaries of human existence.[5]

Greenfield is correct when he maintains that educational organizations are interpretive constructions of reality which are dependent upon the perceptions of those viewing the educational process. The way a leader perceives the organization and the practice of education determines how an educational organization will appear and how the parts will be related to each other. Theories of educational leadership have not begun to understand the meanings of organizations which are intended by the leaders and followers in the educational process. If organizations are socially constructed realities, educational organizations are the conceptions of how the participants in education view the educational process and how the participants are related to each other. Traditionally, the organization of schools has revolved around the transfer of knowledge from the teacher and the textbook to the learner. Achievement or effectiveness of traditional schools is measured by the amount of data which the learner receives, retains, and utilizes.

Anthropological research methods and concepts can be applied to educational leadership to gain a comprehensive and holistic view. Each instance of educational leadership resides within a multilayered and interrelated context of social realities. Various methods and hypotheses ensure that all angles are considered and that a holistic picture is developed. Throughout the interpretative process cultural anthropologists attempt to maintain a nonjudgmental orientation, to suspend personal valuations, and to set aside their own cultural biases.[6]

The cultural baggage of educational leadership which must be bracketed can be viewed as having three different levels: artifacts, values, and basic assumptions.[7] The most visible level of the culture of an educational organization is the level of artifacts and creations, i.e., those deposits which are the result of the process of education. This level includes the physical space of the educational process, its creations, language, and overt behavior. Thus, the school, principal, teachers, students, curriculum, textbooks, classrooms, the school district and board, policies and rules, budgets, learning resource centers, extracurricular activities, homework, taxes, field trips, state legislature, federal government, and parents are all visible parts of the educational process. Bracketing this cultural baggage focuses on the interdependence of education and the total culture and should caution us not to limit education to schooling, the curriculum, textbooks, and other elements of the formal structure of the educational process. The culture of educational leadership includes all the visible, but sometimes non–decipherable, constructions of the social and physical environment of the educational process. Educational leadership cannot be understood by looking at only one facet of the artifacts of the educational culture. Acknowledging that the visible artifacts of the educational leadership culture hang together is indispensable to understanding educational leadership.

A set of organizational values, beliefs, and principles of operation make up a second level of an organizational culture. Whereas the artifacts reflect what is, the set of values reflects what affirms the common life and what ought to be in the organization. Every organization possesses a formal and/or informal set of values about the importance of individuals, how people relate to each other, how power and authority are defined, what is right and wrong, beautiful and useful, successful and ineffective, how organizational membership is achieved, maintained, and limited, how the organization relates to the larger culture, and other values which have to do with the happiness and welfare of the organization. These values form the philosophy of operation for the organization and serve as the basis of formation, maintenance, identity, and mission of the organization.

In educational organizations leaders are the creators, managers, and destroyers of organizational cultures. In fact, Schein contends that one of the primary functions of education itself is to create, manage, transform, and limit values of civilization.[8] Further, the central role of educational leaders in the organizational culture of educational organizations is even more significant. To recognize, describe, and analyze the crucial role of educational leaders in the whole process of education helps us to understand the nature of educational leadership.

To understand the deeper meanings of the organizational culture of educational leadership we must understand the third level of organizational culture which Schein calls the "basic assumptions."[9] These underlying assumptions are so taken–for–granted that they are common to the larger cultural unit. These basic assumptions are the implicit assumptions that actually guide behavior, determine how group members think, perceive, and feel about things. These assumptions could also be viewed as frames of reference, models of reality, or world views. These taken-for-granted, invisible, preconscious basic assumptions about life in general have to do with: the nature of reality, time and space; the nature of the world and how one relates to the environment; the nature of human beings and how to achieve a meaningful human existence; the nature of knowledge and evidence for truth; and the nature of the good, beautiful, and useful in the lives of individuals and in society.

In an educational context these assumptions have to do with the nature of the teacher and the learner, the aims and purposes of education, the content and curriculum, the teaching-learning process, the organization and administration of education, and the nature of educational evaluation. In other words, these basic assumptions are our philosophy of education. Educational leadership is understood against the underlying assumptions about all of life, in the context of a philosophy of education. Does a teacher believe that all kids learn to read at the same rate, in the same way, and for the same reason? Are kids unconsciously evil and forever trying to escape responsibility, or are they inherently good and always attempting to learn more about their life situation? Is education the transmission of data about nature and culture, or is education a process of becoming aware of meanings of human existence? These and other similar questions are basic to the nature of educational leadership.

Educational leaders are those leaders whose own artifacts, productions, values, and underlying assumptions are congruent with the artifacts, productions, values, and basic assumptions of the educational constituency. Educational leadership grows out of shared assumptions, values, and projects of an educational culture. This model of educational leadership is in sharp contrast to the prevailing approach which begins and ends with the appropriateness of knowledge, behaviors, skills, and styles of leadership in given situations. The educational culture is the source of the identity of the leader as well as of the educational organization. What educational leaders are, stand for, and communicate is rooted in the linkages among the productions, values, and basic assumptions of the educational culture. Thus, the cultural baggage must be bracketed in the process of understanding what educational leadership is.

BRACKETING OTHER THEORIES

The major theories of educational leadership today can be traced back to older philosophical positions. Although bracketing these philosophical presuppositions is not an attempt to deny the reality of leadership, bracketing does identify and label the philosophical assumptions in order to recognize, if not neutralize, these presuppositions and to focus on that which is basic to the nature of educational leadership.

An idealistic tradition of philosophy can be identified in the "leaders are born" model of leadership and can be traced back to the ancient Greeks. According to Plato's *Republic*, social life is stratified into classes: philosopher–kings who rule rationally, guardians who protect the kingdom, and slaves who produce goods and services. Leaders under this view strive to think and to understand the way things are and assume the power to demand subservience to the ideals which are understood by the philosopher–kings. Thus, leaders are born, not made, and they can be identified by traits and qualities which all leaders have in some form. If leaders know the truth and what is good for the followers, they do not hesitate to demand absolute obedience. Whether the ideals are understood as laws and principles of the Greek philosophers, the Roman government, the Church, or the policies and procedures of a modern corporation, all subjects are obliged to obey the leaders who are endowed with authority and power from an absolute, eternal source. Whether the leader assumes the position by inheritance, election, or anointing by the gods, the focus is on the authority and power which the leader represents.

Thus, in the idealistic tradition, leadership is identified with authority, self–confidence, quick decision, intelligence, toughness, and physical superiority. The assumption behind idealistic theories of educational leadership is that the leader possesses the truth and principles of a transcendent order of reality. Therefore, the leader has the right and responsibility to command obedience to the ideals of the culture which the educational process is obligated to transmit to future generations.

The importance of bracketing the idealistic bias resides in the fact that an idealistic presupposition about the world and reality profoundly informs the organizational culture of educational leaders. Especially does idealism influence the goals, values, conduct, and relationships of educational leaders when the idealistic bias is expressed through religious dogmas and commitments. However, religious commitment is not restricted to the Judeo–Christian ethos; individuals can worship power, fame, careers, wealth, glory, honor, success, sexual gratification, an automobile, a spouse, a position, and many other things. An effective idealistic leader is one who embodies the ideology of the followers.

Naturalistic, scientific, behavioristic biases are the dominant assumptions of educational leadership today. The rise of the industrial state was accompanied by an increased use of the scientific method, objectivity, and empirical research. Philosophical positivism and psychological behaviorism are powerful biases in the study of educational leadership today. The positivist believes that an independent reality exists apart from our consciousness and that the world can be known as it really is. Thus, leaders can be studied as objects: traits and behaviors which are effective in leaders are identified; the cause and effect relationship between behaviors and responses are observed; then, future behaviors and responses are proposed; finally, the success of leadership behaviors is evaluated in light of anticipated objectives and goals. Leadership behaviors, human relationships, leadership style, and leadership effectiveness are examined by means of the scientific method. According to the positivistic view, individuals learn how to become a leader, what techniques are successful, and how to act in a given situation.

The positivistic bias influences leadership in education in a way which is similar to idealism. In order to get beyond positivism, behaviorism, and empiricism in educational leadership theories, the phenomenological reduction must be performed, and the biases of these theories must be bracketed and labeled in terms of the world views or frames of reference which they reflect.

A third group of educational leadership theories can be identified with a neo–humanistic, existential bias. Abraham Maslow and Carl Rogers are proponents of neo–humanism and emphasize the need to become a responsible, self–directed, actualized individual who can relate to others effectively in the social context of educational leadership. Maslow arranged the psychological needs of humans in a hierarchical order which ranged from the lowest physical and security needs through the higher level needs for social acceptance and self esteem to the highest level needs for self–actualization. Being an educational leader in a social situation creates group dynamics in which the democratic concerns of the leaders and followers are related to the group's concerns for the being needs of the educational organization. For example, an educational leader will not have much of a following by attempting to teach the merits of reading Latin to kids who are living out of garbage cans.

The bracketing of all theoretical biases is a necessary exercise in a phenomenological analysis of educational leadership. Bracketing does not raise questions about the truth or falsity of the theories; it simply identifies the biases for what they are, labels them, and proceeds to analyze and interpret the experience of educational leadership itself.

BRACKETING OTHER MODES OF LEADERSHIP

A phenomenology of educational leadership performs the invaluable exercise of setting aside models of leadership which are derived from business, politics, the military, and religion. Contemporary educational leadership theorists have brought over intact the ideals and models of educational leadership from the field of business.

The nature of education really has very little in common with business, in spite of the fact that business terminology, theories, principles, strategies, and practice are commonplace in the research, professional training, and practice of educational leadership today. Researchers in the field of educational leadership apparently have not paid much attention to just how different business and education actually are.

Whereas the aims and end results of business are to produce a product or render a service for a profit, the aims and purposes of education are viewed in terms of attitudes, competencies, states of knowledge and being, desired behaviors, moral capacities, life skills, self awareness and acceptance, personal freedom and responsibility, and relationships with others in an orderly society. Yet, how often have we heard education depicted as a business which produces kids who act according to patterns of behavior which have been programmed and orchestrated by classroom managers. I once heard the head of a large metropolitan teacher organization defending the need for higher salaries by stating that the "product" of the teachers' efforts was so important that teachers deserved more pay.

Consider also the differences between education's content and curriculum and the product which is manufactured and marketed or the service which is offered. Business really has little to compare with a curriculum or a content, although some products are marketed as if they are abstract qualities like happiness, self esteem, etc. While business and industry have a product or service to develop, education has an intangible, as well as a tangible something to teach in addition to an experience to create and to interpret. Education is so much more than a book, a classroom, a student, a teacher, pencils, and other things in a school. Yet an insurance executive who was serving on the Texas State Board of Education once tried to convince me that Texas' schools had failed because high school graduates he had recently hired could not do what his business wanted them to do. Whether high school graduates are better people, more creative individuals who are happier and more productive citizens did not seem to be included in the business perspective of education which was articulated by the insurance executive.

Again, the business perspective can be detected in the teaching–learning process when advice is offered on "managing" kids in a classroom by the same principles and techniques which a shop foreman utilizes in managing a work force. Likewise, kids are manipulated, modified, and molded by programs, techniques, and devices in a way not very different from a worker manipulating raw materials to produce a product. If we took seriously a lot of statements about education today, we could easily conclude that education is taking the raw materials of kids, processing them in our educational factories, pouring them into our predetermined molds, and then marketing them to professional, governmental, industrial, civil, religious, business, agricultural, educational, and other consumers of education.

When educational organizations try to pattern themselves after business organizations, the result is often humorous if not tragic. Jokes abound which exploit the ludicrous situations which result from organizing and administering schools as if they are businesses. Higher education forth–rightly retains marketing experts to train their admissions counselors to sell their product (curriculum). Large universities often are operated in a way which is very similar to a large corporate business. The organized sports programs of universities literally bring in millions of dollars for their coffers. The principles around which many colleges and universities are organized and administered have more to do with business than with education.

Evaluation principles and techniques are borrowed wholesale from business. Policy analysis in education employs cost–benefit analysis, market research, risk analysis, and other methods which have been developed in the business community. The fact is that many facts of education cannot be measured or evaluated on the basis of empirical evidence using the scientific method.

Both political and religious organizations have a lot more in common with education than do business and military organizations, yet the thing which makes educational leadership unique is "education" itself. Therefore, other models and patterns of leadership should be set aside in order to look at what educational leadership is in itself, apart from what leadership is in other types of organizations.

BRACKETING THE FICTION OF POWER

The relationship of the phenomenon of power to leadership is a major consideration in almost all modern theories of leadership. The monumental survey of leadership theory and research by Bernard M. Bass and Ralph M. Stogdill devotes four chapters to power and authority.[10] James MacGregor Burns begins his important study on leadership by discussing a "preoccupation," "near–obsession," and "over–emphasis" on power,[11] and Gary A. Yukl claims that there is more conceptual confusion about influence, power, and authority than any other facet of leadership theory.[12] In most leadership theories power refers to an assumed cause–effect relationship between something a power wielder does or knows and the manipulation, coercion, control, and influence of other people which results.

A phenomenological analysis of the phenomenon of power brackets the ambiguities and presuppositions associated with the concept of power in leadership. A thorough phenomenological analysis of power would require bracketing and labeling the various philosophical, sociological, psychological, anthropological, theological, and scientific views of power, and this is beyond the limitations of this study. However, a phenomenological examination of the conceptual meaning of power will show the need to bracket the meanings of power and authority which are attributed to educational leadership.

In current usage, the term "power" refers to a human capacity to do or to influence something; "power" also refers to natural or social forces to effect change. Thus, in leadership theory, the English term "power" can refer either to a human capacity or to the exercise of natural or social forces in order to achieve control and influence over other people. Some writers recognize this ambiguity by referring to the "personal" and "position" power of a leader. The personal power of a leader refers to the human capacity which certain personal traits give to an individual, and position power is the power of leaders to dominate, control, coerce, and manipulate those whom they are leading.

The ambiguity of the English word "power" can be traced back through an Old French word *poeir*, "to be able," to its Latin root *possum*, which is a compound of *potis*, "able, capable," and *sum*, "to be." The Latin root *potis* is borrowed from the Greek word *posis*, "husband, master, lord, ruler." The root of the Greek word is *potis* as seen in the compound of *des-* ("bonds, chains, fetters") and *potes* ("master"). Thus a *despotes* (Eng. "despot") is "a master of those in chairs," or "a slave-master." Clearly, the Greek root of the English word "power" refers to the domination or rule of a master or lord over his subjects.[13]

However, the Greeks used *dunamis* ("power, energy," or "domination") with a meaning similar to "power" in English. A review of *dunamis* in Classical and Hellenistic Greek literature reveals a dynamic view of the whole of human life and the life of the cosmos, and *dunamis* is an absolute cosmic principle.[14] Plato on one occasion declares *dunamis* to be an absolute mark of being. In Posidonius, a Stoic philosopher who worked about 150–135 B.C., a whole system of powers which fashions the world and operates in it is based on *dunamis*. In Greek, as well as ancient Near Eastern and early Christian thought, this cosmic principle is equated with deity. Thus, "power" is viewed as a mysterious force in everything in the universe. The manipulation of this cosmic power is achieved through ritual, magic, religion, mental exercises, and physical laws. A leader in such a culture is one who is blessed with gifts (*charisma*) from deities who give this power (*dunamis*) to the leader. A charismatic leader thereby shares in the powers of the deity, which probably explains why so much mystery is associated with so-called charismatic leaders.

However, modern physical science understands the universe to be in a state of dynamic change and describes power in terms of natural forces which cause changes in the physical world. In quantum theory the dynamic aspect of matter arises as a consequence of the wave-nature of subatomic particles in which the unification of space and time implies that the being of matter cannot be separated from its dynamic activity.[15] Energy is the capacity of a body to do work and is derived from the changes which occur in the form and state of particles in the universe. The theory of relatively further shows that mass is a form of energy. Thus, mass is no longer considered as material substance but as bundles of energy because the nature of subatomic particles is intrinsically dynamic. The existence of matter and its dynamic activity cannot be separated.[16] Natural power can be defined as the organization of energy to produce change in the universe.

If power in the physical world is the capacity to bring about change, researchers who possess a positivistic bias are likely to understand power in a leader as the ability to produce change in followers according to scientific principles. To the positivistic theorist the power of leadership to produce change in followers is rooted in the principles of the natural order.

Those who attribute the power of leaders to physical laws assume that power is a substance "in" the leader or is a force "outside" the leader on which the leader is dependent and to which the leader must submit. According to this view, leadership focuses on the behaviors of the leaders and the followers. Robert A. Dahl claims that most definitions of power include an element which indicates that power is the capacity of one social actor to overcome resistance in achieving a desired objective or result in another social actor.[17] Dahl concludes that power relations are casual relations in which the leader tries to produce desired results by applying appropriately force on the relevant causes.[18] Dahl equates power with cause; the power–holder causes the power–recipient's behavior. Thus, by defining the causal relation, one can define influence, power, or authority in leadership and vice versa.[19] The leader causes the follower to do something that the follower would not have done otherwise.

Pfeffer defines power as the "force to change the probability of the power–recipient's behavior" in a way in which it would have been without the application of the appropriate force.[20] Burns concludes that power and leadership become part of a system of social causation; he views the power process as a social dynamic in which power holders who possess certain motives and goals have the potential to cause changes in the behavior of a respondent.[21] The empirical definition of power assumes that power is a force which can be organized to control the behavior of a leader and consequently the behavior of followers.

This positivistic bias is quite prominent in the treatment of the concept of power in contemporary theories of educational leadership. The positivistic bias is very clear in Hoy and Miskel's definition of the power of a leader as an ability to cause others "to do what you want them to do."[22] Observation of what actually happens in today's schools confirms the prominence of the positivistic bias concerning the concept of power and the need to bracket this bias.

How different from the empirical definition of power is the phenomenology of power which brackets other biases and focuses on the subjective experience of power and the structures of the actualization of power in a leader. Phenomenologically, the leader takes the powers which thrust forward toward the pursuits of life into the constitution of the self concept and either affirms or rejects them. The more centered a leader is in the powers of the being of the followers, the more power of being is embodied in the leader. The more completely centered, self–related, and self–aware a leader is, the greater is the power of being of the leader. The nearer to the center the leader is to the needs and desires of the followers, the more the leader participates in the power of the being of the followers. No better example of this phenomenon could be cited than Gandhi; he was able to tap into the very heart of the needs of the masses in India and consequently helped his country to make dramatic progress in human rights. More recent examples would be Mandella of South Africa and Walesa of Poland, individuals who embody what the populace wants to become.

The power of being an educational leader becomes manifest in the actualization of the pursuits of life of the educational leader, since life itself is the dynamic actualization of being. The power of educational leaders is real only when the leaders choose the life values of the potential followers; only when the leader's intentions, desires, hopes, and dreams actualize the needs and choices of the followers is the power of a leader real.

Nietzsche's "will to power" is a designation of the dynamic self–affirmation of life. To live is to be able to actualize the powers to be and to become all that is in humanity; to live is to be able to do what is necessary for life. Life is the actualization of the power of being. The drive of every living thing is to realize its capability. Still following Nietzsche's concept of power, the power of being is the possibility of self–affirmation of being a human in spite of the internal and external possibilities of non–being.[23] An educational leader achieves power by affirming that which makes for authentic life for self and other human beings whose lives are actualized through the process of education. One either transforms the resistances to education–life, or one is controlled by the powers of non–being.

That which is sometimes called "personal power" of educational leaders is rooted in the basic purposes and intentions of human beings to strive for happiness and fulfillment in being an educator, not in the character traits, personality types, or behaviors of educational leaders. An educational leader can extend his or her influence to followers to the extent that the power of the being of the followers, or educational constituents, is affirmed by the power of the being of the educational leader. If education–life itself is identified and defined by the impulse by which life thrusts itself toward happiness and fulfillment, the power of the educational leader is that educational impulse by which the leader is defined and identified. Whatever the educational leader chooses, affirms, and pursues to be happy and fulfilled is what leadership will become for the educational leader. The degree to which the educational leader chooses to be what potential educational followers want to become is the strength of the educational leader's relationship to the educational constituency.

If power is real only in actualization, then power is essentially a social concept, and the power of educational leadership is real only as the relationship of power is structured in the consciousness of the followers. Burns states that power is a relationship among persons, but he explains the power relationship empirically in terms of cause and effect.[24] The studies of French and Raven assume that the relationship between the leader and follower is one in which the leader can cause the followers to behave as the leader wishes.[25] Thus, leadership power is exercised by controlling resources or needs of followers, by threats of punishment, by reward, by possessing expert knowledge, or by occupying space, location, or an office. In contrast to these views which consider each element of power by itself and which seek the "cause" of controlling behavior, phenomenology views the power of leadership within the context of the entire experience of power.

Michael Foucault makes a very important point when he analyzes political power from a phenomenological perspective. He claims that power in the substantive sense, "*le pouvoir*," does not actually exist. Neither is power an institution, a structure, nor a certain force with which certain people are endowed; it is the term assigned to a complex strategic relation in a particular social process.[26] Actualization of power is a state of being of a leader in relationship to a group of followers, but power as it is usually understood in leadership theory does not really exist.

The relationship of power between a leader and followers can be viewed empirically as a leader's ability to dominate or control the follower, or the relationship can be viewed phenomenologically as a state of being of a leader in which the followers are taken into the being of the leader. Consequently, the exercise of power in a social situation will result in either a state of domination of followers by a leader or a state of the followers becoming happy and fulfilled.

Power in the sense of domination is a perversion of the power of being of the human group which is in the power relationship. Power over other people is an expression of the ability to withhold or control something which others need or desire. Certain individuals exhibit a desire for more power than is necessary to lead followers toward common goals. An "authoritarian" leader seems to localize the origin and authority to use power solely in the person of the leader. This relationship of dependence is rooted in the ability of the leader to control the behavior of followers.

Thus, social engineering, behavior modification, power politics, and other accepted management practices which depend on a leader's control of the behavior of followers should not be classified as leadership. On this basis the influence of a Hitler is described as exploitation, despotism, and pathology, while a Gandhi is viewed as a genuine leader.

Legitimate authority results when followers consent or voluntarily choose to be governed or controlled by others. In a democracy the people delegate power to leaders by means of a social contract. Employees often permit their employers to control aspects of their behavior at work by means of a bargain for compensation. Individuals often delegate the power of limited control to leaders who can provide protection, health services, or general social benefits of government. Athletic teams delegate power to leaders with a view to achieve victory in competition. These examples of the authority of leaders are drawn from the freely given consent of the followers, and the governed or controlled persons have participated in determining their own welfare.

Chester I. Barnard understands that power in the phenomenon of leadership is a fiction. He points out that the ultimate authority rests with the commanded rather than with the commanders.[27] That is, the follower can accept or reject the power relationship with a leader. Douglas McGregor maintains that legitimate authority is always relative, never absolute.[28] Power is a fiction which is derived from the perception of the followers. If a person is willing to accept the consequences of disobeying a superior power or is able to exist without the benefits or resources over which the superior has control, the "leader" cannot control the behavior of the follower. The basic dynamic of any actual instance of power depends on the particular conception with which the theorist starts.[29] The "zone of acceptance" of the orders and actions of leaders recognizes that followers are willing to go only to certain self-determined limits of compliance. Political revolutions result when the governed perceive the laws, policies, and practices of government leaders to be beyond limits which are established by the followers. The learners' perceptions of their leaders are no different; everyone has limits beyond which they will not go even if it means death.

However, Stanley Milgram has demonstrated that the willingness to obey directives from a respected institution (in this case Yale University) is quite pervasive. Milgram found that subjects would inflict severe and dangerous electric shock upon victims simply because a "leader" ordered the subjects to shock the victims.[30] This strange phenomenon relates to the institutionalization of power. The subjects had bought into the common values and beliefs of the culture of which Yale was a part; thus, the subjects trusted the "leaders" to do what was best for the uninformed victims. If the subjects had perceived that the laboratory "leaders" were ordering them to do something which was beyond what the institution would allow, the power of the "leaders" would have been undermined.

In primitive cultures and in certain religious societies power is related to a force beyond normal human capabilities. As stated earlier, the deities possess power which they can transfer or convey through chosen people. Persons who use these divine powers often become leaders of tribes or religious groups. A further development of this view of divine power occurs when the representatives of the divine power become leaders in an organized social group or religious body. The representative of the divine power might be a king, prophet, priest, magician, witch doctor, fortune teller, etc. The ancient Romans organized respect for the founding of Rome as a power in the brotherhood of all the people of Rome. Everyone was thought to participate in the brotherhood of the Romulus and Remus myth about the beginning of Rome. A strange respect and outright fear has always accompanied representatives of sources of power which transcend the powers of ordinary humans.

The institutionalization of power operates today when a certain position or office is seen to possess powers and influence over people. In reality, institutions and organizations of business, government, education, religion, and the military have only those powers which are assigned to them by a group of people to whom the subjects belong. For example, the President of the United States has only those powers which Congress, the Courts, and the People have allowed him in and through the Constitution. The office or position has no power of its own, although people are willing to delegate great powers to certain people in the culture of which they have their identity and being.

Attributing power to offices and positions is a very ancient view of the government and control of the universe by divine powers. Some contemporary ministers are perceived to be occupying an office or position which has been given to them by God. Occupying the office of a minister means that the minister represents a divine power which operates through the office, or "calling," of the minister regardless of who occupies the office.

So-called charismatic leaders are set apart from ordinary persons and are treated as persons who have been endowed with supernatural powers. Charismatic powers are not thought to be accessible to the ordinary person, but are regarded as of divine origin; on the basis of these supposed powers the individual concerned is treated as a leader.[31] The divine power attributed to the office of a religious functionary is based on a presupposition of faith in the divine world order.

Delegating power to corporate, educational, and political offices is borrowed from this idea that transcendent powers operate in the universe. Myths with accompanying rituals are created to explain how these powers are related to the practical affairs of everyday life in the universe. Offices and positions possess power only if those who are being led by the office holders perceive the offices and positions to have power. Power is in people, not in offices and positions themselves.

Any power which leaders claim to possess is always relative to the powers which the followers permit the leader to have either directly or indirectly through the institutionalization of power. Thus, the fiction of power means that leaders do not possess power in themselves, nor is there power in any in any office which leaders occupy; rather, power is in the perceptions of the followers. Bracketing the bias of the leader's power helps us to separate the phenomenon of power from what leadership really is. Power really has nothing to do with the nature of leadership, although an understanding of what power is may help one to manage the environment of leadership. But let us never forget that the power to lead learners in an educational setting exists only in so far as the learners delegate power to the leader.

CONCLUSION

The first step in understanding educational leadership is to clear away the contradictory and confusing presuppositions and prejudices which have grown up around the concept of educational leadership. A need exists to re-invent, or re-vision, the concept of educational leadership within the context of what education is in today's world. Peeling away some of the meanings which have attached themselves to the concept of leadership leaves a core of meaning which refers to "a state of being in which `learners' have freely chosen to follow, to believe in, to want to become like, an educator." Although behavior modification, management, skill development, and knowledge of situational contingencies have a real place in the educational process, educators should re-define what educational leadership is within the etymological contents of the word "leadership."

Educators are some of the world's worst, or best, myth and ritual developers and users. One has only to observe a graduation exercise, a faculty promotion hearing, or an alumni gathering to see just how many myths and rituals have encrusted the concept of educational leadership. Much of what roams under the guise of educational leadership has been imported from military, political, religious, and business settings. A new vision of educational leadership is needed within the parameters of the process of education.

Closely related to the myths, or really the basis of the myths, are the beliefs and values of the culture in which educational leadership operates. This cultural baggage which educational leadership carries is a vital aspect of what it means to be a leader in a given social situation. Thus, the subjective dimensions of educational leadership are more fundamental than are the actions, projects, behaviors, and skills of a person who has been described as an educational leader.

All theoretical and philosophical assumptions which are basic to the beliefs and values of an educational leader need to be set aside temporarily and acknowledged. Regardless of what labels are used to refer to these educational philosophies and world views, re-visioning educational leadership means that the whole picture of educational leadership is set within a comprehensive, logical, realistic, and consistent frame of reference. There is no special philosophy of educational leadership apart from a philosophy of life in general.

As much confusion exists about the role of power in leadership as in any consideration of educational leadership. Setting aside both the positive definition of power as a physical force which can be manipulated and the idealistic view of power as a transcendental, mysterious force, we must conclude that followers have limits to compliance with requests and commands of so-called leaders. In a very real sense power is a fiction which is socially constructed within the lived-world in which it occurs. The power of leading is derived from the identification and acceptance of the leader's values and actions by the followers, or learners, i.e., within the followers' "zone of acceptance." Re-visioning educational leadership requires that a serious study of the nature of power in leadership be undertaken.

Certainly all of the biases and presuppositions of educational leadership have not been considered in this chapter. This is only a beginning, but bracketing is a necessary step in the re-visioning of the concept of educational leadership.

NOTES

1. James MacGregor Burns, *Leadership* (New York: Harper and Row, Publishers, 1978; Harper Colophon Books, 1979), 2.

2. *Webster's Third New International Dictionary of the English Language: Unabridged*, 1967 ed., s.v. "lead" and "-ship."

3. Ibid., s.v. "educate."

4. H.A. Frankfort, et. al., *Before Philosophy* (Baltimore: Penguin Books, 1949), 26.

5. Thomas Barr Greenfield, "Theory about Organization: A New Perspective and Its Implications for Schools," in *Administering Education: International Challenge*, ed. M. Hughes (London: Athlone Press, 1975), 73–75.

6. Cf. David M. Fetterman, *Ethnography Step by Step*, Applied Social Research Methods Series, Vol. 17 (Newbury Park, CA: Sage Publications, Inc., 1989).

7. Edgar H. Schein, *Organizational Culture and Leadership* (San Francisco: Jossey–Bass Publishers, 1985), 14–21.

8. Ibid., 2.

9. Ibid., 18–21.

10. Bernard M. Bass, *Stogdill's Handbook of Leadership*, revised and expanded edn. (New York: The Free Press, a Division of Macmillan Publishing Co., Inc., 1981), 167ff.

11. Burns, *Leadership*, 9, 11.

12. Gary A. Yukl, *Leadership in Organizations* (Englewood Cliffs, N.J.: Prentice–Hall, Inc., 1981), 10, 18.

13. *A Greek–English Lexicon*, compiled by Henry George Liddell and Robert Scott, 7th ed. (1883), s.v. "*posis*" and "*despotes*."

14. *Theological Dictionary of the New Testament*, ed. Gerhard Kittel and Gerhard Friedrich, trans. Geofrey W. Bromiley, vols. 1–9 (1964–74), s.v. *"dunamai/dunamis."*

15. Fritjof Capra, *The Tao of Physics* (New York: Bantam Books, 1977), 178.

16. Ibid., 189.

17. Jeffrey Pfeffer, *Power in Organizations* (Boston: Pitman Publishing Inc., 1981), 2.

18. Robert A. Dahl, *International Encyclopedia of Social Science* (1968), vol. 12, 406.

19. Ibid., 140.

20. Pfeffer, *Power*, 3.

21. Burns, *Leadership*, 13.

22. Wayne K. Hoy and Cecil G. Miskel, *Educational Administration: Theory, Research, and Practice* (New York: Random House, Inc., 1978), 48.

23. Paul Tillich, *Love, Power, and Justice* (London: Oxford University Press, 1954), 6–8, 35–53.

24. Burns, *Leadership*, 12.

25. J.R.P. French and Bertram Raven, "The Bases of Social Power," in *Group Dynamics*, 3rd ed., ed. by Dorwin Cartwright and Alvin Zander (New York: Harper and Row, Publishers, 1968), 259–69.

26. Michael Foucault, *Power and Knowledge: Selected Interviews and Other Writings 1972–1977*, ed. Colin Gordon, trans. Colin Gordon. et. al. (New York: The Harvester Press; Pantheon Books, 1980), 235–36.

27. Chester I. Barnard, *The Functions of the Executive* (Cambridge: Harvard University Press, 1938, 1972), 174.

28. Douglas McGregor, *The Professional Manager*, ed. Caroline McGregor and Warren G. Bennis (New York: McGraw–Hill Book Company, 1967), 140.

29. Steven Lukes, "On the Relativity of Power," in *Philosophical Disputes in the Social Sciences*, ed. S.C. Brown (Atlantic Highlands, N.J.: Humanities Press, Inc., 1979), 261.

30. Stanley Milgram, "Behavioral Study of Obedience," in *Contemporary Issues in Social Psychology*, ed. Lawrence S. Wrightsman, Jr. (Belmont, Calf.: Wadsworth Publishing Co., 1968), 141–49.

31. Max Weber, *The Theory of Social and Economic Organization*, trans. and ed. Talcott Parsons (New York: The Free Press, a Division of Macmillan Publishing Company, Inc., 1957), 358–59.

Chapter 3

Consciousness of Educational Leadership

After the shades of the dark room of biases and presuppositions about educational leadership have been raised by means of the exercise of bracketing, what does the light reveal about the arrangement and contents of the room of the consciousness of educational leadership? Setting aside temporarily the philosophical, cultural, linguistic, and other biases of educational leadership enables us to focus on what educational leadership is in itself. Seeing and seeing clearly what educational leadership is requires a radical shift in perspective away from logical and empirical evidence and toward subjective, intuitive, personal, symbolical, and hermeneutical interpretations as they appear to the consciousness of educational leaders. What is the meaning of educational leadership to the individual leader and what is the meaning of educational leadership to those who are being led?

Examining the consciousness of educational leadership requires an analysis of the phenomenon of educational leadership before administrative science or other theoretical presuppositions are employed to define and interpret its meaning. Collecting lists of traits of persons who have been successful educational leaders or studying the lives of great educational leaders assumes that a set of educational leader traits already exists and that these traits can be known by rational thinking. If a set of traits does not preexist, how does a researcher know what to look for in a leader? Setting aside these theories about discovering who and who does not possess these educational leadership traits draws us closer to the consciousness of educational leadership, i.e., what being an educational leader means to those experiencing it.

Further, the phenomenological method of examining educational leadership does not attempt to identify actions or behavior patterns which are associated with successful leaders. Observation of behaviors which result in successful educational leadership also presupposes a definition of successful educational leadership; on the basis of some predetermined goals or expected results certain educational leadership behaviors are judged to be appropriate or inappropriate. "Good" educational leaders become those who are able to get others to do what the leaders want them to do. Thus, behavioral, or empirical, theories of educational leadership focus on the methods of getting the followers to behave according to the wishes of the leader, but empirical theories presuppose that certain behaviors in an individual can be identified as "leadership behaviors."

Bracketing both the trait theories and the behavior theories of educational leadership uncovers a dimension of educational leadership which has not been researched adequately. The ontological ("experience of being") realm of educational leadership is fundamental to a proper understanding of educational leadership. If educational leadership is a condition, a state, or a quality of being someone whom others desire to follow in the process of education, the phenomena of educational leadership include the subjective experiences, as well as the objective data, of educational leaders. According to Husserl, this internal condition is fundamental to one's consciousness of anything. By one's living, experiencing, thinking, valuing, and acting, one can enter no world other than the one that gets its sense and acceptance or status in one's own consciousness.[1] The phenomenological approach to educational leadership shifts the focus from born–traits and observable behaviors to the being of an educational leader.

The question is not so much what are the traits and behaviors of successful leaders in education, but what is the nature and meaning of being an educational leader. Educational leadership becomes a reality in self–growth, in teaching and learning, in schooling, in relating, and in the whole educational process. Thus, the being of an educational leader is central to what educational leadership is and means.

The goal of this chapter is to pull back the curtains of the accepted theories of educational leadership and to examine the subjective dimensions of educational leadership. What does it mean to exist and to live in a state or condition of leading in the educational process? How do educational leaders structure the meaning of being a leader in their consciousness? Why do people choose to follow this educational leader and not that one? Do values determine what leaders and followers do? Why do great leaders seem to be visionaries and dreamers? Does intuition play a part in decision making and communicating of educational leaders?

SELF CONSTITUTION OF EDUCATIONAL LEADERS

The consciousness of educational leadership emerges in an individual as the "leader" identifies with actions, images, words, hopes, goals, and values which followers desire to internalize, so that the educational leader could not be true to his or her identity without being an educational leader.[2] Educational leadership becomes a part of the self of the educational leader to the extent that being an educational leader cannot be thought of apart from the individual's total self concept.

An educational leader becomes aware of being regarded as a leader as the experience of leadership is actualized. The constitution of the consciousness of educational leadership in a person happens as the leader incorporates, takes in, or internalizes the images, actions, ideals, hopes, and values of the educational process; this consciousness becomes an integral part of a self with whom others desire to identify. The self of an educational leader crystallizes around a set of identifications which represent the self which others want to become. Educational leadership is not a reality until these identifications of the self are actualized. The actualization of an individual whose self concept is integrated around a set of educational identifications brings an educational leader into existence. Being an educational leader is not something which is forced upon the self concept, nor is it due to some outside pressure; educational leadership is something which the individual desires, chooses, and actualizes.

However, being an educational leader does not mean that the self concept is fulfilling an inherited set of educational leadership traits. Rather, the self of an educational leader is constituted as a dynamic process; some perceptions, interpretations, and meanings are taken into the self while other perceptions of the self are sloughed off or discarded. Thus, the primary condition of educational leadership is the definition of a self concept which includes values, goals, and cultural traditions of the educational constituency; educational leadership is the acting out of that identity. Identification is logically prior to the actualization of educational leadership, and leadership is not derived from a definition imposed on the individual from outside the norms or behavioral definitions. The primary prerequisite of educational leadership is a perception of self which the individual wants to be acted out in the arena of education. Therefore, conscious choices, intentions, values, dreams, and attitudes are foundational to educational leadership.

Each individual, looking at the same educational situation from his or her unique point of view, angle of vision, or frame of reference, perceives the situation in a way which no other person sees it. Whether a person constitutes a self consciousness which includes educational leadership is determined by how and by whom the educational situation is perceived. The self concept of an educational leader includes how the individual feels, thinks, believes, likes, dislikes, seeks, understands, values, loves, fears, hates, and hopes about educational leadership. These self perceptions in turn shape what the individual defines to be educational leadership.

Strip away every presupposition, theory, attitude, and frame of reference of an educational leader, and an educational leader is a person existing as one whom others desire to follow. Thus, educational leadership does not begin with what a leader ought to be or ought to do; neither does it begin with the competencies or skills of a leader. The given is a person existing as a person whom an educational constituency desires to follow.

The most basic experience of an educational leader is what appears to that person in the totality of being an educational leader. Maslow's "being-leaders" are self-actualizing leaders who have internalized being a person whom others choose to follow.[3] This consciousness of leadership is in one sense the beginning of educational leadership.

Educational leaders in a very real sense are doing things, saying things, and exemplifying aims and values which the educational constituents want to incorporate in their own self consciousness. The self system, or self constitution, of an educational leader is the process of becoming an educational self whom others want to become. Harry Stack Sullivan recognized that true leadership does not emerge until a person can be confident and secure enough to reach out and incorporate, internalize, or constitute other views, aims, goals, beliefs, and values as part of the self system.[4] The reverse side of this coin is that followers who cannot identify with their leader's goals and values tend to become like infants who relate to leaders as parents who represent power and sustenance. The infant follower does not view the authority figure as a leader but as a parent who holds the key to survival and security. The infant followers seek the approval of the parental "leader" only to receive the appropriate reward for being "good."

Thus, the beginning of educational leadership is a state of being, not behaving, knowing, or training. Granted, educational leadership should not be considered apart from the social context where it occurs. Nevertheless, the subjective and intuitive experiences must be considered to be foundational in educational leadership theory.

Viewing the constitution of the self of an educational leader as a process is in sharp contrast to the trait theory of leadership which assumes that certain leadership traits are genetically or divinely transmitted to the individual. According to the trait theories, educational leadership resides hidden deep within the self of a potential leader only to be revealed through self reflection and exposure to situations of discovery of the leadership traits. All leaders are expected to exhibit these leader traits. The self is constituted within a prescribed pattern which has been inherited; an educational leader develops as the individual becomes aware of his or her possession of the leadership traits. Becoming aware of leadership traits involves rational and reflective endeavors. The educational leader gives up all other claims on the self and "surrenders" to the ideals and traits of leadership which are transmitted and revealed rationally. The trait theory minimizes the role of the will, intentions, commitments, beliefs, value judgments, and intuitive experiences in the constitution of the self of a leader. Leadership, according to this view, is a body of knowledge or a set of traits over which the individual has very little control. All but the true, inward, genuine components of self constitution must be emptied in order for the inherited traits to be discovered and nurtured into conscious awareness.

The constitution of the self system in behavioral theories of leadership is practically ignored. According to the behavioral views, the identity of an educational leader is based on neurological, biological, psychological, and technological factors which determine the success of selected behaviors to accomplish desired goals. Thus, educational leadership becomes the selection of appropriate behaviors which achieve the goals of the leaders. The apparent result of the behavioral theories is that attention is focused on successful means to achieve the leader's goals without much thought given to the values which the leader's goals represent. "Good" leaders are those who are able to cause the followers to do what the leaders desire them to do. According to this view, Hitler would be judged a "good" leader. Power, authority, control, management, manipulation, threat, intimidation, reward, and punishment become important factors in selecting appropriate behaviors in a given leadership situation. The self system according to these presuppositions is totally dependent on the principles and laws of the natural order of which the human organism is a part. Thus, anyone can become an educational leader if the prescribed training is followed.

A phenomenological approach to educational leadership denies neither the genetic nor the behavioral factors, but seeks to view the experience of leadership both subjectively and objectively. The meaning of the experience of educational leadership is determined by the perceptions of the leader and the followers, and what the leaders and followers perceive is determined by the constitution of the self system of the leader and the degree of identification of the cultural values which the leader represents to the followers. An examination of educational leadership begins with the dynamics of the personal identity of the leader, or the constitution of the self of the educational leader.

The particular qualities of the self of an educational leader can never be known since the ways a person perceives self are limitless. Each educational leader develops a large number of more or less discrete perceptions of self which are characteristic of his being a person whom others choose to follow. The self perceptions of an educational leader constitute an organization of consciousness which represents his own conception of himself in all its complexity. This organization is not a mere conglomeration of isolated concepts of self, but a patterned interrelationship, or Gestalt, of all the self perceptions. For this reason, someone cannot devise a given set of personality traits or behaviors which are characteristic of all educational leaders.

An educational leader constitutes a self image the same way an infant develops a self concept. The organization of the self perceptions of an infant is not a simple, standardized process, but rather a long and involved matter of exploration and experimentation probably beginning with the differentiation of "me" and "not me." Bit by bit the child organizes perceptions on the basis of differentiations between self and the remainder of the phenomenal field. Thus, educational leaders are continually constituting self concepts from the beginning to the end of their involvement in the educational process.

However, the constitution of the consciousness of an educational leader is also a social product which arises out of interaction with others, inferences about ourselves which are made as a consequence of the feedback which we get from the reflected appraisals of followers. Does this mean that an educational leader can experience educational leadership apart from followers? No. The intentionality, or interconnectedness, of consciousness holds the entire complex of perceptions of self together as a Gestalt of leadership in education. Both the behaviorists and the trait theorists reduce the self concept of an educational leader to either the traits or the behaviors while the phenomenological approach tries to view the totality of the experience of educational leadership.

The constitution of consciousness is each educational leader's basic frame of reference and is the point of orientation for all behavior. Jan is a third grade teacher in a large metropolitan school system. Her classroom is unlike any other in the entire system. Animals and fish and plants and bacteria abound. Her classroom reeks with odors which the kids seem not to notice. In the absence of desks of any kind large appliance boxes which have lots of paint and doors and windows occupy one end of the room, signs of all types hang from the ceiling, a television is on in one corner, some books are on the floor in another area, a microscope is on a table surrounded by laboratory equipment, and a computer is located in another section. You get the picture. At first Jan's peers considered her odd and radical, a "poor" teacher. This concerned Jan, but she did not know anything else to do. She loves kids and wants to see them learn about themselves and their world, and she wants them to be happy in her classroom. The laughing which often escapes from her room irritates both her peers and her principal.

After an inservice program on personalizing classroom instruction is presented in Jan's school system, an intense interest in personalized instruction develops throughout the entire school system. The two consultants who conducted the inservice program discovered Jan's unusual classroom and praised it as an excellent model of a personalized classroom. Slowly but surely Jan's peers and her administrators develop respect and admiration for her. She is selected as outstanding teacher. The more she talks about her love for kids and the marvelous things which occur in her classroom, the greater is the desire of her peers to become like her. Other schools in her district invite her to speak about her ideas of schooling, and teachers from other schools want to visit her classroom. Consequently, she is asked to chair a curriculum study committee to develop plans for personalizing instruction in the whole school system. Although remaining faithful to her first love of being a third grade teacher, Jan is writing, talking, teaching, dreaming, promoting, reflecting, researching, living, and breathing personalized instruction. In one sense, the entire school system revolves around Jan and her ideas of personalized instruction. Jan is an educational leader.

Surely Jan's position as a third grade teacher did not make her a leader. Neither did any personality traits insure that she would become a leader. One would be hard put to identify a set of behaviors which made her a leader. What made Jan an educational leader was her love for kids, her desire to see them happy, her belief that learning about oneself and one's world would be good for all students, and her commitment to values and goals which were shared by others in her school system. As she affirmed and lived out the concept she held of herself, she became a person whom the other teachers and administrators wanted to affirm and to follow. Jan's constitution of her consciousness of being a teacher became an image of herself which in turn determined that she would be an educational leader. The fact that her organization of self perceptions included those ideas, values, and goals of education and schooling which the school system shared is fundamental to explaining the emergence of Jan's educational leadership.

HUMANITY OF EDUCATIONAL LEADERS

In every educational leadership situation leaders have made broad assumptions about the followers, and the followers have made assumptions about other followers and about their leaders. These assumptions operate as a general theory which determines how the educational leaders will deal with their peers, their followers, and their superiors. These views about leaders and followers in educational contexts by and large reflect philosophical positions on the nature of human beings and serve as the foundation of the phenomenon of educational leadership in institutions and in society as a whole. The age-old questions about human nature figure prominently in all theories of educational leadership. What does it mean to be human, as opposed to being anything else? Is the human being ultimately free or determined, social or selfish, good or evil, spirit or body, supernatural or natural, economic or altruistic, behavior oriented or knowledge oriented? Philosophical anthropology provides various answers to these questions, whether one is reading Plato, the Bible, Decartes, Rousseau, Hobbes, Locke, Kant, Hume, Marx, Freud, Skinner, or Maslow.

The nature of educational leadership rests squarely on the nature of the human beings who become the leaders and the followers in the educational process. In the Western world, the nature of human beings has been explained from various perspectives: as creatures who are limited and determined by natural laws, as spiritual creations of divine beings, as rational beings who realize their humanity by reasoning and speculating, as social members of a collective whole, and as a blank form which can be filled in by willing and by personal choice. In accord with each one's presuppositions and world view, the naturalist tends to see the human being as totally natural, the religious theorist sees all as spirit, the rationalist sees everything as ideas and transcendental realities, while the existentialist sees human beings as totally will and choice.

As we have already seen, the naturalistic point of view focuses on the behaviors and the cause–effect, observable dimensions of educational leaders; the idealistic perspective sees leaders discovering traits and characteristics which make them into leaders; the religious perspectives identify visible signs of favor by deities, such as, ecstacy, visions, and supernatural feats in leaders; the social perspective is concerned with the human relations between leader and followers, and existentialists rely on the subjective and personal choices which make leadership meaningful.

In 1966, Frederick Herzberg published an instructive analysis of industry's view of work and the worker.[5] According to Herzberg, the worker has a dual nature which includes a physical and psychological needs system. The physical needs stem from the human being's animal disposition which is centered on the avoidance of the loss of life, hunger, pain, sexual deprivation, and on the primary drives, in addition to the infinite varieties of learned fears that become attached to these drives. The other segment of man's nature is his compelling urge to realize his own potentiality by continuous psychological growth. Thus, workers are motivated and managed either by the set of physical needs or by the set of personal actualization needs.

The importance of Herzberg's study resides more in his philosophical assumptions than in his conclusions, which are based on the determination of psychological attitudes. He illustrates the result which a view of the nature of human beings has on industry's approach to workers and managers. The two sets of human needs are traced all the way back to the contrasting stories of the biblical characters of Adam and Abraham. Although his philosophical interpretations are rather naive, Herzberg shows us the need to examine the philosophical assumptions of the different views of the human nature of workers and managers. Herzberg points out that what managers believe workers are affects how they relate to the workers and in turn determines what is expected of the workers. Needless to say, how the workers view the managers (or leaders) influences what the leaders do.

Assumptions concerning the nature of human beings which are reflected in contemporary theories of educational leadership are not significantly different from those of Herzberg. On one end of the continuum the individual is viewed as lazy, evil, dependent, physiologically motivated, immature, authoritarian, directive, manipulative, power wielding, selfish, irresponsible, distrustful, task–oriented, security conscious, and mechanistic. These assumptions about the nature of the person are consistent with McGregor's Theory X leader,[6] Argyris' immature leader,[7] Likert's System leader,[8] and McClelland's low achievement motivated leader.[9] In an attempt to integrate all the major leadership theories into their Situational Leadership theory, Hersey and Blanchard have divided the theories into four groups, and Group I, which they call S1, includes Theory X and the other assumptions mentioned above.[10]

On the other end of the continuum is McGregor's Theory Y, Argyris' maturity model, McClelland's high achievement motivation, Likert's System 4, and Hersey and Blanchard's S4 assumptions which are characterized by responsibility, self esteem, adulthood, openness, participative decision making, trust, care, love, delegation, interpersonal relationships, people orientation, creativity, cooperation, goodness, optimism, industriousness, and self–motivation. Although the various theories may designate two or more intermediate positions between the opposite extremes of the continuum, most of the theoretical positions fall closer to one of the two sets of assumptions about people.

Several leadership theorists, such as Hersey and Blanchard, have tried to introduce a third dimension of the leadership phenomenon which focuses on the selection of certain leadership behaviors for a given leadership situation. Essentially what the "situational leadership" theories have introduced into a "behavioral approach" is the cognitive dimension. Effective leadership in education, or in any other organization, is "knowing" which style of leadership to use for each given situation. Choosing the appropriate style of leadership depends on a scientific description of the organization, the influences and needs of the decision makers, and the goals or outcomes which are desired by all concerned. Each decision involves factual and value elements which lead to an understanding of what a "correct" decision is and clarifies the distinction between policy questions and questions of administration. Herbert Simon grounds these questions in analytic philosophy. His philosophical assumption is that a particular school of modern philosophy, logical positivism, was accepted as a starting point for his theory of decision making and leadership.[11] According to logical positivism, propositions are true if they correspond to empirical observations of natural phenomenon. Determining whether a proposition is correct means that it is compared directly with experience, "with the facts," and leads logically to other propositions which can be compared with similar experiences. According to Simon, ethical terms cannot be reduced to factual terms, and values can be considered only to the degree that value choices can be empirically verified.[12] Therefore, questions concerning the nature of the human person must be limited to scientific descriptions of individual human beings. The person is in one sense a collection of observable facts which can be rationally tested, but in another sense the person is a physical organism which can be studied and manipulated as any other natural phenomenon.

The "man as a machine" view has broad implications for educational leadership. First, power and control become central concerns in the consideration of effectiveness of educational leaders. What knowledge and techniques are required to influence followers to do what the educational leaders desire them to do? If "nice guy" behaviors will cause followers to adopt a certain curriculum, then the human relations style of leadership is appropriate. But "strong arm" tactics may be just as appropriate if exerting one's authority causes the followers to adopt the desired curriculum. Thus, knowledge and behavior modification techniques are major tools which educational leaders need to control and to change the behaviors of the biological organisms who are the followers.

Empiricists and positivists view the educational leader as a physical phenomenon; the person of the leader is identified with the physico–chemical phenomena of the person who is able to cause educational followers to do what the leader desires. Educational leadership is reduced to knowledge and techniques which allow the leader to influence, control, and manipulate the followers according to the wishes of the leader.

The picture which contemporary theories of educational leadership present of the nature of the human being is deterministic, pessimistic, animalistic, positivistic, and mechanistic. Many within the human relations school of educational leadership also hold this view of the human being. For some human relations theorists the individual person is still a physical organism to be studied and manipulated by psychological principles and behavior modification techniques to secure desired changes in groups of persons.

However, some theorists within both the Theory X and the Theory Y schools view the individual as a "ghost in the machine." Taking their cue from Descartes, these theorists see the human being as a spirit–mind which inhabits a body. Thus, educational leadership is a set of non–physical characteristics which occupies a physical body. The non–physical reality of leadership is expressed in the physical body as ideal traits and characteristics of educational leaders; at the same time, the bodily functions of the leader are to be studied and controlled by the rational aspect of the person. The "ghost in the machine" views acknowledge that the behaviors of any person (or leader) can be considered quite apart from any other dimension of the person. The goal of the behaviors may be related to the accomplishment of an organizational task or directed toward human relationships, but the nature of the person assumed is that the physical reality is a part of the person which can be separated from the subjective mind.

Just as no reputable textbook on the philosophy of education will omit questions about the nature of the learner, consideration of the nature of educational leadership must not omit questions about the nature of both parties in the leadership situation: the leader and the followers. Granted that in the last analysis no theory will, or can, fully describe and explain what a human being is, statements about the nature of human beings function as the foundation on which educational leadership is fashioned. The most reasonable position is one that does not oversimplify the various aspects of being a human while being able to accommodate new data about the human condition. Although a clear statement of the nature of a human being, or a leader, is a philosophical demand that far exceeds the limitations of this book, there is a cluster of interrelated concepts, principles, and features which help to distinguish an educational leader from one who is not an educational leader.

One feature of the nature of an educational leader is the unity of the experience of a consciousness of followers who voluntarily choose to follow a leader with whom the followers desire to identify. There are no leaders without followers and no followers without leaders. The concepts of theorists whereby the knowing mind of leaders can be separated from leadership behaviors must be overcome by phenomenological intentionality, i.e., the unity of experience which recognizes that consciousness is always consciousness of . . . something. Consciousness of educational leadership is consciousness embodied, the totality of the experience of being an educational leader in a real world through the medium of bodily existence in the world. Man taken as a concrete, total being is not a psyche joined to an organism, not a mind in a body, but the movement back and forth of existence which at one time allows itself to take corporeal form and at other times to move towards personal acts. Psychological motives and bodily occasions may overlap because there is not a single physical impulse in a living body which is directly related to analogous psychic intentions; there is not a single mental act which has not found at least its germ or its general outline in physiological tendencies.[13]

To limit the nature of the human being to a set of behaviors or the description of physico-chemical phenomena in an organism is just as short sighted as to equate humanity with intellect, mind, or subjectivity. Being human is a unified, meaningful experience which involves every dimension of existing in a world where other "human" organisms exist. The meaning of the totality of human existence cannot be reduced to biology, psychology, sociology, science, or philosophy. A watch cannot be defined by the description and scientific analysis of each part; the meaning of a watch is related to a concept of time which is built into the machine. Neither can Beethoven's Fifth Symphony be defined by examining the notes, the instruments, or the paper on which it is written; a symphony is the totality of all the techniques of music which are an extension of all that the artist is. In fact, the Fifth Symphony cannot be separated from who Beethoven is as a person. All that a person feels, does, hopes, believes, values, wants, needs, experiences, knows, wills, and perceives is a dimension of the nature of a person.

Being an educational leader is not limited to behaving in a way that causes the followers to obey the leader. Neither is an educational leader someone with a given set of character traits which have been observed in successful leaders. Nor is knowing which style of behavior to apply in a given situation a definition of an educational leader. Rather, being an educational leader is more like being an artist than being a technician. If the nature of a person is like a fabric which is composed of many and various colors of threads, the nature of an educational leader is a multifaceted phenomenon which involves a total experience within the context of the educational process. Educational leadership is a comprehensive, unified experience which is woven from the various threads of the existence of an individual in an educational process.

Thus, an analysis of the nature of an educational leader must include evidence from anthropology, psychology, sociology, biology, philosophy, and from all the other social and physical sciences, as well as insights from theology, fiction, mythology, biography, poetry, prose, and reflections from all the arts. Further, the evidence is obviously unlimited, and the results will remain incomplete and always changing.

The nature of the humanity of education leaders cannot be based solely in the psycho-physical realm. Such things as pride, courage, integrity, dignity, honesty, ambition, altruism, love, patience, dependability, sense of humor, sobriety, faithfulness, kindness, gentleness, openness, and cooperation are central to what an educational leader is and cannot be ignored in a study of educational leadership. A study of the human nature of the leader hopefully will help to interpret the relatively new, but quite prominent role of women as educational leaders.

The best that we can hope for here is to call attention to the need for general directions which research in the human nature of leaders should proceed. First, anthropologists share with behavioral psychologists the principle that human beings must be interpreted in terms of their corporeality and their observable behavior. Whatever a human being is uniquely can be described in terms of personality, of relating to others, and of relating to the environment. Human beings, unlike animals, are not completely limited by their instincts and by their environment. The completely dependent state of human infants, the primitive state of human organs, and the exaggerated development of the human cerebral cortex and its synapses are related to the creation of language and culture to compensate for the deficiencies of the human species. Humanity is created as humans subdue and control the world in which they live. Certain innate behavioral dispositions, such as weeping, smiling, clutching, sucking, and babbling and the universal occurrence in all cultures of certain modes of behavior, such as eye contact, can be traced back to innate behavioral schemata proper to the species. These dispositions set no final limitations on human freedom nor on the capacity to alter or transcend one's historical situation, but they do describe a direction in the process of existing in the human mode, a process through which alone a human being takes form as a self and acts to create a "humanity" which can alter and transcend antecedent conditions of the human organism. Since the innate dispositions and the historical situations vary from individual to individual, an attempt to define the essential essence of humanity is doomed to failure. Existing in a human mode is determined by the totality of the process of self-realization. [14]

Further, every human being experiences his or her environment in a way peculiar to the individuality of the person in question. Identically similar physical stimuli can elicit divergent physical and psychological responses when diversely interpreted by the one responding. [15] A response to a given stimulus is determined by a subjective interpretation of the stimulus by each individual. Although the structuring of the consciousness of any experience is related to the peculiar character of the bodily organs, the forms of intuition and the categories of meaning assigned to experiences are not directly dependent on experience. Beyond a person's vital needs, the satisfaction of which is necessary if the individual and the group are to survive, there are some nonvital, basic needs which must be satisfied if the organism is to develop toward its potentiality. Ashley Montagu maintains that certain values for human life, such as cooperation and love, are not matters of opinion, but are biologically and socially determined.[16] Individuals and societies live according to a set of values which recognize a line below which no person can exist and still be called human. Granted what is human varies from culture to culture and from age to age, but humanity itself is thoroughly grounded in a set of species–encompassing values.

Basic to what it means to be human is the fact that all humans are communal and dependent on others. That people can exist totally independent of all others is largely fantasy.[17] To paraphrase the immortal words of John Donne: No one is an island, entirely on his or her own; every person is a piece of the continent, a part of the whole; if a clod be washed away by the sea, the whole continent of Europe is the less. Any person's death diminishes me, because I am involved in humanity; never ask for whom the bell tolls which announces a death; it tolls for every person. Just as no plant or animal is totally self–sustaining, no person can be other than vitally involved with other human beings. The person is involved in interpersonal relationships; every person is socially bound to some group. A fundamental postulate of what it means to be a human is to relate to other humans in meaningful communal existence.

To be an educational leader means to transcend instincts and drives which seem to determine the entire existence of other animals, to make conscious value judgments and to extrapolate goals and intentions from these rational choices, and to cooperate and interact with other humans in meaningful life projects.

VALUING: ESSENCE OF EDUCATIONAL LEADERSHIP

What sets apart educational leadership from all other experiences of leadership? An educational leader values and is a perception of a person whom the educational constituents want to identify with and to follow. Therefore, the nature of educational leadership is fundamentally a question of the educational values of the leader and the followers. Whether or not people follow an educational leader depends much more on what the leader believes and values than on the knowledge, the training, the personality, the behaviors, or the skills of the leader.

Business and industry are beginning to recognize the importance of values in the management of organizations. After studying sixty-two of the most successful companies in the United States, Peters and Waterman offer one all-inclusive maxim of advice for management: Determine what the value system of the organization is.[18] IBM's purpose statement reveals a profound concern for values when it states that a sense of accomplishment and pride in one's work often goes hand in hand with a basic understanding of both individual and company identity.[19] Thomas Watson, the founder of IBM, considered that any great organization, i.e., "one that has lasted over the years," owes its vitality and longevity not to its form of organization or administrative skills, but to the power of some basic beliefs and the appeal these beliefs have for its people. Watson's firmly held thesis was that any organization, in order to survive and succeed, must have a sound set of beliefs and values on which everything in the organization is based.[20]

Selznick claims that values are the central concern of organizational leadership. He states that an institutional leader is predominately an "expert in the promotion of values." The very survival of institutions is, according to Selznick, a matter of maintaining and encouraging the values and the distinctive identity of those institutions.[21] The foundation of a corporate philosophy is a set of values from which leaders exist and operate. Ouchi maintains that the development of a meaningful organizational philosophy must begin with a basic set of values and beliefs that are consistent with each other and with the realities of the economic and social environment.[22]

Values play a key role in determining whether subordinates follow their leaders. The stereotype of the American executive as a power broker overlooks the fact that executives are driven at the deepest level by their values. Executives have something deep inside that supports them, something they trust and stand on when the going gets tough; something ultimate and meaningful; something personal; something beyond reason and empirical data.[23] Thomas Watson, Jr., the son of the founder of IBM, said in a speech at Columbia University in 1962 that the basic philosophy, spirit, drive, and values of a leader have far more to do with the achievements of an organization than do technological or economic resources, organizational structure, innovation, or timing; he concluded that values transcend everything else in determining the success of a leader.[24] A philosophy of leadership must deal with values if it is going to deal with the nature of leadership. Affect, motives, attitudes, beliefs, values, ethics, morals, will, commitment, preferences, norms, expectations, responsibilities are the basic concerns of leadership philosophy. Leadership is intrinsically and fundamentally valuational.[25]

Calling attention to the negative effect of a manager's holding a single value or viewpoint, Reddin claims that a manager will distort reality so that it fits his or her established set of values, or point of view.[26] All of the views which a leader holds concerning the organization, its goals, and its people are determined by the leader's values. Therefore, the values of leaders are established prior to their decisions and their behaviors. An examination of educational leadership which does not consider the values of the leader and the followers will not begin to explain the nature and meaning of educational leadership.

Educational plans, policies, aims, objectives, content, curriculum, methods of instruction, organizational structures, evaluation procedures, and reform endeavors are all based on the values of the leaders in the educational process. Values of educational leaders and followers may be implicit or explicit, written or oral, verbal or non-verbal. Even though educators are reluctant to acknowledge their value system or may even be unaware of what their value system is, values determine what educational leaders do in educational settings. At the very center of educational leadership is a core of those values on which educational leaders and followers ground their being, their actions, their knowledge, their skills, and their behaviors.

Educational Values as Meaning-Intending

Since values have no meanings other than those intended by the valuers, the values of educational leaders are the values of education which are intended by the leaders in the educational process. Educational aims and purposes of educational leaders rest squarely on the educational values of the leaders and followers. Husserl comments that having a meaning, or having something "in mind," is the cardinal feature of all consciousness.[27] Every intentional experience has its "intentional object," or its objective meaning. Similarly, the objective meaning of the values of educational leaders are those meanings which are intended by educational leaders themselves. Values have meaning for educational leaders only as they are experienced existentially by the educational leaders themselves.

Therefore, the foundations of educational leadership rest squarely on the educational aims and purposes of the educational leader. Studying the nature of educational leadership phenomenologically involves the analysis of the educational aims and purposes of an individual educational leader. Further, the aims and purposes are grounded in the belief system and values of the leader.

Effectiveness and success of the educational leader is in large part determined by how closely the aims and purposes of the leader correspond to the educational aims and purposes of the followers who have their own set of aims and purposes which in turn are based on their own values, beliefs, and needs. Uncovering both the leader's and the followers' values, therefore, becomes the critical exercise for achieving success and effectiveness of educational leaders.

All beliefs, values, desires, and goals are meaningful in a consideration of educational leadership, whatever their source is. Sometimes values are couched in dreams, illusions, religious beliefs, legends, myths, rituals, slogans, and irrational notions, as well as physical, emotional, and social needs and desires. The strength of a leader's values is determined by the meaning given to them by each particular leader and his or her followers.

For example, the totally irrational and psychotic values and beliefs of Jim Jones drove him to lead over 900 of his followers to commit mass suicide. The nature of Jones' leadership cannot be considered apart from his irrational beliefs and values. In colonial days witch hunters could burn young girls at the stake and feel a sense of satisfaction as the flames seared their tender flesh because the witch hunters believed the threat of being possessed by witches was real, and everyone knew that the only way to kill a witch was by burning their spirits. Dealing with the threat of witches was valued more than the life of the young girls. Even today, children in India can starve to death in sight of the nourishment of beef because the adults value the spirits of dead ancestors which may inhabit the cows more than they value the lives of children or their own lives. The dreams and values of Martin Luther King, Jr. had more to do with achieving equal educational opportunities for Blacks in America than have all the behavior modification programs and federal grants combined. The nature of educational leadership involves the totality of the human consciousness, including all the rational and irrational aspects of human experience.

Whether values are good or bad is a moral question which must be decided by all persons involved in a given situation. However, the meaning of the values of an educational leader is determined by the intention of those participating in the educational process, and the illusions, dreams, myths, rituals, beliefs, and irrational conceptualizations of education are important "facts" in educational leadership.

Value–Audits for Educational Leaders

To be an effective educational leader requires that one know as much as possible about his or her own values, about the values of the followers, and about the values of the culture, or larger community. Hodgkinson suggests the use of a value–audit to uncover one's philosophy of leadership.[28]

The obvious places to look for the values of educational leaders are in admonitions and prohibitions contained in speeches, policy manuals, personnel policies, student and staff handbooks, curriculum materials, graduation standards and requirements, departures from stated practices and policies, conflicts, rewards and penalties, budgets, and resource allocations. In contrast to a positivistic approach which claims to be value–free, a phenomenological approach examines these empirical data as extensions of values within human consciousness.

However, subjective and intuitive evidence can be included in the value–audit. One of the educational leader's maxims of responsibility is to know oneself, including values and psychological needs. This Socratic maxim equally applies to the exercise of self reflection to bring to light an educational leader's own values. A self reflective value–audit asks such questions as: Who am I? Why am I here? What is a human being? Where am I going? What is worth dying for or living for? What is worth knowing and forgetting? What is education to each individual? What is teaching and learning? What is each person supposed to be doing in a school? What are good and bad schools? What is evaluation? Reflections of a leader might take the form of a personal journal and become a part of the value–audit.

A similar kind of reflection on the values of others is a worthwhile contribution to the value–audit. The interview technique, the case method, and field method help to bring out the values of leaders and followers. Many corporate organizations have used discussion of corporate goals and objectives, sensitivity training, brain storming, role playing, therapy groups, playbacks of audio and video tapes of meetings, games, and psychological, projective exercises to uncover values and beliefs. Values tend to surface in the presence of personal conflicts, displays of positive and negative emotions, distractions, sudden changes, signs of discomfort or pleasure, and preoccupation with certain topics. When applied to educational followers, the value–audit raises questions about the aims and purposes of the educational process in which the followers are involved. Through reflection on the questions raised about the meanings which the followers bestow on the aims and purposes of education, the value system of the educational followers begins to unfold. Values which surface from such exercises and interviews are openly acknowledged and reflected on again and again in order to continue the process of values clarification.

Like the ethnographer, the educational leader should dig into the educational constituency's innermost secrets, fears, strengths, and weaknesses. The educational leader's role is to be a most personal scientist who has a professional respect, admiration, and appreciation of the values and beliefs of the educational constituency's way of life. To know and to respect the cultural values and beliefs of learners is the flip-side of a leader's knowledge of her or his own values.[29]

Not to be overlooked in the value-audit for educational leaders is a consideration of the cultural and moral values of the political constituency which directly or indirectly supports the educational process. The successful educational leader may be at variance with the secondary or peripheral values of his or her own constituency, but the basic values of the leader's constituency are reflected in the aims and purposes of the educational system's constituency.

The leader of a church school or religiously supported college may hold beliefs about minor doctrines of the church group which supports the school, but will find it difficult to lead the school if his or her beliefs are very different from those of the constituency. Often the beliefs of a faculty leader or administrator lead to the leader's dismissal from the school. Thus, the sphere of an educational leader's influence could be enlarged or constricted, depending on whether the basic beliefs of the leader find reception in the larger context of the educational process.

The Is-Ness of Educational Values

The nature of educational leadership centers in the nature of the values of education itself. The qualifier of educational leadership pertains to the "process, state, or result" of "drawing out" or "bringing out" what education is, not merely changing behaviors or acquiring a body of information. Education is the total process of helping others to make sense out of life for themselves. Education is enabling others to learn how to learn. Moreover, education refers to the process of "development" (Dewey), or of "growing up, and being brought up."[30] Growing up involves physical development, acquisition of beliefs, values, and knowledge, establishing communication, relating to others, becoming conscious of one's self, and accepting responsibility for being human. Learning about growing up is a person coming to know about his or her own consciousness of growing up. Knowledge acquired through this learning must be known in a way which is appropriate to the knower. Only that is really known which is learned through experience and that which is personally appropriate. Therefore, one could say that life itself is education.[31] Whitehead maintains that the only subject matter of education is "life in all its manifestations."[32]

Just as education is never neutral, impartial, or disinterested, the consciousness of being an educational leader always leans toward the values of the leader and the followers. Education is not simply the transference of knowledge, facts, and data from the brain cells of the teacher to the receptacle of the student, the brain cells of the student. Rather, education is a "knowing" in which both the knower and the learner participate in the reflection and action implicit in the knowledge. All knowledge is personal in the sense that our understanding of any fact is predicated on our construction of reality in which the situation of "knowing" occurs. We are always committed to a form of knowing which is consonant with the values and goals implicit in what is known.

Thus, an educational leader "draws" the followers into his or her construction of reality, and both the leader and the learners join in the quest of actualization of their common values. Neutrality of leadership is not possible. The very essence of leadership is a common search for information, reflection, and action which is based on common values.

The essence of educational leadership is founded on those values and aims of education which make education meaningful to the leader, as well as to the followers and to the general constituency which is served by the educational process. Studying the nature of educational leadership involves a clarification of those basic values which determine the aims and purposes of the educational process of which the educational leader is a part.

Moral Excellence in Educational Leaders

Today there is a great deal of interest in the problem of moral excellence in educational leaders. Educators are uncertain about their values orientation; values which were once associated with the Judaeo–Christian religion have lost their influence in the schools; and leaders in the educational systems are unsure and troubled as to what is right and wrong and which goals and principles are to be esteemed and valued.

This uncertainty and uneasiness about the values of educational leaders became apparent to me when I tried to determine how values were being taught in the Nashville Tennessee Metropolitan School System a few year ago. After several telephone inquires I was directed to the Social Studies Curriculum Coordinator who reluctantly admitted to being responsible for the teaching of values in the Nashville public schools. During my initial interview of this person, I was confidently informed that the Metro School System "did not teach values."

In fact, the coordinator told of an incident where a group of Jewish parents accused his Protestant teachers of imposing non-Jewish religious values on their kids by conducting Christmas programs in the schools. "No-sir. We just can't afford to teach values," the coordinator emphasized. Acting on some prior knowledge of the system, I then enquired about the Drug Awareness Program and the Holocaust Studies Program, of which the coordinator was obviously proud.

After the coordinator admitted that these programs were promoting values which the educational constituency esteemed, I asked if students were allowed to smoke tobacco or to use alcohol or any controlled substance on school grounds. "Certainly not!" The student handbook spelled out the consequences of such student "misbehavior," including the use of profanity. However, both faculty and administration were not restricted from using tobacco, profanity, or alcohol as long as no state statute was violated. Further, the faculty and administration selection processes of the central office did not provide for any screening, educating, or promoting of any particular values in the system. It was agreed that the values of a free-enterprise system, a democratic society, and the cultural values of the Metro area citizens would be supported through the curriculum, teaching methods, and administrative processes of the system. Yet, the Social Studies Coordinator was clearly uneasy, talking about how these values would be promoted and taught in the schools.

Just as Ghandi and Lincoln were "good" leaders and Hitler and Stalin were "bad" leaders in the political arena, educational leaders can be described as good or bad according to commonly held values, human decency, and moral standards. Moral leadership concerns actions and states of being which are good or bad or right or wrong according to standards, rules, and ideals of the public or according to preferences and needs of individuals which relate to the common good of the public. What educational constituency would not say that lying, cheating, stealing, killing, polluting, raping, prejudice, and hating are wrong, while love, courage, honor, justice, honesty, and respect for others, property, and the environment are good?

Values are not objects "out there" which are assigned to leaders and followers by a subject. Neither are values measures of satisfaction of human desires or needs; if this were true, values would consist in what is pleasurable or painless, and the world could be considered to be value-free. Values are neither given to leaders nor imposed on others by leaders in some absolute or transcendent form; values are created out of the concrete situations in which humans become fully functioning persons of worth and dignity to themselves and to others collectively. Values which followers want to see in a leader are closely associated with what it means to be fully human; determining what is human cannot be prescribed, assigned, or codified apart from the total, concrete situation of the individual. Morality is the quality of life which the human race is willing to accept as a basis for being human and for maintaining human existence.

Barnard makes a strong case for what he calls "moral excellence" as an integral quality in leaders. He identifies moral excellence with an aspect of individual superiority in determination, persistence, endurance, courage of a leader. It determines the quality of a leader's actions and often is most inferred from what is left undone or ignored. It is that in leaders which commands respect, and reverence. In Barnard's own words, moral excellence in leaders is:

> . . . the power of individuals to inspire cooperative personal decision by creating faith: faith in common understanding, faith in probability of success, faith in the ultimate satisfaction of personal motives, faith in the integrity of objective authority, faith in the superiority of common purpose as a personal aim of those who partake in it.[33]

One way to view educational leaders is to analyze what they perceive the goals and values of educators to be in a given educational setting. What is "good education" for a given educational leader? Educational leaders act according to a set of values in an educational setting whereby the educational constituency chooses to identify with what the leader symbolizes or represents. Educational leadership is strengthened or restricted to the degree that the followers identify with the values which the leader embodies.

Certain minimum biological conditions must be met by humans if they are to survive and remain human, i.e., breathing, eating, drinking, excreting, sleeping, avoiding pain, and reproducing. Likewise, several nonvital needs must be met if the human organism is to develop and maintain physical and mental health. One's biological and psychological natures determine the direction which self-constitution will take. "What is" shapes "what ought to be," as well as "what will be." Certain values for human life are not matters of opinion, but are determined biologically. Within this milieu of biologically based values, the human being is directed toward love, trust, and cooperation with other humans.[34] Humans cannot be reduced to any quality, ideal, trait, or behavior other than a state of being a human organism. Thus, one of the most basic questions of human existence is analysis of the meaning of being-in-the-world, i.e., "what is the meaning of being?" The most basic mode of being-in-the-world is concern and responsibility for oneself, for the world, and for others. Existence is authentic when one freely chooses how he or she will be-in-the-world, but inauthentic when other forces are allowed to shape his or her being-in-the-world.

Educational leadership is a mode of being a human in an educational situation. Compare two people who are participating in an AIDS awareness program in the local school system. An unbiased analysis of the total concrete situation of the two "leaders" will reveal the good and the bad leader. The question of goodness is not what ought to be or what is right, but what is the meaning of following either of these leaders. What is the meaning of being a leader in this educational situation? The two individuals being compared may possess similar personality traits, may perform identical behaviors, and may relate to the school organization in the same way, but what does each leader become in this situation in relation to self, the world, and others? Do the followers become tools for concerns of a leader or do the followers become more of what they are individually? Only as the AIDS program unfolds can the authentic leader be determined.

Values are essential to educational leadership, but what moral leadership is cannot be declared beforehand; nor can the educational situation be value-free. Being an educational leader evolves out of the total situation of the process of education in a given context where the goals of the educational constituency are anchored in what it means to be human.

GENETICS OF LEADER DECISIONS

Whatever else an educational leader is which learners choose to follow, an educational leader is a decision maker. All theories of leadership consider decision making as fundamental to leadership. Herbert Simon even contends that decision making is synonymous with management and that management can be equated with leadership.[35]

The literature on leadership does not neglect decision making. In fact, the assumption in the literature is that decision making is a scientific technique which poses a question or sets a goal, collects facts about alternatives, evaluates the data favoring each alternative, and then chooses an answer or solution which "probably" will be most effective or satisfying. The scientific method of decision making focuses on the solution to a problem or an answer to a question which results in the "right" answer or the "one" correct solution to the problem. Little wonder that today's educational leaders are taught to employ "decision science" and quantitative evaluation methods. These methods rely on computations of variables, cost–benefit analysis, correlation determinations, probability curves, validation checks, and outcome measurements.

Although quantitative research and decision science can provide data for evaluation, how is the data structured and interpreted in the consciousness of the leader? In what way is the choice presented to the consciousness of the educational leader? Schutz begins an article on genetics of decision making by claiming that decision making is the analysis of the whole process by which an individual in daily life determines his or her future conduct after considering several possible alternatives.[36] Whereas scientific decision making is linear, objective, logical, and systematized, genetic decision making is a process which can be exposed, analyzed, and described, but is not a step–by–step method for making decisions. Scientific decision making is quantitative, while genetic decision making is qualitative.

The sergeants in the military are fond of contrasting the styles of decision making of recent West Point graduates and combat–seasoned sergeants. The sergeant is said to make decisions on the basis of experiences of survival in combat situations, whereas the inexperienced officers rely on their textbooks and classroom experiences in "war science" at West Point. Although the sergeant's evaluations are biased, decisions in actual combat are based on global, holistic views of the total situation, and the young officers are at a disadvantage, not having the holistic experiences of survival on which to draw for decisions. Genetic decision making would consider both approaches to decision making in combat situations and would look to a combat-seasoned graduate of West Point as the better decision maker.

An analysis of decision making begins with the daily life situation of the educational leader in the natural attitude where the world is taken for granted and where the leader possesses an inherited stock of knowledge, cultural biases, beliefs, attitudes, and values. Past experiences, present anxieties, beliefs, and biases are tacit, but real and dynamic elements in the process of decision making of educational leaders. The amalgam of taken-for-granted knowledge, suppositions, and beliefs assumed in the natural attitude determines how a leader perceives evidence, sense data, alternative solutions, and possible conclusions.

I once knew an educational administrator who had served as a missionary to Africa, but was forced to return to America because of the health of his wife. He seemed to experience a great deal of guilt about his inability to fulfill his desire to be in Africa. Almost all of his major decisions were shaped by his unresolved guilt. For instance, he wanted to turn the school he served into a missionary training institution to "send missionaries to Africa," since he could not go himself. Also, he became a "soft touch" for any foreign student whom he thought he could train to return to the "mission field." The presuppositions and biases which he brought to the decision situation shaped many of his decisions. The thing is that all of us bring a host of presuppositions to the decision making event.

Although the decision maker cannot completely withdraw from the thesis of everyday life, acknowledgment of the reality of the biases and presuppositions of the natural attitude is a necessary step in the analysis of genetic decision making. The techniques of simulation, gaming, brainstorming, and other free variation exercises help to weaken the impact of the natural attitude. By bracketing, or setting aside, the natural attitude, the decision maker can focus more clearly on the real issues in the choice. Also, involving other people who possess expert knowledge of decisional factors and who do not have vested interests in the possible outcomes and conclusions of the decision can increase the reduction of the everyday biases and assumptions.

Every decision involves experiences of doubt, questions, or incompleteness in a future state of affairs. An analysis of the meaning of those experiences of doubt and anxiety poses questions about the nature of the problem to be solved or the questions to be asked. What is the real question being asked? What is the proper time, place, method, and situation to ask the questions? Is a solution to the problem even possible, or are you wasting time trying to answer the question at this time? What will happen if the question is ignored or delayed?

Peter Drucker claims that Japanese managers spend ninety percent of their time asking the right questions and very little time searching for the right answers.[37] Genetic decision making focuses on the right questions, although the best answer is not ignored. The experiences of doubt and incompleteness are as much a part of making a decision as is the collecting of data and evaluating alternative solutions.

Genetic decision making looks at the aims and projects which are necessary to bring about the anticipated state of affairs from the leader's and the followers' perspectives. Through a dramatic rehearsal by means of imagination and fantasy the leader can visualize the state of affairs to be brought about by a future choice or action. Schutz observes that one has to have some idea of the structure to be erected, metaphorically speaking, before he or she can draft the blueprints of a project. In order to project one's future action as it will unfold, one must by means of imagination or fantasy place himself or herself at a future time when this action will already have been accomplished, when the resulting act will already have happened. Only then can one reconstruct the individual steps which will have brought forth this future act.[38] Thus, the future act is anticipated in the future perfect tense by means of an exercise of imagination and fantasy.

Projecting oneself into a future state of affairs has important consequences for a leader's decision making. For one thing, the decision maker is personally involved in the process at the critical point of the final choice. This involvement contrasts sharply with scientific decision making. Being personally involved in the process of making choices encourages others to choose to follow the leader's proposed solutions or suggested answers. The imaginative rehearsal of the future choice or act is based on the leader's previously performed judgments and actions which are typically similar to the proposed choice or act and on the leader's biographically determined situation. For example, an educational leader imagines what a five percent salary increase will mean to several faculty members, what the salary increase will mean to himself or herself, and what the salary increase might mean to faculties which are similar to the one being considered.

In order to make a decision the educational leader considers the possibilities and alternatives available to bring about the future act. The leader must select subjectively those elements relevant to the deliberation of the potential state of affairs. Alternatives and possibilities are established in a unified system of potentiality in order for a choice to be created. No form of evidence is excluded from these acts of deliberation and choosing. The point here is that better decisions are possible when more options and alternatives are available.

Thus, genetic decision making is "poly-option" decision making. The focus is on the number of options available, rather than on the strength of the evidence for the correct answer. The leader who is able to draw the followers into his or her perspective will offer more options for authentic and meaningful knowledge to take place in the leadership situation.

In making a decision the educational leader considers the possibilities and alternatives available to bring about the future states or acts. The leader selects subjectively those elements which are relevant to the deliberation of the potential state of affairs. Alternatives, options, and possibilities create a broader system of potentiality from which choices are made. No form of evidence is excluded from these acts of deliberation. However, Schutz notes that deliberation of options includes limitations of practicability. He points out that all knowledge taken for granted in the natural attitude is socially constructed and thereby biased.[39] Husserl contends that even logic and mathematics are limited by pre-predicative judgments, i.e., the acceptance of numbers and common sense are based on prior assumptions.[40] Beliefs which conflict with other beliefs, possibilities which are not within the control of the decision maker, and views and interpretations of proposed actions by potential followers also have a bearing upon the practicality of the deliberations. Each conflicting value, feeling, aim, project, or proposed action is played out upon the screen of the leader's imagination to create a clear choice. From out of all the competing alternatives choice emerges as a unified preference of the decision maker.

Whereas the goal of scientific decision making is to explain causes and predict outcomes, genetic decision making intends to understand the multiplicity of meanings of the deliberative situation. Genetic deliberation questions the questions and interprets the conclusions. From what perspective is the deliberation being conducted? What values, attitudes, intentions, hopes, dreams, and biases are shaping the perceptions of the decision maker? What is the nature and reliability of the evidence presented? Would the questions and the answers be the same in a similar situation or in a different context?

The techniques of genetic deliberation are not the same as the methods of decision science, but rather are similar to the methods of depth psychology, qualitative research, field studies in anthropology, or phenomenological analysis in philosophy. The techniques of genetic deliberation include participant observation, in-depth interviewing, qualitative field notes, gaming, simulation, fantasizing, sensitivity training, transactional analysis, philosophical analysis and synthesis, and pragmatic questioning. Genetic deliberation focuses more time and attention on asking questions and analyzing meanings than on formulating answers or solutions.

Time constraints, exhaustion of knowledge sources, presentation of available alternatives, and consideration of other factors finally call for deliberation to cease and for a choice of projects to be made. The word "decision" etymologically means "to cut off." Deliberation and debate is ended, the question is called for, and the process of cutting off, or rejecting, that which is not desired begins: decision making is in progress. Choosing among the possible projects of action always takes place within the total decision making process. Every time something is chosen, one or more possibilities are excluded, or "cut off." Choosing one thing means that one has chosen to exclude thousands of other things. When a leader chooses to make a speech to the faculty, he or she chooses not to write a letter, make an announcement over the P.A. system, make a video tape, ask someone else to speak, or a thousand other things which may be available as a means to communicate with the faculty.

What, then, constitutes a "good" choice or a "right" decision? The basis of selecting one answer, conclusion, or act instead of another is not necessarily the result of deductions drawn from quantifiable, verifiable data of the scientific method. The problem of positive and negative weights of each possible choice evolves out of each situation of choosing, thus avoiding both the "value-free" stance of positivism and the absolute value system of idealism.

Schutz points out that choosing between two projects implies a previously chosen system of connected projects of a higher order.[41] However, higher order choosing is based on the projected state of affairs from the leader's perspective and on the biographically determined situation of the leader. Thus, the "right" choice has no standard format which holds true for all purposes and situations, but rather is valid if the decision maker perceives the multiple realities of the anticipated state of affairs of the choice within the context of the purpose at hand. That purpose at hand also is set in the context of the leader's interests, motives, values, ends and means, and pre-experienced situations and decisions. Further, the test of truth proceeds to higher and higher orders or anticipated states of affairs of yet other situations, of an individual's entire life, of the lives of others, of society, and of human beings as a whole.

An educational leader may be called upon to decide whether to end the school lunch program. Decision science would seek to determine the costs and benefits of the program to the school system. In contrast, the genetic method of decision making would begin by trying to envision what ending the program would mean to the students, faculty, and the system as a whole. Is the question really whether to end the lunch program or is it a local political issue? Are there alternatives to the lunch program, or must the program be continued or stopped immediately? Who is opposing the program? Who is really benefiting from the program, needy kids, the local food stores, or the tax payers? Is the issue a school problem or a community problem? Or, are we dealing with the hunger issue? What will ending the program do for the physical health of the students? How will the physical health affect the learning of the students who are being served by the lunch program? If the problem is a matter of money, should you go to the civic clubs, churches, and other funding sources to seek assistance? Could the program be discontinued for a week or cut back to a smaller number of days per week? On and on the questioning goes until the leader and the followers are confident that the question is the proper question, that the alternatives have been surveyed, and that the consequences and results have been interpreted. The issue is not settled, but is finally raised to a consideration of how the lunch program is set in the context of all humans.

The experience of the "right" choice moves the decision maker toward the anticipated state of affairs. Thus, the decision process is not complete until the decision maker commits himself or herself to the fulfillment of the anticipated action which the decision proposes. Not until the decision maker says, "I will . . . ." is the process of the decision experienced totally from the actor's perspective. Self commitment of a leader to his or her decision minimizes the possibility of leaders selecting answers and solutions to problems and finding little support from followers to carry out the decisions of the leader. When the leader is personally involved in the decision process and has drawn the followers into the realm of the purposes at hand, the followers are more likely to participate not only in decision process, but are more likely to participate in the actions which result from the decision and which lead to the purposes at hand.

An educational leader who is personally involved in the entire process of decision making will spend more time on analyzing the questions and problems than on selecting the correct answer or conclusion. The genetic process of decision making is based on qualitative considerations rather than quantitative deductions. The process of the formulation of alternative directions to approach problems and questions moves the whole decision process toward the purpose at hand.

Spending more time on asking questions and posing more possible solutions to the problems force leaders to spend more time on what is really important and less time on the peripheral issues. Spending more time on the questions encourages leaders to ask whether many of the questions are valid or whether they really need to be answered. By the time a critical choice is required in the decision process, the potential followers often are already convinced of the validity and quality of the possible answers or conclusions. Genetic decision making tends to identify more real questions, more alternative solutions, and will result in more commitment on the part of both leaders and followers. Finally, the acknowledgement of biases and presuppositions which leaders and followers bring to the decision making situation will ultimately promote more authentic questions and more possible solutions in the decision making process.

The objection may be raised that genetic decision making is inappropriate for emergencies, e.g., when the house is on fire and a child needs rescuing; obviously, there is not time to go through an endless process of analyzing what to do. However, the genetic method immediately raises the issue to the highest realm of what is needed in the context of all children of the world. If the genetic style of decision making permeates the community, someone is more likely to "see" the need to try to rescue the child. Following the method of decision science would require that a person calculate the risk to the rescuer and the probability of saving the child. The truth is that emergencies often require an intuitive, heroic style of decision making. Further, the question of what is the purpose at hand is very quickly answered in the case of a child who needs help; the question in this case focuses on the values and attitudes of those who are present in the situation of need. A leader is one who will raise the question to the highest level of human values and meaning in the shortest amount of time. People will follow that kind of leader.

In education, leaders are needed who will raise questions and needs of learners to the highest level of analysis in the shortest period of time on behalf of the educational goals. Genetic decision making involves the educational leader personally in the choices which are presented in the educational situation. The leader and the learners are bound up in the same milieu of seeking knowledge and understanding of problems, questions, human life, and existence.

However, genetic decision making is not a splitting of consciousness and reality as an idealistic perspective tends to do, as if reality is constituted by consciousness and judgement is a construction of consciousness apart from reality. Neither is decision making a dichotomy of consciousness and reality from a mechanistic frame of mind, whereby consciousness is structured to correspond to the physical reality which is in turn judged to be real according to available empirical evidence and deductive reasoning. Genetic judgment exists only when we not only recognize but also experiment with the dialectic between objectivity and subjectivity, reality and consciousness, practice and theory, action and reflection, thinking and judgment. Genetic decision making is the analytic, reflective process of recognizing as many biases as is possible, of uncovering the most alternatives, of introducing the maximum empirical and subjective evidence, of evaluating and interpreting the solutions and conclusions from multiple perspectives, and of keeping the decision process as open and as critical as is possible.

One of the most encouraging developments in leadership studies is an emphasis on qualitative research in the field of education. Although little has been done in the area of decision making, the principles of quality research obviously apply to decision making as it relates to educational leadership. David Fetterman has collected several articles on qualitative approaches to educational evaluation which note a "shifting of allegiance to a phenomenologically oriented paradigm."[42]

In order for educational leaders to practice genetic decision making, they must develop intellectual, emotional, and personal capacities which the liberal arts curriculum should promote. Educational leaders who are genetic decision makers need broad experiences which are common to constituents in the educational process; they need general knowledge of educational curriculum; they must be able to think clearly, analytically, scientifically, critically, imaginatively, creatively, abstractly, concretely, personally, holistically, etc.; and they need to be aware of their own and their constituents' cultural beliefs and values. Thus, genetic decision making is more an art than it is a science or a hereditary endowment.

COMMUNICATION AS EXTENSION OF LEADER

All great leaders have been great communicators. Communication is a vital aspect of the leadership process. In fact, to be a leader and not be a communicator is impossible. Communication is simply an extension of the person of the educational leader. Although leadership theorists have considered the formal aspect of the communication process, the subjective dimensions of the communication process need to be analyzed. What does the educational leader experience during the communication process? Very little attention has been paid to the relationship of social theory to communication theory. What is the nature of the experience of the educational leader who is communicating to followers?

The communication process includes at least three parts: a message, a transmitter, and a receiver. A message moves through three stages: encoding, transmitting, and decoding. The communication process of educational leaders can be analyzed according to what the leader experiences during the encoding of the message, how the transmission is experienced, and how decoding and listening are experienced. What happens in the consciousness of an educational leader during the communication process? What are the internal phenomena of communication? What are the subjective aspects of the three phases of the communication process?

Excellent studies have been done on the formal elements of the communication process. Theorists have examined the selection of the proper words, the length of messages, the grammatical construction of the language, the proper medium to transmit the message, psychological analyses of the sender and the receiver of the messages, content of the message, how messages are sent in formal organizations, and how messages can be clarified and verified throughout the communication process. How painfully we are aware of confused messages which are misunderstood because receivers made assumptions on the basis of their prior experiences, beliefs, and feelings. The absurd results of miscommunication is the source of much of our humor. For example, a young mother who believed in parental sex education was delighted one day when her young son asked, "Mom, where did I come from?" She tried to make the most of the opportunity. When she finished her detailed lesson, she asked if he now knew where he came from. The son, looking very puzzled, said, "No, Mom, I meant, did we come from England or some other country?"

Definitions of communication in books on educational leadership almost exclusively focus on the transmission aspect of communication. For instance, Hoy and Miskel in a standard textbook of educational administration cite the definitions of Merrihue and Davis as standards. Merrihue defines communication as "any kind of behavior" on the part of the sender which conveys a desired meaning to the receiver and which causes desired response in the receiver, and Davis defines it more simply as a process of passing information and understanding from one person to another.[43] These representative definitions are concerned with the formal structure, the signification, the verification, the medium, the language of communication. When applied to educational leadership, this view explores the channels of communication in organizations, the behavior of leaders, the criteria of effective communication, the results of good communication, formal and informal communication in organizations, the timing, the flow, the volume, and the environment of communication, and other such formal aspects of the communication process.

What is missing in the literature on leadership theory is an analysis of the internal phenomena of communication of educational leaders. Communication is first a subjective experience of the leader.

Effective leaders seem to be aware of the subjective elements of communication as well as the formal aspects. Educational leaders have the ability to transmit intelligible messages and the ability to understand messages sent by others. Thus, the subjective aspects of the communication process of educational leaders are significant for a theory of educational leadership.

Creating and Encoding Messages

The leader who creates a message is very much a part of the message which is created. Marshall McLuhan points out that messages are "extensions" of the person creating the message.[44] The person of the leader is embodied in the message which is created. In fact, the leader cannot be separated from the message which is communicated. When a leader is communicating effectively, someone says, "She was really into her message, wasn't she?" Recognition of the inseparability of the message and the leader is the first step in understanding the nature of the communication of an educational leader.

Recently, I had the privilege of hearing a blind musician give a concert. The instrument which he used literally became an extension of his person. He communicated through the instrument unlike any musician I had ever heard. He was so intimately acquainted with the instrument that he made the instrument say exactly what he wanted it to say. I was never so aware of how a person can put himself into a piece of music. In the same way the cane is an extension of the blind person; the brush is part of the artist; and a pen is a part of a journalist.

The message of an educational leader is an extension of the person who created the message. The fears, loves, values, goals, and biases all attach themselves to the message of a leader like filings cling to a magnet. How easily we forget this fact and try to get our messages across "objectively" or "impartially." The college president who uses incorrect grammar ten times in a speech does not convince very many people of his concern for academic standards even though "Academic Standards" may be the theme of his speech.

Likewise, the educational administrator who claims his or her door is always open and who wants participative decision making is fooling no one when subordinates cannot get in to see him or her or when decisions are made without involving those who are affected directly. Subordinates get the message: the administrator does not care, period. Asking for input and then ignoring the suggestions offered may give a stronger negative message to the educational constituency. You are the message you are communicating.

Communication begins in the leader as thinking, articulation, and symbolization. Verbal messages are created by the mental processes of thinking; thinking is based on conceptualization, reasoning, and argumentation; mental exercises are made possible by language; language is based on words, sentences, and syntax; and words are based on the symbolization of objects, events, ideas, actions, and feelings. Language has no meaning apart from that which the subject, or leader, assigns to it. Neither do scientific signs, symbols, and formulae nor the symbols of logic have meanings apart from that assigned by their subjects. Thus, the leader is subjectively involved even in the creation of scientific statements and messages.

However, not all messages are articulate or verbal. Inarticulate data can be communicated to animals. Rats and pigeons can learn to press levers which communicate the presence of food by accidentally hitting the lever which drops the food. Dogs can see a light or hear a bell which communicates the availability of food or the presence of danger. Also, a chimpanzee can reorganize the sign and event sequence and recognize the coherence of the positions of boxes in relationship to climbing in order to obtain food. This same inarticulate communication occurs in literate persons both consciously and unconsciously.

Before children learn to speak, they operate exclusively at the pre-language, inarticulate level. However, no one questions whether the baby can communicate effectively without language. Cries, screams, grunts, giggles, coos, and general babbling can summon an anxious parent in an instant. Also, the baby's facial expressions, gestures, and other body movements can communicate pleasure (e.g., the social smile), fear, and pain.

The field of nonverbal communication is too broad to discuss here, but the point must be made that people are always communicating some message, both verbally and nonverbally. An educational leader cannot help but communicate something. The question is what is being communicated and what is the meaning of what is communicated. Good leaders are able to "read" both the verbal and nonverbal messages of themselves and others better than non-leaders.

The subjective experience of the communication of the educational leader includes the intentions of the message maker. The intention of the creator of a message can be considered in terms of one of the four functions of language. First, does the leader intend to convey information, data, and facts? Second, does the leader intend to establish rapport or communion with followers, such as greetings, well-wishing, small talk, colloquial expletives, etiquette, or politeness? Third, perhaps the leader desires to express emotions, feelings, attitudes, beliefs, values, or beauty. Or, finally, the leader may intend to affect the follower's thought or behavior by means of questions, commands, requests, persuasive remarks, wishes, or other directives. Intentions of an educational leader who communicates a message are private and subjective and can be known directly only by the one who is intending to communicate a message.

One of the major goals of sensitivity training, and other reflective techniques, is for the message creator to become more aware of this inner space of intentions. Even at its very best, the intentions of the creator of a message are often quite different from the message which the follower receives. Therefore, a leader must give careful consideration to gaining insight into this inner world of intentions, desires, and purposes of his or her messages.

The encoding of a message is so bound up with the personality of the leader that the encoding process expresses the leader's view of reality. Messages which are put into words are significations and representations of what the world means to the message maker. Heidegger maintains that talking is the way in which we articulate meaningfully the intelligibility of what he calls "Being–in–the–world." [45] For example, the verb system of the ancient Hebrew language does not express linear time. Since the concept of time in a semi–nomadic culture would be limited to whether a project, action, or event was either completed or incomplete, the Hebrew verb system expressed either "perfected" or "imperfected" action. Whether something occurred in the past, present, or future time would only be determined by the context of the verb used. A semi–nomadic culture would find little use for explicit measurement of time in a linear fashion.

Thus, the encoding of a message is bound up inextricably with the message maker's perception of himself, the world and others. The structure of the message which is encoded is constituted by the leader's understanding of his or her existing in the world. Since the encoding of the message constitutes the structure of the ideas and thoughts included in the message, the message is in a very real sense a perception of the message maker's values, attitudes, intentions, and world view. Who a leader is will be communicated through the encoding of the message.

The Medium Is the Leader

Even the transmission phase of the communication process is bound up with the message maker's self perception, as well as his or her view of the world, and others. The fact that the person is embodied in a message makes the leader the medium of the message. Who a leader is will be communicated through the message and through the medium of the message. Those who have studied the use of the body as a medium of language have pointed out how certain body postures and movements transmit psychological messages. Although body language definitely is a means of nonverbal communication, the interpretation of these body signals can be very confusing and misleading if one looks no deeper into the transmission process than observing what certain behaviors seem to mean. The question remains as to how meanings are assigned to certain behaviors of the body. Are crossed legs universally interpreted as a defensive behavior? What meaning is intended by the message creator? Did the recipient of the message miss a cue or misread a certain gesture? Thus, the internal and subjective dimensions of the transmission phase of the communication process of educational leaders need some attention.

The symbolization of language, flags, codes, machines, gestures, and tools have no power in themselves to communicate anything other than the meaning which is assigned by their creators, transmitters, and receivers. Michael Polanyi sees the use of these media as extensions of the person who is using them. He observes that individuals assimilate these media to our body by pouring ourselves into them. Thus each time we use a tool our identity undergoes some change, and our self concept expands into new modes of being.[46] A person "dwells in" the medium of the message; the person becomes a very real part of the message. The message comes from the forces of the being of a person. This perspective is in sharp contrast to the view of a subject who constructs a message out of empirical data and transmits the message via a mechanical process, i.e., the stimulus-response pattern. From a phenomenological perspective leaders create messages out of their own states of existence and dwell in the media of transmitting the message.

All the body parts are interrelated in a peculiar way. They are not spread out side by side, but are enveloped in each other. The person is in undivided possession of the body and knows where each part is through a phenomenal body image in which all the parts are included. The phenomenal body is to be understood as an expressive unity, a synergic system, to be compared not to an object but to a work of art. Thus, the sightless person's cane is no longer an external object, but is an extension of the phenomenal body of the blind person who is able to feel the pavement, as the keyboard of a computer is incorporated into the body of an experienced operator.[47]

Messages of educational leaders are transmitted as a holistic act of communication. The medium, or leader, is embodied in the message. Reflection on the transmission of educational messages calls for appropriate gestures, attitudes, emotions, language, vocabulary, attire, environment, etc. For instance, reading a formal lecture in a monotone, subdued, growling voice is not the best method to transmit a leader's strong feelings to encourage teachers at the beginning of a school year. I know a teacher who thinks that the very presence of students in a classroom is a message to the students that spontaneous learning is not to occur. Therefore, this teacher immediately finds a way to get the students out of the classroom where learning can take place. Similarly, educational leaders must be aware that the "intercom" is the "Anti-Christ" to teachers; teachers are not likely to hear what a leader says by such a method. Thus, educational leaders must be creative and thoughtful about "how" they choose to transmit messages. Further, leaders should look at the total communication process and choose and use media which are appropriate for the intention of the message creator.

Leaders in the Listening Mode

The third phase of the communication process is the reception of the message which has been created and transmitted. The only physical phenomena which actually pass between the sender and the receiver of a message are sound waves and light waves. The sender creates sounds, symbols, signs, pictures, and other configurations of language and gestures which are received primarily by the follower's eyes and ears. And Richard Hubbell has declared without equivocation that ninety-eight per cent of all that we learn in our lifetimes is learned through our eyes and ears.[48] And the ancient philosopher, Zeno, said, "We have two ears, but only one mouth, that we may hear more and speak less." One way to improve the reception of messages is to improve the clarity and accuracy of the physical and linguistic aspects of communication. Better reception of the message would depend on better speakers, better letters, better fax machines, better channels of communication, better reading and listening skills.

Ralph Nichols and Leonard Stevens, experts on the art of listening, cite a busy executive who claims to spend eighty per cent of his time listening to people.[49] Realizing that the average person can retain only twenty-five per cent of the information which he or she hears, many organizations are making serious attempts to improve listening skills. Listening training programs have been developed to identify bad and good listening habits, but these listening skills, techniques, and devices are merely devices and techniques which do not get to the heart of the problem of listening as it relates to educational leadership.

Before my grandmother died, she developed some ear problems. My dad and mother carried her to Vanderbilt University Hospital to try to identify her problem. While they were waiting for the extensive tests to be run, Mom persuaded Dad to have the doctor examine him also, since Dad seemed to be having some hearing problems. After performing a series of tests, the doctor called Dad and Mom into his office and went over Dad's tests. The doctor explained Dad's problem in layman's terms as "selective hearing." Dad was hearing only what he wanted to hear. Selective hearing is basic to the problem of listening and is central to the problem of educational leadership. Listening as understanding goes far beyond the formal and neurological phenomena of creating, sending, and receiving messages.

Alfred North Whitehead, commenting on the indeterminateness of all language, wrote:

> But no language can be anything but elliptical, requiring a leap of the imagination to understand its meaning in its relevance to immediate experience . . . no verbal statement is the adequate expression of a proposition.[50]

Nothing is meaningful until it is interpreted within the experiential consciousness of the hearer. Just as words have no meaning in themselves except the meanings which are agreed upon by a group speaking the same language, just so, messages have no meaning except that the hearers supply the imaginative link between the sign and symbols of the message and the hearer's store of experiences, beliefs, attitudes, and values. Thus, the subjective phenomena of listening and understanding messages in an educational leadership situation are fundamental to the process of communication of educational leaders. What happens when the message as a totality is received by all the senses and acknowledged within the consciousness of an educational leader during the communication process? What are the internal phenomena of communication? What are the subjective aspects of the three phases of the communication process?

Beyond following the few basic rules of formal speech construction and transmission, what can an educational leader do to improve communication? Without question, the most important thing a leader can do is to listen to the followers before he or she begins to speak. A speaker can do very little to cause an audience to listen to what he or she is saying. A leader must communicate something which the followers want to hear, and how does the leader know what the followers want and need to hear without first listening to what the hearers are saying. St. Francis of Assisi advocated this important attitude in his prayer when he said, "Lord, grant that I may not seek so much to be understood as to understand." The one aspect of the communication process over which I have the most control is whether I am willing to listen to those to whom I am trying to communicate.

Carl Rogers called this attitude toward his clients, "active listening." As a therapist Rogers believed that he must take responsibility for what he heard from those whom he was counseling. He claimed that we could not be active listeners until we are able to demonstrate a spirit which genuinely respects the potential worth of the individual, which considers that person's rights, and which trusts his or her capacity for self–direction. [51] An active listener tries to grasp the speaker's point of view, to get inside the speaker, and to convey to the speaker that he or she is really seeing things from the speaker's point of view. In order to test whether you are seeing things the way the speaker is seeing them, the listener reports to the speaker what has been heard. This restatement of the speaker's message should be accurate enough to satisfy the speaker. Listening behavior is contagious; listening demonstrates respect for and interest in the thoughts, feelings, and welfare of the speaker.

The listening attitude is indispensable in the communication process of educational leaders. An educational leader is bound up with the listeners to the extent that the common language of both the leader and the followers is rooted in the values and beliefs of both parties in the communication process.

To distinguish this kind of listening from the formal and technical aspects of listening without ears, the expression "listening with the heart" might be helpful. Listening with the heart is "being–with" the speaker in such a way that you are caught up in a common existence, a common life. Shortly before he died, Carl Rogers wrote that really hearing a person put him in touch with a client, enriching his own life. Rogers described listening to others as "listening to the music of the spheres," elevating the listening situation into a universal realm. [52] Listening with the heart is wanting the best for the speaker. You not only hear what is being said, but you respond in an appropriate way. You feel responsible for what is said. You take the message into your life and react to it in order that the other person is helped by what is communicated. In short, listening with the heart is loving the other person. We build up a relationship of trust, sharing, openness, and respect.

An educational leader can control only what he or she does in the communication process. Trying to control what the followers hear is likely to result in misunderstanding, rejection, and reduction of the content of a message when it is remembered.

David Johnson has examined the effectiveness of expressing different variations of warmth and anger on obtaining cooperation in the speaker and the listener. He found that more cooperative behavior in listeners resulted from the invariant expression of warmth and love, and the least cooperative behavior in listeners resulted from the invariant expression of anger and disrespect. However, the expression of anger followed by the expression of warmth resulted in the greatest "public" agreement of listeners with the speaker. [53] This study suggests that the educational leader who expresses love, warmth, concern, and respect for the listeners will have the greatest influence on the listeners' attitudes and behavior.

Communication basically is a process in which there is some predictable relation between the message transmitted and the message received. Realistically, communication does not occur without some indication that the intended receiver has been listening to the message which is sent. A speaker can perform all the formal and physical phenomena of transmitting a message perfectly, but if the message is in a foreign language, communication probably will not occur. The accuracy of the communication process can only be checked by ascertaining what the listener has heard. Systems theory has emphasized the importance of the feedback processes to verify the accuracy of communication. Since almost all processes of communication are cyclical, the communication circuit or loop is not complete until the sender of a message receives some reaction from the recipient of the message. Thus, communication is a two-way process that requires some kind of closure of the set of communicative acts involved in the transmission, reception, and reaction to a message.

An educational leader who is communicating effectively is careful not to overlook the two-way dimension of communication. Failure to provide feedback and to listen to feedback is to cut the communication loop and to interrupt the communication process. Providing feedback which clarifies meanings and is useful demonstrates respect and concern for both the speaker and the listener. Feedback, in turn, will strengthen the influence of a leader on followers.

Thus, communication is not just a series of communicative acts which occur between a message sender and a recipient, but is a cyclical process which occurs in relation to a social system. The structures and functions of a given social system will be reflected in the frame of reference and way of thinking of the communication of the members of the social system. The communication process must be viewed as a whole and not as isolated acts of individuals.

The subjective dimensions of the communication process are vital factors in educational leadership. Those often overlooked subjective factors set educational leaders apart from non-leaders.

HERMENEUTICS AND UNDERSTANDING MESSAGES

Hermeneutics recognizes the ambivalence of the communication process. A message transmits meaning, but it can also cover up the meaning and deceive the recipient of the message. Heidegger's discussion of truth treats the relation of language to reality in terms of the "unconcealing" (Greek *alethia*-- "truth"), of that which is communicated. [54] That which is communicated is not a picture of reality, but only a representation of the message of the messenger. The medium of the message may conceal or cover up the verbal meaning of the message, and thereby, may deceive or mislead the recipient. Thus, the central issue of hermeneutics is the integrity and intention of the message maker rather than the logical accuracy of the language or the formal techniques of transmission of the message. Sometimes speech is little more than idle talk; words are passed along, but the meanings of the messages are concealed and misleading. Hermeneutics is an attempt to expose the intended meanings of the message sender rather than the meanings of the words of the message content.

The intentionality of the communication process also involves how the hearer interprets the message. Sociologists of knowledge have tried to clarify the relationship between the experience of knowing and the interpersonal experience of sharing knowledge. Meaning in a social exchange is a function of what has been called *Verstehen*, the interpretive understanding through which the individual comprehends the person speaking. [55] A sociology of knowledge is based on a phenomenology of the social location of knowledge (German, *Sitz im Leben*). The predefined reality of the individual, as it is subjectively understood and socially expressed in everyday life, has been one of the major concerns of sociologists of knowledge. The sociology of knowledge must of necessity explore the structures of social interaction and communication. Thus, communication plays a vital role in the social construction of reality.

How the receiver interprets the message is influenced by the social construction of the meaning of the message, as well as by the receiver's perception of the meaning of the message. The meanings of words, syntax, and language are definitely socially determined. Edward T. Hall, an anthropologist, regards culture itself as a medium of communication and says that man's total life ("the silent language") is a form of communication. [56] What the hearer understands in the communication process involves the way society impacts on the meaning of the message.

Once while visiting an inner city high school in Louisville, Kentucky, a principal talked to me about one of those end-of-the-school-year crises which had consumed most of his morning. A senior Black girl had been sent to his office with a message from an irate teacher who said that the student had called her an S.O.B. and that she never wanted to see the student again. After finally calming the angry, weeping student enough to be rational, the principal said he asked the student why in the world she had called the teacher an S.O.B., realizing she only had a few days before graduation. The student said, "I did not mean anything by the remark. My father calls my mother that all the time, and my mom doesn't react the way the teacher did." Obviously, what S.O.B. meant in the teacher's culture was entirely different from what it meant in the student's culture.

A whole realm of tacit knowledge, the context, the horizon, the milieu, the environment, and the setting, affects how an individual understands a message. The person may not be aware of the total surroundings of everything on which his or her attention is fixed, but the context colors how the person sees and interprets the thing observed. While focusing on a nail which one is attempting to drive with a hammer, one is also subsidiarily aware of the hammer, the board, the movement of the arm and body, and the whole environment in which the nail is being driven. While viewing this page you are now reading, you are seeing it in a particular setting with certain lighting conditions, on a desk, with other books around it, etc. All these peripheral objects in the field of vision affect what is seen to some degree. Similarly, the meaning of a message of any sort is conditioned and shaped by the context and social situation in which the message is received.

Communication of an educational leader is a total process which includes the subjective experience of creating or encoding a message, but also includes the action or project of transmitting or expressing the message verbally and nonverbally. The communication process encompasses the receiving, hearing, understanding, and decoding of the message by the follower. The educational leader is the message, the leader is the medium of the message, and the leader is the meaning of the message.

EDUCATIONAL LEADERSHIP AS DIALOGUE

The outcome of effective communication between educational leaders and their followers is an interactive relationship. Looking at the complex transactions which occur between leaders and followers, we begin to see just how important is the consideration of the dialogical nature of educational leadership. The meaningful relationships between educational leaders and their constituencies are fundamentally dialogical.

What is dialogue? Dialogue as described by Martin Buber is the total communication and response between persons in which there is an exchange of meaning between the persons in spite of the barriers which tend to block the relationship. In dialogue, each person experiences the other person as an individual of worth and potential and not as a subject over against an object. The principle of dialogue is an openness of the other person, with a willingness to respond to what is heard, as well as to speak. Dialogue not only takes the other person seriously, but also takes responsibility for what transpires between persons. Realizing that a person is significantly determined by human choices, dialogue advocates that educational leaders make choices which respect, support, and encourage learners in the total process of education.[57]

"Being-with" the Educational Constituency

Both Heidegger and Buber emphasize the impossibility of human existence without the existence of others. Existence implies not only being-in-the-world, but also being-with-others. Just as there is a world of things apart from which humans cannot exist, a personal environment of other people is assumed in human existence. One cannot envision human existence without the existence of other people.[58] The existence of others is a necessity of thought, not a problem of thought. As the book implies an author, a meal implies the cook, and police imply laws, so does the constitution of the being of one person imply the existence of another person. The nature of being a human (*Dasein*) is a being-in-common, a shared human existence in which the social interdependence of our everyday experience is primordial and constitutive. One's full self-consciousness, self-affirmation, and identity derive from the consciousness of others.[59]

Reflection on what it means to exist as a human being indicates that the existence of one individual as a person of worth, dignity, and human identity is delusive without the existence of another human being. In other words, personal identity is established by recognition of kinship with other humans and by the response of commonality by other individuals. Social or communal reality makes selfhood and personal identity possible. Both sexuality and language development confirm that no individual is complete without other humans. The male is only half of the human reproductive system, and the solitary existence of all human beings would obviously result in the biological extinction of the human species. Similarly, the presence of language implies an agreement with others on the meaning of symbols and language patterns. Without this implied dependence on others, language and communication would be impossible, and human existence would not be possible.

Thus, social relationships between educational leaders and their followers are grounded in what it means to exist meaningfully in the world. The very nature of being–in–the–world spatially and temporally is being–with–others socially. The foundation of all interpersonal relationships is the recognition that each human being is more like other humans than anything else in the world. The values and beliefs which are common to what makes human existence meaningful are the foundational stones of interpersonal relationships between educational leaders and followers. Being–in–the–world in the sense of being constituted by one's projects and by one's relations with objects which one makes use of and develops as tools for realizing them involves being–with–others who are also in the world in the same sense.

One can free oneself from this or that preoccupation but not from preoccupation itself. In the same manner one can free oneself from dependence upon this or that person but not completely from social relations.

In contrast to those theories which assume that interpersonal relationships can be explained in terms of conformity to externally originating, absolute patterns (bureaucracy) or in terms of stimulus–response patterns which conform to natural laws (behaviorism), the dialogue principle explains both the leader's and follower's behavior and organizational structure in terms of the meanings intended by the subjects who are involved. The meaning of interpersonal relationships is the holistic movement which gathers together self, others, and the environment in the subjectively structured consciousness of the subjects. Thus, the very foundations of educational leadership rest on the dialogical principle.

The educational leader who is following the dialogue principle does not tell a learner that a light will appear someday at the end of the dark tunnel, nor does the leader just reinforce those behaviors which lead toward the light at the end of the tunnel, but rather the educational leader takes the learner by the hand and experiences the darkness and the light at the end of the tunnel by "being–with–the–learner." A knowing subject is brought face–to–face with a knowing subject, and all subjects involved in the educational process readjust their knowledge to meet the shared view of reality.

Leaders Experiencing the Other Side

Buber's description of the relationship between the teacher and the learner is relationship of "pure dialogue."[60] Dialogue is an interaction between two persons in which each tries to give and to receive out of the fullness of the Being and Presence of both subjects. The dialogical relation is characterized more or less by the element of inclusion.

"Experiencing the other side," "mutual inclusion," and "friendship" are Buber's ways of identifying the nature of the dialogical relationship. Thus, the educational leader tries to feel what it means to be a follower, and the followers try to feel what it means to be a leader. Each tries to feel from "over there" the acceptance and rejection of what is presented to the subjects. The leader empathizes with the followers who in turn empathize with the leader; the leader is aware of the meaning of policies and procedures from the followers' points of view just as the followers try to see the policies from the leader's perspective. Only as the leaders know the followers and are known by them in dialogue will people follow a leader without being compelled or tricked. Dialogue implies an openness to the other side with a willingness not only to speak and to act, but also to respond to what is heard and experienced. True educational leaders draw their followers into an implicit dialogue in such a way that the leader's goals and values become the catalyst which activates similar values in the followers.

Sartre includes a classic description of the nature of dialogue in *No Exit*, when one of its characters suggests that each person try to forget the presence of the other. Inez replies:

Forget? How silly can you get! I feel you even in my bones.
Your silence shrieks in my ears. You can nail up your mouth,

cut your tongue out, but how can that keep you from being there? Can you stop thinking? I hear it, ticking away like an alarm clock, and I know you hear me thinking . . . You are everywhere, and every sound comes to me soiled, because you've intercepted it on its way.[61]

Humans are so inseparably bound in community that others are obstacles to the fulfillment of existence. Thus, Sartre declares in the interchange above that "Hell is other people." Educational leaders and followers are so bound up in a common existence that dialogue is a fundamental characteristic of educational leadership.

Friendship, trust, respect, love, forgiveness, honesty, patience, joy, humility, faithfulness, and praise and support of learners are imperative ingredients of educational leaders. Learners will be happier, will learn faster, and will score higher on tests in an environment characterized by the dialogue principle. However, these human virtues are not to be mistaken for the "hands off," "do-what-you-want," undisciplined atmosphere which some educators advocate. Dialogue is a basic respect for the welfare and value of others as participants in the same humanity. Both leaders and learners are subjects who are bound up in the same human existence. Teachers are not simply passing along knowledge nor reminding learners what they have learned but forgotten; neither are teachers manipulating and managing the behavior of learners; rather, teachers are sharing in the knowing and changing of the learners as participants in the educational process.

Dialogical Schools

A society which is formed on the basis of dialogue is distinctly personal. Subjects who are met in the world are persons, not objects belonging to the world. Persons are acknowledged as co-existents in the world. The other person is a center of concern in terms of which the world is structured in the same way that the I-subject is in the world. Thus, the nature of the social structure which grows out of dialogue is community and not coercion, manipulation, or compulsion.

Dialogical leadership binds the individual and the collective into a community. Neither the leader nor the learners are solitary individuals who are totally separate from each other. Community cannot be one-sided; community consists of openness and willingness to listen and to receive as well as to speak and to give advice. Neither is the dialogical leader an authority over a collection of individuals where pressure, force, and threat are employed to mold individuals into whatever type of person the leader desires. Personal identity is swallowed by the mass-production dynamics of crowds and collectives. Dialogical educational leaders do not control, dominate, oppress, intimidate, or manipulate learners; they live-with the learners.

Paulo Freire applied dialogical leadership to the education of peasants in Brazil. Freire's revolutionary leadership concept recognizes the need for leaders to dialogue with the potential learners. Freire maintains that a truly revolutionary leader must be "in communion" with the people who are being led.[62] He insists that learners must find themselves in the emerging leaders, and the leaders must find themselves in the learners. Going to the people in a dialogical manner produces an almost immediate empathy between the learners and their leader. Commitment between the learners and the leaders is almost instantly sealed. This sense of community creates a fellowship of co-equal discontent with those forces which dominate and oppress the people. Once the sense of community is felt among the leaders and learners, the practice of dialogue between the leaders and the learners is almost unshakable. When the people feel that they are able to control their own destinies, they know that they have come to the power of being human as a community.

Dialogical leadership does not lead to laissez-faire, extremely individualistic leadership patterns. In dialogue the leader and the learners are respected and trusted for their being-with-each-other in their being-in-the-world. Trust in the leader is simply a mirror of the leader's trust of the learners. Dialogical leadership results in communion and trust between the leaders and the learners.

Freire notes that revolutionaries are fused in a genuinely human action. He says that communion elicits cooperation, and cooperation brings leaders and people to the fusion. This social fusion exists only if revolutionary leadership is really human, empathetic, loving, communicative, humble, and liberating.[63] The unity expressed by this kind of communion occurs at the human level, but not at the level of things and ideas. Dialogical communion is desperately needed in the educational leadership process. Much that is wrong with education today could be improved by applying the dialogical principle.

Brian was generally disinterested in what was happening during the first six weeks of third grade, staring out the window day after day. Miss Parks invited Brian's parents in for a conference. Brian's second grade teacher, Miss Adams, had entered in his personnel folder, "Brian is slow and has a learning disability." Miss Adams had told Brian that he was a slow learner so many times that he had begun to believe it, although Brian had been in the top five students in his class the prior two years in another school system. The mother explained to Miss Parks that Brian had been in an open classroom arrangement for the first two years and was confused by the "military" atmosphere of Miss Adams' classroom which was governed by "The Ten Commandments for Students" which was prominently displayed in the front of the room. The day after the conference with Brian's parents Miss Parks told Brian she wanted to see him after school. Miss Parks talked to Brian about his lack of interest in class; she told him that she believed that he could do everything they would be doing in third grade. Then, Miss Parks reached down and put her arms around Brian and told him she loved him and wanted to help him have fun in school in third grade. Brian's performance dramatically changed without any other special attention. Later in the school year Miss Parks recommended that Brian be placed in the gifted and talented program. Brian's parents to this day believe that a little love and care from Miss Parks totally transformed Brian's entire school career. The tragedy of this true story is that it could be multiplied thousands of times, but without the same fortunate outcome. Many students never get the benefit of love and concern which Miss Parks provides her students.

Miss Parks was in communion with her students; she shared their desire to become better persons. Leaders like Miss Parks would turn a school into a community of learning where students and teachers participate in a common life.

Blessed Are Those in Dialogue

How does one reconcile the fundamentally communal nature of educational leadership with the fact that the human relations movement in administration has been individualistic almost to the point of "anything goes" or that scientific management has been collectivistic to the point of exploitation and dehumanization of employees? Analyzing human relations in the dialogue principle results in the conclusion that social relations are sadly distorted among humans. The everyday relations with one another are inauthentic; these relations do not involve the selves of those who are taking part in social transactions and do not flow from the whole selves of participants. The togetherness we normally observe is not real community. What we find more often is a distortion of the communication between parties and a hiding of the real significance of social transactions. The individual needs to take responsibility for his or her own authenticity in social relations.

Kierkegaard has warned us that the individual can be swallowed by the concept of "crowd" and can become completely irresponsible, sold to the collective mass. Nietzsche followed with the idea that the "herd" will allow the individual to exist only as a part of the whole, only in favor of the whole. The herd concept tends to reduce all members to the lowest common denominator, to the level of the mediocre, the familiar, the harmless. The faceless, anonymous "they" (*das Man*) of Heidegger removes choice and responsibility and deprives the other of true selfhood. This third–person perspective of others implies that "they" are objects out there twice removed from the dialogical relation which exists between "I" and "You." Thus, being–with–others as if they were objects is an inauthentic mode of being human because it deprives the others of their rightful estate as persons of worth and respect. Inauthentic relationships suppress the genuinely human and personal identity of humans. To try to remove care from the Other and put oneself in place of the Other, i.e., "to *leap in*" for the other is to put the Other out of the position of respect and dominates and subordinates the Other.[64] Any kind of relating to others which depersonalizes and dehumanizes them is an inauthentic mode of human existence and cannot be called community. Authentic relating is that mode of relating which promotes human existence in its fullest sense, i.e., humans stand out as humans who are responsible and free to become what they have the potential to become.

Dialogical leadership in education is an authentic mode of relating. The dialogical leader responds with his or her whole being, listening with the heart and hoping for the Other's best. Willing and able to disclose himself or herself to others, a dialogical leader makes openness, honesty, trust, and love a way of relating. Just as the leader meets, draws out, and forms the followers; in like manner, the followers transform the leader. Followers in a dialogical relation tend to become leaders.

Dialogical leaders work hard to make others participants in decision making and policy formation because others are trusted and respected as participants in a common existence. At the same time, dialogical leaders accept the limitations of relating authentically. Finally, the nature of dialogical leadership is based ontologically on those values and aims of the educational leaders and their constituents to the extent that the educational process contributes to the human individual's authentic and meaningful existence.

A lawyer once came to Jesus of Nazareth and said, "Teacher, what can I do to inherit eternal life?" (Lk. 10:25) Or, as reported by Matthew (Mt. 22:36), "Teacher, what is the greatest commandment in the law?" To both questions Jesus responded, "You should love God with all your heart, soul, and mind, and your neighbor as yourself." After the lawyer seemed to agree concerning the importance of loving God, he was still puzzled and asked, "And just who is my neighbor?" The Teacher of Nazareth told the lawyer an immortal story ("The Parable of the Good Samaritan") of a man who fell among thieves, was beaten, and was left on the side of the road to die. A priest and then a Levite (both religious functionaries) came by and saw the injured man, but did not stop to help. A hated Samaritan also came by and stopped to help, carrying the man to an inn and paying for his lodging. The point of the story is that those who can see themselves in the ditches of life when they see others in ditches have seen a part of that which is eternal in human beings.

Dialogical leadership is "Seeing oneself as the person in the ditch" in the sense of "being the victim in the ditch." The happiness and welfare of others is a part of the world in which the dialogical leader participates. The bottom line is that the dialogical leader is happy and fulfilled when the follower-learners are happy and fulfilled as persons.

In his brilliant discussion of what it means to be human in this world, Ashley Montagu postulates the indisputable existence in organic life of deep-seated potentialities toward socialization. He presents evidence which indicates that isolated animals will, in general, be retarded in growth, be irremediably damaged, or even die; whereas, animals living communally with others will grow faster and bigger, will recover from greater wounds, and will survive more often. Montagu cites research which indicates that planarian worms which are exposed to ultraviolet radiation disintegrate more rapidly when alone than when associated in groups. He cites another experiment in which ten goldfish are placed in a tank of colloidal silver which would kill any one of the fish, but together the ten fish secreted a slime which neutralized much of the toxin in the water, allowing the ten fish to live in the water. Thus, Montagu argues that social life confers a distinct biological advantage on its participants,that the dominant principle of social life is not the struggle for existence, but cooperation, and that some form of social life is coeval with life itself.[65]

Dialogical leadership operates on the basis of the social nature of both educators and learners. What happens in a educational leadership event is the participation of all parties in a form of social existence which is greater than the individual existence of either the leader or the learner. All parties are caught up in a common existence of which the educational community is only an event in a chain of existence.

LEADING IN THE FUTURE–PERFECT TENSE

Peter Drucker notes that the one thing which growth enterprises have in common other than growth and defiance of economic stagnation is an entrepreneurial leader.[66] And the one thing which all leaders have in common is a vision of a desirable future as if it already exists in the present (the nature of the future–perfect tense of the verb in English). The Danish philosopher, Soren Kierkegaard, said that life must be lived forwards, but it can only be understood by looking backwards. Leaders want to know what life in the future will be; what it will mean; what we can know about the future; what we ought to change in the future; what we can reasonably hope to come true in the future. Whether it is a vision of a spherical universe by Copernicus, a dream of a just society by Martin Luther King, Jr., a Utopia by Plato, an image of a man on the moon by John F. Kennedy, an ideal way to fry chicken by Harlan Sanders, or what the United States might be if public education were free by Horace Mann, all leaders envision a possible, preferable, and probable future state of human existence. Former President Ronald Reagan is reported to have told students at Moscow State University in June of 1988: "To grasp and hold a vision, to fix it in your senses––that is the very essence, I believe, of successful leadership not only on the movie set, where I learned about it, but everywhere."

Passion for the Possible

Central to the definition of leadership is a person who has been variously described as charismatic, visionary, entrepreneur, messiah, guru, innovator, magnate, miracle–worker, revolutionary, genius, etc. An educational leader is one who foresees the unforeseen, who conceives the inconceivable, who penetrates the unknown, who takes the path not taken, who fuses the finite and the infinite, who immortalizes the mortal, who sees visions and dreams dreams, and who brings the future into the present. Merleau-Ponty, a disciple of Husserl, describes political leadership as a human quality that causes leaders to animate the political process and that makes their most personal acts the affairs of everyone.[67]

A twenty-eight-year-old William Paley took over a debt-ridden, station-less CBS in 1928 and in ten years had turned it into a 114-station, $27.7 million business. According to David Halberstam, Paley started only with a vision, a sense of what might be, and he envisioned an audience at a time when there was in fact no audience with radios.[68]

Leaders not only are able to conceptualize a possible and preferable future for the followers; they also formulate solutions for the troubles and fears of the followers; and then they personify the emotional, physical, economic, spiritual, and social benefits which the followers perceive the leader to be capable of accomplishing. Both the leader and the followers are addressed. Leaders in a very real sense are doing things, saying things, and exemplifying aims, values, and goals which the followers want to incorporate in their own self constitution.

Hadley Cantril studied Hitler's rise to power and concluded that Germany needed an image of a person with whom they could identify, a leader to whom they could give their troubles and by whom they could be saved. Hitler personified the goals and desires of the future Germany. Hitler shouted, "You are Germany! We are Germany!" The people responded, "You are our man. You are a working man. You are giving your whole being to Germany." In fact, Hitler himself used the greeting, "Heil Hitler," because he had become an image, a personification, of the desirable future of Germany.[69]

James M. Kouzes and Barry Z. Posner found that hundreds of the leaders whom they studied shared a common characteristic of "envisioning the future, of gazing across the horizon of time and imagining that greater things are ahead."[70] Business leaders are expected to paint the big picture of what the whole puzzle will be when all the pieces are in place. Educational leaders, no less, must become futurists.

Educational leaders are those individuals who personify the goals, values, and desires of those who have bought into the process of education as a way of realizing a desirable future. Thus, one of the central functions of an educational leader is to conceptualize, dream, and contemplate what the aims and values of the educational constituency are and what they ought to be. Call this intuitive capacity whatever you wish, but great educational leaders will be great dreamers, visionaries, speculators, prophets, and futurists.

Educational leaders, as all leaders, think in the future perfect tense, but "thinking in the future perfect tense" does not refer to speculation without foundation, crystal ball gazing, fortune telling, or predicting what will happen. Although dreams, visions, wishes, possibilities, and potentialities are very much a part of futuristic thinking, thinking in the future perfect tense is not a leap toward the future without realizing the connectedness of the future with the present and the past. Leaders who are thinking in the future perfect tense are trying to actualize the future in the present, not trying to live in the future.

Some educators are beginning to see the relevance of probing the possible. Instead of building curriculum on the traditions, ideals, values, and societies of the past, educators need to be exposing learners to alternative futures. Learners need to engage in divergent and creative thinking. Thinking in the future perfect tense is not optional with educational leaders; a passion for the possible is integral to being a leader. To paraphrase a very old prophet, "Where there is no vision, the people have no leaders and soon perish."

Planning for the Probable Future

The difference between fortune telling and educational leaders who are thinking in the future perfect tense is one of knowledge, connectedness, systematization, commitment, and concern for the learners. Whereas predicting the future is concerned with what will happen, futuristic thinking tells us what can happen, what we can change, and what we can do to encourage change to happen. The ultimate goal of most thinking in the future perfect tense is to provide images of where we want to go and how we can get there. Thus, leaders are involved in planning how the future is actualized in the present.

Leaders envision plans to bring their dreams to fruition, while fortune tellers try to guess where we will be in the future without any way of telling us how to get there. Churchill envisioned a victory during the Second World War, but not without "blood, sweat, and tears." Lech Walesa envisions a free and democratic Europe and is willing to wait and pay for it with hard work and imprisonment. Bishop Tutu and Nelson Mandela see an end to apartheid in South Africa, but not without a realization of what freedom will cost them and their people.

Successful leaders are armed with knowledge of their followers and their goals, as well as plans, programs, and strategies to get there.

Philosophically, anyone who claims to predict what will happen in the future assumes that the future is predetermined by some power in the universe. The astrologer or fortune teller must obtain knowledge of how this power determines what will happen. However, a natural determinism also assumes that physical principles are fixed to the extent that the future can be predicted. The effective leader, on the other hand, is not so concerned with predicting what will happen in the future as "interpreting" how future events and trends impact on the present. Knowledge of the context of the leadership situation is essential to leadership. Plans for the future are made on the basis of an interpretation of a probable image of the future.

Successful leaders do not wait until they are struck by a "bright idea" or are inspired to revolutionize the world, or to change education. They go to work on what is a probable future. Peter Drucker, the father of innovation in management, says that systematic innovation consists in a purposeful and organized search for changes, and in a systematic analysis of the opportunities which such changes offer for innovation. Drucker identifies seven sources for innovative opportunities: unexpected successes, failures, and outside events; incongruities between reality as it actually is and as it "ought to be"; innovation based on need within a field, such as education; changes in the structure of a field that catches everyone unawares; changes in demographics; changes in perception, mood, and meaning within a field; and new knowledge, both scientific and nonscientific in a field of innovation. And contrary to what most think, science-based innovation is the least reliable and least predictable source of successful innovations, whereas the mundane and unglamorous analysis of unexpected successes and failures is less risky and more certain to result in innovation.[71]

This intellectual construction of a probable future has developed into a full-blown, academically recognized science called "futurology," (different titles are used in other disciplines). Futurism has invaded education and is taught as a separate discipline in schools of education throughout the United States and the world.

Educational leaders must be involved in shaping alternative ways of thinking about the future. Albert Szent-Györgi noted that the very survival of human beings will depend on how successful we are in changing our ways of looking at the future and planning for a probable future:

> We live in a new cosmic world which man was not made for. His survival now depends on how well and how fast he can adapt himself to it, rebuilding all his ideas, all his social and economic and political structures. His existence depends on the question of whether he can adapt himself faster than the hostile forces can destroy him. At present, he is clearly losing out.
>
> We are forced to face this situation with our caveman's brain, a brain that has not changed much since it was formed. We face it with our outdated thinking, institutions and methods, with political leaders who have their roots in the old world and think the only way to solve these formidable problems is by trickery and double talk.[72]

Leaders in the schools of tomorrow do not think of the future as simply an extension of past or present trends. Change and uncertainty have become an integral aspect of our culture, and educational leaders must imagine a future which is probable and is manageable. Certain forces in our world are threats to the survival of life on this planet. Therefore, education must participate in visions of the future which extend beyond the limits of conventional thinking and interpretation of the facts. Just knowing about the future does not guarantee its reality. Unexpected knowledge and events over which we have little or no control will have a major impact on our future. Envisioning a probable future has never been as important in educational leadership as it is today.

Alvin Toffler, a noted futurist, advocates a "practicopia," instead of a utopia, as a vision of the future. A "practicopia" is a realistic and practical view of the future, but is not a utopia. A practicopia offers a positive, revolutionary alternative, which lies within the realm of the attainable.[73] The practicopia allows for individual differences and embraces racial, regional, religious, and subcultural differences. It is built primarily around the home and is pulsing with innovation. The new civilization will emphasize art and will need new ethical and moral standards to deal with new and complex issues, but it has the potential to be humane and democratic without dependence on exploitative subsidies from the rest of the world. Present changes point to a workable counter civilization, an alternative to the present trends. Two things cut through everything as the Third Wave thunders in our ears. One is the shift toward a higher level of diversity in society--emphasis on individualization. Second is a faster pace at which historical change will occur.

Images of the future, knowledge of past and present trends, emotional and affective sensitivity, demographic trends, emotional and affective sensitivity, demographic settings, and value structures are essential to planning for a probable future. One of the very useful tools for planning the future is the scientific method. In fact, the scientific method is uniquely suited to the prediction of a probable future, but just predicting what will likely occur is not nearly enough. Educational leaders must do something to plan and prepare for the future. Visions and images of the future must include how life and education will mix in everyday life.

Educational leaders participate in a shared vision of the future. An effective educational leader will envision how the followers will contribute to the vision of the future and will be caught up in the future of those who are following the innovative leader.

Pursuing a Preferable Future

"The time has come for educators to find their own voices, tap their own experiences, and decide what they want things to be," said Maxine Greene at the third annual Maycie K. Southhall Distinguished Lecture Series during the 1987–88 academic year at Vanderbilt University. Greene is echoing what business leaders are saying loud and clear: new leaders must win the trust of followers in part by making clear that they have certain values and that these values will shape what the leader wants the future to be. John McHale contends that the question is not whether we can change the world, but what kind of world we want.[74] Of all the possible and probable futures an educational leader may envision, what is the preferred state of affairs? Alice learned from the Cheshire cat that if she did not know where she wanted to go, it did not matter which path she took. If educational leaders do not know which goals and values are preferred, they are likely to perpetuate what has been or what others pressure them to become.

Educational leaders should not rely only on descriptive analysis of present or past trends and predict what is going to happen; leaders must attempt to envision future needs and goals to determine what norms and goals will lead the followers to the preferred state. After imagining carefully what we want the future to be, then we should work backwards toward the present, determining what values and actions will move us toward our desired future. Leaders who are able to envision a reasonable and desirable future are more likely to lead the followers in a desired direction than those leaders who simply try to predict what will happen so that followers can adjust to predetermined principles or natural laws or those leaders who try to lead the followers backwards to the past traditions and goals of earlier schools.

The process of choosing a preferred future implies a commitment of energy and self to the direction which the leader has decided to move. Investing self and other personal resources in the image of the desired future will draw the leader into the fulfillment of the image. What leader in society is in a better position to envision a desirable future and to then become a part of the fulfillment of that vision than is an educational leader? It is no accident that the utopian schemes developed by Plato, Augustine, Rousseau, and others include a system of education. Those systems of education imply a whole series of values and ideals about what it is that the utopian architects hope for human beings and for a future society. Hanna Holborn Gray, President of the University of Chicago, made the following comment at a symposium, "Corporations at Risk: Liberal Learning and Private Enterprise," held by the Corporate Council on Liberal Arts on September 3, 1986, Cambridge, Massachusetts:

> In other words, thinking about education is a way of reflecting on the future, and the future that one would like to see; it is a way of thinking about the present, and what it is that is deficient within the present; and finally, it is a way of thinking about the past, and seeing what it is within the past that needs either to be repudiated or renewed. Education then becomes the instrument, or the vehicle, for this way of thinking about a larger world and about the essence of what human possibility, human personality, and human competence might ideally become within a social order.[75]

In a discussion of entrepreneurship in the service institutions, Drucker contends that innovation is needed more in service institutions such as schools than in any business. The rapid change occurring in today's society presents both great opportunity and great danger for service institutions. Drucker concludes that the public school exemplifies both the opportunity and the dangers. Unless schools take the lead in innovation, they may not survive this century, except as schools for the minorities in the slums.[76] Allowing for innovation in the public schools may be the foremost social challenge of the next generation. Educational leaders must know what kind of future is best for us, and they must be involved in bringing that future to the present.

Educational leaders have a unique responsibility to create and cultivate visions of a preferred future. They must serve as models of the very best that our society has to offer. They must aggressively promote values and standards which are basic to a good and meaningful life for all. Most of all, they must dream and articulate means, as well as ends, that will call people away from exploitative, meaningless, degrading, disruptive, and inhuman projects and raise their sights to unifying, fulfilling, liberating, and life-enhancing pursuits which are worthy of the best our world has to offer.

THE ART OF EDUCATIONAL LEADERSHIP

If educational leadership is based on being more than acquisition of an organized body of knowledge and performance of a set of behaviors, then educational leadership is very much an art. Indeed, being a leader in an educational setting is an art which requires great discernment, vision, empathy, love, values, skills, as well as scientific know-how not unlike an artist who paints in oil or an architect who designs buildings. Heidegger's concept of being-with-others is an expression of the whole being and is similar to what creative and performing artists do when they practice their art. Artists express who they are in and through their art media. A painting by an artist is often referred to by the name of its painter, e.g., "a Picasso." Who would deny that Frank Lloyd Wright is deeply and personally identified with the style of architecture he designed? Wright is reported to have said, "A doctor can bury his mistakes, but an architect can only advise his clients to plant vines." Is not the same true of what a leader does? Look at the leaders in your school. That elusive, yet unmistakable, dimension of leadership which goes beyond personal traits, scientific methods, and behavior styles is the same process required of the practice of an art form or a craft. Being an educational leader is an art form if practiced as a total experience of the leader.

The art of educational leadership is certainly not the antithesis of leadership as a science. A recent textbook on management displays the contrast between management as an art over against management as a science. The result, which is typical, sets up a continuum with pure art on one end and pure science on the other end. On the artistic end, management is characterized as visionary, whimsical, intuitive, visceral, naive, highly subjective, fanciful, impulsive, biased, unorganized, and idealistic.[77] Interestingly, the problem of viewing leadership as an art developed after administrative scientists (following the positivism of Herbert Simon) judged it to be "unscientific."

Some of the very best educational leaders I know are artists. In fact, when I think of the best teachers I have ever known, the overwhelming majority are teaching fine arts. To classify any one of them as "whimsical, visceral, naive, fanciful, impulsive, biased, or unorganized" is unthinkable and careless. These artists bring together a delicate balance of scientific knowledge and subjective experiences, logical reasoning, and creativity that results in followers who are exemplary in creation and promotion of the fine arts and of life in general. These artist–leaders are in the tradition of John Ruskin who said that fine art is that in which the hand, the head, and the heart of man go together. What higher compliment could be ascribed to an educational leader than possessing a delicate balance of practice, knowledge, sensitivity, creativity, lover of life, and aesthetic awareness?

Combining craft, vision, and communication is indispensable in the artistic process and is recognized by some to be important in responsible business management. Pascale and Athos characterized the kind of management practiced in Japan as an "art."[78] More to the point, Peter Vaill describes managing as a "performing art."[79] As an artist, the educational leader engages and involves the students and followers in the work of education itself. An educational leader is just as involved with followers as an artist is involved with viewers, listeners, or readers.

Educational leadership requires an imaginative grasp of the psychological, anthropological, sociological, philosophical, biological, and scientific aspects of the educational process. Whereas science focuses on analyzing, classifying, evaluating, and generalizing, the artist strives to find meaning in patterns, extrapolations, harmonies, contrasts, and wholes. A whole is more than the sum of its parts; that "more" is constituted by something internal, some inwardness of structure and function, some specific inner relation, some internality of character or nature. The educational leader as a total being is more vital than any collection of the leadership behaviors or personality traits. Educational leadership is a process of valuing, choosing, rejecting, relating, knowing, and acting, very much like an artist. The subjective, holistic, phenomenological dimensions of educational leadership are not mysterious or fanciful; rather, educational leadership requires a serious consideration of the values and visions of both leaders and followers. Educational leaders are those who can take the fragments of the educational process and form a meaningful whole, an educational process where students and other constituents learn how to live a meaningful and worthwhile life.

THE "IS-NESS" OF EDUCATIONAL LEADERSHIP

The nature, or "is-ness," of educational leadership is primarily ontological, i.e., an experience of "being" something. Now, what is it that an educational leader is "being?" The qualifier of the type of leadership which sets it apart from all other leadership is "educational," which implies a quality pertaining to the process, state, condition, or result of "drawing out" or "leading out" what individuals can become at their best. In contrast to changing behaviors or acquiring data, education is the whole process of making sense out of life. Education is "learning how to learn." Education refers to the state or condition of growing up and being the best one can be, not conforming to a predetermined standard, except in the sense of the minimal standards which qualify as a human being.

Growing up involves physical development, acquisition of beliefs, values, and knowledge, establishing communication, relating to others, becoming conscious of one's self, and accepting responsibility for being human. Education is becoming aware of the process of growing up. Learning in the educational process should be appropriate to the interest and welfare of the learner. Only that which is really known is learned through experiences which are personally appropriate. In that sense, life is education. The only subject-matter for education is Life in all its manifestations. [80]

Educational leaders need to be reminded of the nature of that which they are leading. Educational leaders are not trying to produce goods, make a profit, or market a gadget; therefore, care should be exercised not to impose business characteristics on educational leaders. By the same token, educational leaders are not preparing their clients for battle with hostile forces as a military establishment. Neither are religious causes parallel to those of educational leaders. Educational leaders are not trying to mobilize a body of people to support a particular view of government. However, the nature of political and religious leadership is closer to educational leadership than is the nature of business and military leadership. The uniqueness of educational leadership is rooted in education itself.

Just as education is never neutral, the consciousness of being an educational leader always actualizes toward the values which are basic to the educational constituents. Education is not simply the transference of knowledge, facts, and data from the brain cells of teachers to the receptacles of students; rather, it is a "knowing" in which both the knower and the learner participate in the reflection and action implicit in the knowledge. All knowledge is personal in the sense that our understanding of any fact is predicated on our construction of reality in which the situation of "knowing" occurs. We are always committed to a form of knowing which is consonant with the values and goals implicit in what is being taught and learned.

Thus, an educational leader "draws" the followers into his or her own construction of reality, and both the leader and the learners join in the quest of actualization of their common values. Neutrality of educational leadership is not possible. The very essence of educational leadership is a common search, reflection, and action which is based on a common set of values and beliefs.

What we have tried to show in this chapter is that educational leadership needs to be viewed as a total experience. Each facet of the experience can be examined only for purposes of exposing the meaning of the experience, but we experience the consciousness of leadership in education as a totality, not as a decision, communicating, or relating. When we look at the meaning of how we experience educational leadership, we interpret this consciousness in the same way we interpret a work of fine art. Thus, effective educational leadership is the practice of a delicate art.

CONCLUSION

Empirical studies of educational leadership have broken down leadership into skills and behaviors which are appropriate in order to achieve given objectives in the followers, or learners. Behaviors are sequenced in some logical and quantified hierarchy of the behavioral objectives which equal the complex whole. Learners are passive, inert objects which are in need of motivation, manipulation, management, modification, and measurement. Thus, leadership training attempts to equip leaders with knowledge and skills which will enable leaders to cause the followers to behave in accord with the leader's desires. The results of a strictly empirical approach to educational leadership has been disappointing and ineffective.

A phenomenological analysis of educational leadership is an alternative to the empirical approach. Setting aside the presuppositions and prejudices which researchers bring to their study of educational leadership helps us to focus on that which is most basic and meaningful to those who are experiencing educational leadership. Peeling away the layers of biases and presuppositions exposes a core of principles, practices, and interpretations which common to those who are leaders in the process of education.

Among those things which educational leaders experience in common are the following: self constitution of a person whom others want to follow; a view of the nature of humans which demands respect and allows for learning and growth; values and beliefs with which the educational constituency identifies; a holistic decision making process; a communication process which bonds the leader and the learners inseparably; a hermeneutics of understanding the meaning of leadership in an educational setting; a dialogical approach to interpersonal relationships between leaders and followers; abilities to envision a desirable future state of educational affairs; the practice of educational leadership as an art; and a philosophical concern which views educational leadership ontologically, i.e., as a global and holistic state of human existence in the educational process. Yet a consciousness of educational leadership demands that all of these common experiences, attitudes, beliefs, and values be held within an educational frame of reference. Further, that frame of reference must be anchored in the nature, or is-ness, of what it means to be an educational leader.

NOTES

1. Edmund Husserl, *Cartesian Meditations: An Introduction to Phenomenology*, trans. Dorion Cairns (The Hague: Martinus Nijhoff, 1977), 21.

2. Abraham H. Maslow, *Eupsychian Management: A Journal* (Homewood, Illinois: Richard D. Irwin, Inc. and The Dorsey Press, 1965), 122ff.

3. Ibid.

4. Harry Stack Sullivan, *The Interpersonal Theory of Psychiatry* (New York: W.W. Norton and Company, Inc., 1953), 250–51.

5. Frederick Herzberg, *Work and the Nature of Man* (New York: The New American Library, Inc., 1966).

6. Douglas McGregor, *The Human Side of Enterprise* (New York: McGraw–Hill Book Company, Inc., 1960).

7. Chris Argyris, *Personality and Organization* (New York: Harper and Row, Publishers, 1957).

8. Rensis Likert, *The Human Organization: Its Management and Value* (New York: McGraw–Hill Book Company, 1967).

9. David McClelland, et al., *The Achievement Motive* (New York: Appleton–Century–Crofts, Inc., 1953).

10. Paul Hersey and Kenneth H. Blanchard, *Management of Organizational Behavior: Utilizing Human Resources*, Fourth ed. (Englewood Cliffs, N.J.: Prentice–Hall, Inc., 1982), 309–10.

11. Herbert A. Simon, *Administrative Behavior*, Third ed. (New York: The Free Press, 1945, 1976), 45.

12. Ibid., 46.

13. Maurice Merleau–Ponty, *Phenomenology of Perception*, trans. Colin Smith (London: Routledge & Paul, 1962), 88.

14. See the instructive comments on philosophical anthropology in Wolfhart Pannenberg, *Anthropology in Theological Perspective*, trans. Matthew J. O'Connell (Philadelphia: The Westminister Press, 1985), 27–42, from which much of the preceding paragraph was derived.

15. Jurgen Habermas, *Zur Logik der Sozialwissenschaften* (Frankfort am Main: Suhrkamp Verlag, 1970), 107.

16. Ashley Montagu, *On Becoming Human* (New York: Hawthorn Books, 1950, 1966), 52.

17. Ibid.

18. Thomas J. Peters and Robert H. Waterman, Jr., *In Search of Excellence* (New York: Harper and Row, Publishers, 1982), 279.

19. Cited in Richard Tanner Pascale and Anthony G. Athos, *The Art of Japanese Management* (New York: Warner Books, Inc., 1981), 296.

20. Cited in Peters and Waterman, *In Search of Excellence*, 279.

21. Philip Selznick, *Leadership in Administration* (New York: Harper and Row, Publishers, 1957), 63.

22. William G. Ouchi, *Theory Z* (New York: Avon Books, 1982), 112.

23. Warren G. Schmidt and Barry Z. Posner, *Managerial Values and Expectations* (New York: AMACOM; An AMA Survey Report, 1982), 12.

24. Cited in Pascale and Athos, *The Art of Japanese Management*, 296–97.

25. Christopher Hodgkinson, *The Philosophy of Leadership* (New York: St. Martin's Press, 1983), 201.

26. William J. Reddin, *Managerial Effectiveness* (New York: McGraw–Hill Book Company, 1970), 45.

27. Edmund Husserl, *Ideas: General Introduction to Pure Phenomenology*, trans. W.R. Boyce Gibson (New York: Macmillan Publishing Company, Inc., 1937; Collier Books, 1962), 241.

28. Hodgkinson, *Philosophy of Leadership*, 229.

29. Cf. David M. Fetterman, *Ethnography: Step by Step* (Newbury Park, Calf.: Sage Publications, 1989), 120–38.

30. Bernard Curtis and Wolfe Mays, "Introduction," in *Phenomenology and Education*, ed. Curtis and Mays (London: Methuen and Co., Ltd., 1978), ix.

31. Ibid, xxi.

32. Alfred North Whitehead, *The Aims of Education* (New York: The Free Press, a Division of Macmillan Publishing Company, Inc., 1929, 1967), 6–7.

33. Chester I. Barnard, *The Functions of the Executive* (Cambridge: Harvard University Press, 1972), 259–60.

34. Montagu, *On Becoming Human*, 52.

35. Herbert A. Simon, *The New Science of Management Decisions* (New York: Harper and Row, 1960), 1.

36. Alfred Schutz, *Collected Papers I*, ed. Maurice Natanson (The Hague: Martinus Nijhoff, 1962), 67

37. Peter F. Drucker, *Management: Tasks, Responsibilities, Practices* (New York: Harper and Row, Publishers, 1973, 1974).

38. Schutz, *Collected Papers I*, 68–69.

39. Ibid., 74.

40. Cf. Edmund Husserl, *Experience and Judgment*, trans. James S. Churchill and Karl Ameriks (Evanston: Northwestern University Press, 1973).

41. Schutz, *Collected Papers I*, 93.

42. David M. Fetterman, "The Quiet Storm," in *Qualitative Approaches to Evaluation in Education: The Silent Revolution*, ed. David M. Fetterman (New York: Praeger, 1988), 277. These articles contain a wealth of bibliographical references on qualitative research in education.

43. Cited in Wayne K. Hoy and Cecil G. Miskel, *Educational Administration: Theory, Research, and Practice* (New York: Random House, 1978), 239.

44. Marshall McLuhan, *Understanding Media: the Extensions of Man* (New York: The New American Library, Inc., 1964).

45. Martin Heidegger, *Being and Time*, trans. John Macquarrie and Edward Robinson (New York: Harper and Row, Publishers, 1962), 204.

46. Michael Polanyi, *The Study of Man* (Chicago: The University of Chicago Press, 1958), 31.

47. Maurice Merleau-Ponty, *Phenomenology of Perception*, trans. Colin Smith (London: Routledge & Kegan Paul, 1962), 149.

48. Cited in Ralph G. Nichols, "Listening Is Good Business," in *Readings in Management*, 2nd edn., ed. Max D. Richards and William A. Nielander (Cincinnati: South-Western Publishing Company, 1963), 191.

49. Ralph G. Nickols and Leonard A. Stevens, "Listening to People," in The Editors, *People: Managing Your Most Important Asset*, reprints from Harvard Business Review, Copyright 1987, by the President and Fellows of Harvard College, 95.

50. Alfred North Whitehead, *Process and Reality*, corrected edn., ed. David Ray Griffin and Donald W. Sherburne (New York: Macmillan Publishing Co., Inc., 1929, 1978), 13.

51. Carl R. Rogers and Richard E. Farson, "Active Listening," in *Readings in Interpersonal & Organizational Communication*, 2nd edn., ed. Richard C. Huseman, et al. (Boston: Holbrook Press, Inc., 1969, 1973), 543.

52. Carl R. Rogers, *A Way of Being* (Boston: Houghton Mifflin Company, 1980), 8.

53. David W. Johnson, "Effects of the Order of Expressing Warmth and Anger on the Actor and the Listener," in *Readings in Interpersonal & Organizational Communication*, 571–84.

54. Martin Heidegger, *Existence and Being*, intro. and analysis by Werner Brock (South Bend: Regnery/Gateway, Inc., 1979), 306.

55. Maurice Natanson, *Edmund Husserl: Philosopher of Infinite Tasks* (Evanston: Northwestern University Press, 1973), 112.

56. Edward T. Hall, *The Silent Language* (Garden City: Doubleday–Anchor Press, 1959, 1973), 98.

57. John Macquarrie, *Existentialism* (New York: Penguin Books, 1973), 102.

58. H.J. Blackman, *Six Existentialist Thinkers* (New York: Harper and Row, Publishers; Harper Torchbooks, 1952, 1959), 91.

59. Ibid., 90–91.

60. Martin Buber, "The Training and Education of a Child," in *The World of the Child*, ed. Toby Talbot (Garden City: Doubleday and Company, Inc., 1967; Anchor Books, 1968), 442–47.

61. Jean–Paul Sartre, *The Philosophy of Jean–Paul Sartre*, ed. and intro. Robert Denoon Cumming (New York: Random House, Inc., 1965; Vintage Book edn., 1972), 187.

62. Paulo Freire, *Cultural Action for Freedom* (Cambridge: Center for the Study of Development and Social Change, "Harvard Educational Review," 1970), 45.

63. Paulo Freire, *Pedagogy of the Oppressed*, trans. Myra Bergman Ramos (New York: The Seabury Press; A Continuum Book, 1968), 171.

64. Heidegger, *Being and Time*, 158.

65. Montagu, *On Being Human*, 37–45.

66. Peter F. Drucker, *Innovation and Entrepreneurship: Practice and Principles* (New York: Harper and Row, Publishers, 1985), 9.

67. Maurice Merleau-Ponty, *Adventures of the Dialectic*, trans. Joseph Bien (Evanston: Northwestern University Press, 1973), 28-29.

68. David Halberstam, *The Powers That Be* (New York: Dell Publishing Company, Inc., 1970, 40.

69. Hadley Cantril, *The Psychology of Social Movements* (New York: John Wiley and Sons, Inc., 1941), 233-37.

70. James M. Kouzes and Barry Z. Posner, *The Leadership Challenge* (San Francisco: Jossey-Bass Publishers, 1988), 83.

71. Drucker, *Innovation and Entrepreneurship*, 35.

72. Albert Szent-Györgi, *The Crazy Ape* (New York: The Philosophical Library, 1970), 17.

73. Alvin Toffler, "The Third Wave," in *Technology and the Future*, 4th edn., ed by Albert H. Teich (New York: St. Martin's Press, 1986), 68.

74. John McHale, *The Future of the Future* (New York: Ballantine Books, Inc., 1971), 65.

75. Hanna Holborn Gray, "Education as a Way of Reflecting on the Future," Working Paper/1 of the Corporate Council on the Liberal Arts (Norton's Woods, 136 Irving Street, Cambridge, MA 02138, 1987), 7.

76. Drucker, *Innovation and Entrepreneurship*, 186.

77. Cf. Robert Kreitner, *Management*, 2nd edn. (Boston: Houghton Mifflin Company, 1983), 24-25.

78. Cf. Pascale and Athos, *The Art of Japanese Management*.

79. Peter Vaill, *Managing as a Performing Art* (San Francisco: Jossey-Bass Publishers, 1989).

80. Whitehead, *The Aims of Education*, 6-7.

Chapter 4

Landscapes of Educational Leadership

In the preceding chapter, the meaning of educational leadership as it relates to the individual was analyzed in some detail. This chapter will explore the "landscape," horizon, context, milieu, or "lived-world" of educational leadership. The goal is to describe and interpret the consciousness of the educational leader's intentional relationship to the world and to the followers in the educational process. Whereas the previous chapter had to do with the individual's consciousness of education no matter where or how it occurred, the present concern is to focus on the consciousness of educational leadership in the mode of schooling.

How does the individual leader relate to the educational process in an organizational setting? What does educational leadership mean in a school, in a classroom, or in some other organized structure? If we assume a 180-day school year of eight hours per day for thirteen years, the average person will spend about 19,600 hours in a schooling environment before he or she goes to college or enters the work force. Thus, educational leaders who are going to be effective must understand the culture in which schooling occurs and must see that educational organizations are constitutions of reality by those individuals who are involved, which in turn means that they are subject to change.

An educational leader relates to the formal educational organization very similarly to the way an individual relates to another individual. The social reality of a leader relating to a school is that the individual leader constructs the consciousness of his or her own schooling experience in the same way an educational leader relates to an individual learner. In fact, a leader cannot relate to an organization of any kind except to relate to individual persons in the organization, since the meaning of the experience of being in an organization is constructed by the leader and by each follower.

Educational leadership is a way of being in a social context, but it is a way of being as an individual existing in relation to other individuals. In the final analysis those things which make up the social world are individual people who act in light of perceptions of their social situation. Any complex social situation, institution, or event is the result of a particular configuration of individuals, their dispositions, beliefs, physical resources, and contexts. Thorough explanations of large-scale social phenomena require deductions which are based on statements about these dispositions, beliefs, resources, and inter-relationships of individuals.[1]

Leadership in the context of an educational organization implies that the leader relates to individuals who are grouped as a collective according to the educational culture constituted by the leader and the followers. The leader becomes a part of the educational organization as Freire became one with the peasants of Brazil whom he taught to be literate, as Ghandi was one with the masses of India, or as Martin Luther King, Jr. was inseparable from the Black culture of the South.

Values, aims, and purposes of the individual leaders become a vital factor in the total relationship between the leader and the individual followers in the educational process. That same kind of relationship exists between a leader and school groups in regard to communicating, deciding, and methods of teaching. The educational leader relates to members of an educational organization as a total experience of being-with-others.

The educational leader is also interconnected with every other element of the educational constituency. An educational leader brings to the educational situation a stock of common knowledge, norms, values, attitudes, and ways of responding to educators. To be an educational leader involves a knowledge of education and a knowledge of a much broader range of human affairs which are relevant to the educational process. To learn to be a leader requires not only the routines and behaviors necessary to perform in an educational system, but also to be aware of the cognitive and affective layers of knowledge which are directly and indirectly related to the educational leader's roles in the educational process. A very large stock of tacit knowledge is an integral part of the landscape or horizon which affects the roles of the educational leader.

A. F. Davies made a careful study of the relationship between Adolf Hitler and those who followed him. Davies concluded that Hitler's strength as a leader resided in his profound knowledge of other people (a *Menschenkenner* "man-knower"). Hitler seemed to know everyone's secret vices and desires, their hidden ambitions and motives, their loves and hates. Hitler knew who could be flattered, where they were gullible, where they were strong, and where they were weak. All of this Hitler seemed to know by instinct and feeling, an intuition which rarely failed him. He had the same uncanny perception of the inner weaknesses and strengths of his enemies.[2] Although Hitler's aims, values, and actions were those of a power-monger and despot, what he knew about those who followed him in a political and military setting is similar to what an educational leader must know about his or her followers in an educational setting. Educational leadership includes all of the ways of relating to the total context of the educational process. Being-with-others in a Heideggerian sense is to know others in a way which goes far beyond what leaders usually are expected to know and to understand about their constituencies.

Each part of the educational constituency is related personally to every other part of the educational constituency. Thus, educational leaders must be aware of the need to clarify and interpret the values, aims, and goals of the school system for all the participants, most importantly the learners. Interpersonal relationships should be as personal and as broadly based as possible. Communication must cut across bureaucratic lines, and leaders must constantly insure that messages are clear and personal. In the same way, educational leaders should make the decision making process as inclusive as possible and should involve the teacher-learner perspective at every level in the educational process, although teachers and students themselves cannot always participate in the decisions directly.

Awareness of the landscapes, or horizons, of educational leadership contributes to an understanding of the leader's roles in the educational process. The leader's roles and modes of being are played out in the organization of the educational process as a holistic response to the values, aims, and culture of the entire educational constituency.

LEADER'S LIVED-WORLD OF SCHOOLING

The lived-world of an educational leader is the total situation of educational leadership occurring in an educational organization. This statement implies a phenomenological view of social reality similar to that of Alfred Schutz. Schutz sees reality as woven by human will from a constitution of consciousness which is created out of our imagination and which is colored by our personal interests and past experiences. Thus, organizations are not objectively real phenomena; they are constitutions of the human mind and based on views of reality which are socially constructed. Organizations are not presented to our consciousness the same way as material objects are presented and cannot be studied the same way. If organizations are products of human consciousness, they should be studied in the context of human will, human intentions, and human existence.

What is the nature of educational organizations? Are schools a manifestation of a natural order, or are they the products of diverse human invention which renders them not only different from other organizations, but different, as well, among themselves? Are schools everywhere essentially the same, or are they so varied in quality, meaning, and event that we must think of them as different as the people within them who give them life? Schools, like other organizations, are "inside people" and are defined completely by people as they construct ideas of organizations in their consciousness through their actions in the practical world.[3] What the observer sees in a school depends upon who the observer is and what the observer sees. Schools are reflections of self rather than objective, concrete entities to which self must adapt. Theorists have not helped us by objectifying and reifying educational organizations as if an organization can be healthy, "maintain itself" (Bennis), or have a "personality" (organizational development theorists).

Thomas Barr Greenfield insists that organizations are abstractions which we ourselves make, but they are important. The outline of his basic theory of organizations is instructive. According to Greenfield, a theory of organizations as will and imagination may be summed up in two statements: first, he rejects group mind and an overarching social reality thought to lie beyond human control and outside the will, intention, and action of the individual; second, he acknowledges the tumult and irrationality of thought itself. Acting, willing, feeling, fearing, hoping, living, failing humans and the events that join them are always more complex, interesting, and real than the ideas which are used to explain them.[4]

The major propositions of Greenfield's theory about organizations can be summarized as follows. First, it is the individual that lives and acts, not the organization. Organizations cannot act; they are not organisms with a life of their own; they are perceived realities, constructs of the mind. Second, because we live in separate realities, what is true for one person may not be true for another. What is rational for one person may be irrational for another. Third, understanding organizations is as simple or as complex as understanding why individuals act as they do. Fourth, facts and values are closely interwoven and inseparable. Facts decide nothing. It is a person who decides about the facts. Therefore, individuals are responsible for what they do. Thinking in categories about organizations cannot remove the notions of right and wrong. The value dimensions of each organizational member make events and organizations meaningful. Fifth, systems of logic and rationality are themselves fraught with paradox: their validity requires a personal interpretation of the propositions from outside the system of thought itself. The truth of a proposition ultimately depends on a belief in the veracity of the system of logic within which the proposition is framed. Language is crucial. How one defines categories, events, and people has a critical impact on how that person relates to them. Greenfield concludes that "an organization is a set of meanings" which the organizational participants act out from psychological, moral, and physical dynamics.[5]

Individuals make up the social network of groups involved in education, and individuals together form the constructions which we call schools. Educational organizations are composed of individual leaders and followers who value and think and act according to a frame of reference, a landscape, which is socially constructed in the minds of those who are participating in the educational endeavor.

Educational leadership (including action, thinking, wishing, achieving, reflecting, etc.) is a state or condition of a person being someone whom an educational constituency wants to follow, to identify with, and to become like. Some social scientists speak of the field in which a group or institution exists as its "life space" (Lewin). The life space of educational leadership consists of the educational group and its environment as it exists for the group. Phenomenologists refer to this life space, or milieu, as landscape, horizon, or "life–world."

Thus, the institutionalization of educational leadership in our culture is the phenomenon of schooling. But a school is not an objective, real, external entity as is a slide under a microscope; the buildings, books, policies, and people are real enough, but the organization is a construct in the mind of the leaders and the followers in the educational process. The constitution of the concept of schooling is socially agreed upon by those participating in the schooling. As human creations, schools embody the intentions, goals, fears, prejudices, language, myths, and other cultural baggage of the educational leaders and their constituents.

The life-world of an educational leader presents itself as an intersubjective meaning-context and appears to be meaningful in the interpretative acts of the consciousness of each participant in the educational process. The meaning of educational leadership is the result of each participant's interpretation of past lived experiences which are grasped reflectively in the here-and-now from an actually valid frame of reference. Alfred Schutz, who applied phenomenology to the social setting, said that lived "educational" experiences first become meaningful when they are interpreted "after the fact" and become comprehensible to each person as well-circumscribed experiences. Thus, only those lived experiences are subjectively meaningful which are called forth from memory to their actuality, which are analyzed as regards their construction of consciousness, and which are explicated in respect to their relation to the frame of reference of the one existing in the social situation. Subjectively meaningful behavior is not only the currently comprehended action of others or of oneself, but is also the institutionalizations of interpersonal acts in social settings.[6]

The social world of the educational leader is a construction of the human minds of those who make up the educational world, and our ability to attribute meaning to that world is dependent on whether we are members of it and whether we have internalized its symbols. Educational leaders interpret the behavior of others not only in terms of the meanings they attach to the leadership phenomena, but also in terms of the meanings they expect others to infer from their own behavior. Out of these meanings and symbolic interactions educational groups construct their social reality. The social reality of educational groups is the values, beliefs, behaviors, attitudes, and cultural artifacts which are validated through the social consensus of the constituents of a given educational setting.

The institutionalization of the meanings of educational leadership develops out of socialization and the immersion of individuals in the modes of thought customary to the time and place of the educational process, but it is also a consequence of that search for meaning which appears to be a universal human need.

The selection of interpretations of educational leadership in a given educational setting is largely influenced by the requirements of the educational society, institutions, and symbols, given the demands and cultural matrices of individual existence. Educational leadership phenomena are not approached as they are objectively, but as they are assimilated into the Kantian notion of preexisting patterns which have been constructed in the minds of those participating in the educational process. In other words, individuals become educational leaders only insofar as others believe in what they represent and as they conform to the schemata of what the followers understand an educational leader to be and to do.

According to the sociology of Georg Simmel, the educational leader is conceptualized as the "unitary expression" of the educational group. Chester Barnard spoke of the leader as an "embodiment of the central purpose of the organization." Leaders in a sense create the moral order that unifies the group. Schools are built on the unification of people around educational values, and educational leaders are "entrepreneurs for values." Educational leaders have to be committed to certain values which the school's constituents find compatible with their own values and goals.

Each organization has a purpose which is unique. In educational institutions the function of leadership is thoroughly educational, whereas leadership in a profit–making institution is production of a profit. Thus, educational leaders embody the purposes and aims of the educational constituents of the school.

Students as Landscapes

If the institutionalization of educational leadership is the lived–world of schooling, the social reality of schooling cannot exist without students, even though education is a process far broader than schooling. The purpose of schooling implies students. The questions and decisions of educational leaders have to do with what is going on with students in schools. Do we really have to be reminded that schools exist for the purpose of students? Yet, many educational leaders describe what is happening in their schools as if students are "products" which the school is manufacturing. Students are reasons why educators get paid a salary, or, alas, students are obstacles to the educational program the educators are offering. How does one explain teachers who sometimes say that they could have a good classroom if they could just get rid of certain students?

Once I heard Bill Page, an educational reformer from Nashville, Tennessee, addressing about 700 people in Santa Barbara, California, who were involved in a reading curriculum selection project. After eight or ten reading experts had presented their programs and techniques to solve the reading problems, Page reviewed the proposals which had been presented by the reading experts and then received a standing ovation when he asked, "Where do the 'kids' fit into these reading programs?" The horizon of educational leadership includes the presence and needs of students.

In one sense, educational leading and learning are inseparable in schooling. The very practice of leading as an educator involves learning on the part of the student. The leader participates in, as well as influences, the learning of the students. In fact, the leader learns from the student while the student is learning from the leader. Educational leadership is not simply the transmission of data from the leader to the student, unless the student's awareness of the need for the knowledge is presupposed. Neither does the educational leader utilize power and authority to get students to behave in a way which pleases the leader. The students are the center of the educational endeavor of schooling and not an "object" of the programs and policies of the administration.

Schooling is not the articulation of systems of knowledge; it is the construction of meaning for students. Yet some schooling has a way of inhibiting, threatening, enslaving, and generally "putting down" students instead of developing a workable, meaningful concept of the self for the student. My daughter knew how to read, write, and count before she entered school, but soon she had to "unlearn" what she had learned in order to learn how to read, write, and count according to the way the school was teaching these skills. The result was that she regressed in her learning almost two years. Educational leaders should think about schooling from the student's perspective.

If educational leaders are viewing schooling from the perspective of the student, they are thinking about drop-out prevention, rather than ways to eliminate problem kids. They are looking for ways for each child to succeed in the school, rather than doing what is best for all the students. The goals of lesson materials are developed in terms of goals which are meaningful to the student, not referenced to the criteria established by the state or the district office. Educational leaders are asking what all the programs, policies, curriculum, strategies, and lessons mean to the students. Granted, viewing schooling from the perspective of the student is not easy, nor does it mean that the school is turned over to the students. Educational leaders help to raise the consciousness of students to the values and goals which are best for the students and for human life in general.

An educational leader also attempts to explore with students the historical and cultural circumstances of their social world, whether their world is oppressive or liberating, empty or meaningful, fragmented or unified. Students need to be aware of the problems and contradictions in their society and how they can deal with these opposing forces. Each student needs to realize how society will respond to their cultural background, their racial heritage, their gender, and their choices in schooling; at the same time, students should learn what the opportunities and assets of their world are. Dewey believed that the virtues of democracy and the sins of enslavement are learned through experiences in an informed environment. Educational leaders must be willing to participate with the students in the risks and conflicts which are involved in helping students see the limits and entrapments of their society, while showing them how to take advantage of the opportunities which their world offers.

When I went through a "teacher training" program in the early sixties, I was told not to get involved in the lives of the students. "You cannot change the social situation of the welfare kids and problem students. They will just drive you mad, and you will soon give up teaching." How could a program be more misguided?

The student's world is vitally connected with the educational leader's world. The educational leader is a part of the landscape of the student, and the student exists in the world of the leader. Seeing the students within the horizon of the educational leader's consciousness of schooling will go a long way to fulfilling the desired intent of schooling in today's educational endeavors.

Curriculum for Consciousness

How does an educational leader relate to the curriculum and content of schooling? Freire's program for literacy in Brazil is most instructive.

The starting point for Freire's analysis is a critical comprehension of a person as a being who exists in and with the world. Since the basic condition for consciousness of being in the world (as Freire called it, "conscientization") is that its agent be a subject (i.e., a conscious being), conscientization, like education, is specifically and exclusively a human process, a social construction of reality. It is as conscious beings that individuals are not only in the world but with the world, together with other people. Simultaneously individuals transform the world by their projects and actions, and they grasp and express the world's reality in their own creative language.[7]

Freire views textbooks as instruments for "depositing" the educator's words into the learners. Textbooks have very little, if anything, to do with the actual experiences and real needs of the illiterate students whom Freire is trying to teach. In most literacy programs students are asked to read words from books which do not relate to their experiences of reality. For instance, most textbook authors assume that the students are from urban, middle-class, educated families. We saw what problems this perspective causes in our own country when Black students were required to read White words from books which mirrored a White culture with White values, White customs, and White standards of behavior. The words and the language are foreign to the culture of the students. Fundamentalist religious groups in America have formed textbook screening committees to try to remove from the public school textbooks words and facts which are not compatible with their own particular religious beliefs.

In America, students are asked to read school-words, but not reality-words. Schooling in many respects requires that students read and describe the world, but not that they understand the world. Facts are learned, formulae are memorized, language is imitated, art is copied, and culture is transmitted, but rarely are students challenged to reflect on their critical awareness of their situation, their values, their goals, their real world. Schooling involves using mandated textbooks which are taught according to standardized methods in order that students learn the "essential elements" so that standardized scores will be "above average."

The Chicago public school system adopted Bloom's mastery learning approach in their K-6 reading program which is based on an empirical model which assumes that learners are passive, in need of motivation, and reinforcement. Teachers spend their time developing a sequenced, criterion-referenced curriculum and deciding how they will motivate, reinforce, and evaluate the learning of the learners. In the reading program subskills such as beginning consonant sounds, vowel sounds, blends, digraphs, and comprehension were taught in an organized manner until mastery was achieved. By the sixth grade reading achievement scores were high, but decreased rapidly during the junior high years; some learners were actually not reading. Learners were spending time learning test items and completing work sheets, but hardly any time was spent on actual reading, let alone reading for meaning, enjoyment, or needed information.[8]

From Freire's point of view, the educational leader's role is to enter into dialogue with the students about their own concrete situations and simply to create with the students the instruments and perspectives with which they can teach themselves. This kind of leading is not a Subject causing an Object to accept certain ideas or behaviors, but is a Subject entering the world of another Subject and creating a critical consciousness of the joint-world of the leaders and the learners in the educational leadership situation. Thus, the curriculum is identified with the learning process. The text and context are integrated; the word of the curriculum is developed out of the lived-world of the learners. The content comes from inside the world of the students, not imposed from state departments of education by means of teachers.

When does a teacher and a student understand a verb, math, biology, or a lake? One does not understand a subject simply by acquiring facts and memorizing data about it. Understanding means that both the leader and the learners enter the world where the meaning-intending is being constituted by those living within that world view, that frame of reference, or that life-world. Understanding for educational leaders means walking in the shoes of the students, touching their hearts, sharing their joys and sorrows, helping them solve their problems, and channeling their surging aspirations toward fulfillment of the destiny and potential of each student. The leader is so intimately involved in the content of the learning situation that the old Chinese proverb applies which states that a teacher should be jailed if his or her student steals a loaf of bread.

Freire's literacy program in Brazil taught illiterate individuals to read and write Portuguese by showing the students how to grasp critically the way words are formed, so that the students created their own words.[98] The program used fifteen to eighteen "generative words," whose syllabic elements offer through re-combination the basic phonemes of the entire Portuguese language.

First, Freire selected a vocabulary for the illiterates from words which conveyed the greatest existential meaning (i.e., words with high emotional content) and which had the strongest linkage with typical sayings and experiences of the learners. These words reflected the sufferings, frustrations, beliefs, and dreams of the illiterates. Second, the generative words were selected from the vocabulary which was developed. The criteria which governed the selection of the words was their phonemic richness, phonetic difficulty, and pragmatic tone. Among other things, the best generative word corresponds significantly with the pragmatic thing designated, carries a strong potential quality of conscientization, and generates a grouping of sociocultural reactions in the persons using the word. Third, the generative words which represent typical existential situations of the illiterates were then set in "codification." Fourth, fairly general agendas were developed for the leaders. The fifth step involved the preparation of cards which contained the phonemic families which corresponded to the generative words.

The literacy program functioned in what Freire called "cultural circles," where the group itself selected topics to clarity and name situations through group discussion. The codified situation was presented to the group of illiterates through slides, filmstrips, and posters. Only after the students had exhausted the analysis (decoding) of the situation would the leader identify the generative word, encouraging the students to understand (not memorize) the word. Then the word was presented in another context without the object it names; the word was divided into syllables and was presented in phonemic families using "discovery cards"; using the card to reach a synthesis, the students began to create their own words with the phonemic combinations offered by the breakdown of tri-syllabic words.

A similar approach was used by an educational leader in a learning disabled group of children in Nashville, Tennessee. The leader used the *TV Guide* as a text to teach words which appeared on commercial programs on television. When a child could use a word in other contexts and could write and spell the word (the word literally belonged to the student), he or she put the word on used data processing cards and placed it in a shoebox. Kids with very low abilities who would normally not achieve a vocabulary of over 350 words soon developed vocabularies of 500 words. The progress continued at a phenomenal rate to the point that the kids had vocabularies of over 1,500 words (the last account I had of the students' progress).

The point of these illustrations is that the leaders and the learners are participating in the construction of a critical consciousness. The development of this consciousness cannot be separated from the curriculum or the process of the schooling. Educational leaders participate from inside the consciousness of the learners as part of the lived-world of the learners.

Educational leaders would do well to go back and reconsider what John Dewey meant when he discussed his concept of experience-based education. In a very real sense the curriculum and content of the educational process is life in all its ramifications (Whitehead), and the educational process occurs within the life-world of the leaders and the learners.

Dewey insisted that life consists of a series of overlapping and interpenetrating experiences, situations, or contexts, each which has its own internal, qualitative integrity. The individual experience of each student is the primary unit of schooling, as well as of life. Education should be a constant reconstruction of the meaning of experience within the context of a genuine democratic community.[10]

THE LIVED–WORLD OF BIASES AND PREJUDICES

Merleau–Ponty says that the world is not what we think it is but "what we live through."[11] "Living through" the world is the way human consciousness opens itself to the world, i.e., the ways one is aware of being in the world. This perceptual reality underlies our constructions of consciousness and becomes the landscape, or lived–world of the educational leader. But what if the lived–world and perceptual realities are ambiguous or biased against certain persons or groups of persons in the educational process? Biases and prejudices in educational leaders may cause the learners to falsify their self concepts or to see themselves as inferior in their lived–world.

Leaders and learners encounter each other in the everyday world of schooling by means of types and roles and behaviors which are standardized, habitualized through either conscious or unconscious social constructions of reality. The world of the school is interpreted as meaningful for the leaders and the learners on the basis of this consciousness of the lived world. At times the lived–world of the school is oppressive, biased, prejudiced, negative, confused, alienating, frightening, discouraging, or even inhuman. Effective educational leaders must develop an awareness of these biases and contradictions in their lived–world of the school.

Sexist Biases

One of the major biases in the culture of schooling is that educational leadership is defined in terms of male dominance. While the overwhelming number of teachers are women, the number of women in administrative positions are relatively few. There is no question about women in America facing discrimination in educational leadership. Maxine Greene notes that the constructions of reality normally used to describe and interpret the common sense world of everyday life are largely those of males.[12] Male perspectives have dominated the modes of categorizing and structuring the consciousness of experiences of both private and public life (e.g., education), because males have been the ones in power in the Western world. Sex roles are handed down without question as cultural patterns by ancestors, teachers, and other authority figures. These roles are internalized by both men and women and become a significant basis for the inferiority stereotype of women in leadership positions.

Bass' survey of research on how sex roles are developed in leaders explains that socializations occurs in our culture primarily in the nuclear family which defines sex roles as total roles that define one's sense of self and leadership behavior. The stereotype role of the male in all aspects of life is characterized by dominance, aggressiveness, independence, self confidence, strength, and power. The female role stereotype assumes that women are non-aggressive, dependent, subjective, pliable, submissive, non-competitive, emotional, physically weak, insecure, and illogical.[13] These sexual stereotypes which are found in leaders are ingrained in our culture and express themselves in almost every aspect of life.

As a preschool child I vividly recall being teased by older boys while playing after church services. Some older boys delighted in mispronouncing my middle name (Gerald) and calling me "Girl." Their object was to get me angry enough to chase them. My upbringing had so conditioned me to disdain being called a girl that one poor kid who was my own age made the mistake of joining in on the teasing. I easily caught that kid and beat him so mercilessly that my older brother and the other older boys had to come to his rescue. My goal was to prove that I was not a girl even at the expense of injuring the other child.

Sexual discrimination, stereotyping, and prejudice are totally foreign to what we claim the desired outcomes of the educational process are. Sexism is "miseducative" (Dewey) because it prevents open-ended growth, personal reflection, and meaningful communication in a free and value-driven society. And since education does not have a very good record in regard to equality and affirmation of women in schooling, educational leaders have an opportunity to take some positive steps to eliminate sexism in the schools.

Language use in school textbooks. is one of the primary media of continuing and even promoting unfair and irrelevant distinctions between the sexes. That "he" and "man," when used generically, are gender-neutral terms is a myth of our male-dominated culture, and empirical evidence shows that, regardless of the author's intention, the generic "man" is not interpreted gender neutrally. Recognizing the sexist biases in language, many professional organizations, such as the American Psychological Association, American Philosophical Association, and the National Council of Teachers of English, have developed guidelines to help eliminate the use of sexist language.

Sexual stereotyping is also reflected in the textbooks and curriculum of the schools. The presuppositions of the content, examples, theories, human activities, interests, and points of view in textbooks too often reflect a sexist bias in favor of males. Labeling certain roles as predominantly male or female, such as lawyers or homemakers, engenders sexism. Also, omitting women's distinctive interests and experiences perpetuates sexual stereotyping in schooling.

Efforts to improve leadership for women in education will improve education for everyone since the needs of women and men to become human are similar in education. As we saw in the previous chapter, the is-ness of educational leadership involves interpreted experiences and meanings which are common to all humanity and not restricted to either gender. Biases and prejudices which are perceived about women must be addressed as problems of perception and not as problems of women as educational leaders. Do we need to be reminded that absolutely nothing in the educational process of which I am aware could not be done by a women. Thus, a critical need exists to identify and to destroy all sexist biases in educational leadership. [14]

Maxine Greene's insightful discussion of a woman's search for freedom could be applied to education leaders when she declares that truth tears away the masks of convention (biases) and compliance which hide women's being in the world. Using Heidegger's hermeneutics, Greene maintains that "unconcealment" breaks through the masked and falsified labels and categories of prejudices which compose the lived-world, the interpreted experiences of women. Women's self concepts and their ways of thinking are so intertwined that freedom for women requires that they affirm their rights to self-determination and equality as leaders in the educational process. [15] It remains for both men and women to establish a leadership in the educational process where the sexist biases and prejudices are admitted and negated.

Educational leaders who are able to bracket the biases and flag the sexist postures in schooling will be more effective and will understand the nature of educational leadership better. Being aware of the sexist biases is both a responsibility and an opportunity of all educational leaders in today's process of schooling. Educational leaders who do not seek to eliminate sexist biases should not be called "educational" leaders.

Color Biases

One of the most insidious biases in the culture of schooling in the United States is the racial discrimination against Blacks. In fact, the color consciousness was so intense in the slave-owning White culture that a separate sub-culture developed among the Blacks who were the victims of the slavery. Thus, prior to 1954 a consciousness of Black schooling existed along side the preferred consciousness of White schooling. Although numerous civil rights and equal opportunity Acts of Congress and policies and actions of the Department of Justice have attempted to blot out these ugly pages of racial discrimination, vestiges of the color bias still haunt the consciousness of both leaders and learners in the schooling process in the United States.

E.E. Jennings surveyed 359 Black executives in 1980 and found that forty-five percent of them still believed that racial prejudice was the most important obstacle in the path of further career progress. To compound the problem, a lack of proper educational attainment and an inferior quality of educational preparation available result in fewer Blacks than Whites in comparable positions of political, educational, military and industrial leadership.[16] The positive effects of both the 1954 Supreme Court decision of Brown vs. Board of Education, and the Civil Rights Act of 1964 have not eliminated the color bias in educational leadership. De facto segregation of Blacks still lingers in many school settings in the United States, and "White flight" and private schools seem to be increasing. Further, integration closed a number of Black schools and displaced a large number of Black teachers and leaders.

In order to understand and cope with the color bias in educational leadership, we must examine the nature of Black consciousness in American culture. C.T. Vivian points out that Black and White relations have been placed in an economic context since the master and slave days, and freedom for Blacks has meant getting a financial base to operate in a materialistic society. Yet when ordinary Black people began to move upward, it was not an economic force which moved them. "They sought dignity, not dollars; manhood, not money; pride, not prosperity."[17] Today, Black parents and students want to learn Black history, Black values, and Black culture from their own Black perspectives. They want schooling designed by and for those whom it serves. Evidently, what the leaders of the Black movement realized is that leadership derived from both the followers' and the leader's constructions of reality, their basic beliefs and values.

The study of King Davis on the status of black leadership in the early eighties claims that there is a unique role demanded of leadership in groups which are oppressed, denied, or alienated from social institutions which determine their quality of life. Black followers are stimulated by and sensitive to those problems, policies, conditions, values, and needs which influence the quality of life for Black people. Thus, Black organizations are viewed as the formalized structures through which the relationship, interaction, support, energies, resources, plans, activities, and philosophies of Black leaders and followers develop collectively toward seeking the "good life."[18] Further, the fact that personal charisma plays a prominent role in stimulating Black followers is not a mystery. Charisma can be viewed as the result of the consolidation of the elements of the consciousness of the good life.

The relationship between Black leaders and their followers is influenced by this consciousness of leadership, which Davis describes as a complex of variables: (1) identification of mutual problems and a resulting sense of injustice; (2) group identity and need for a sense of community; (3) mutual support; (4) mutual respect; (5) mutual trust; (6) shared expectation of change; (7) communication patterns and methods; (8) recognition of the need for reciprocity; (9) recognition of interdependency; and (10) shared world view.[19] These variables are the structure of the consciousness which is constructed by Black leaders and followers. The nature of the consciousness of Black leadership is very similar to the consciousness of educational leadership which we explained earlier in this study.

Educational leaders must realize that they are dealing with the followers' constructions of reality (their world views). Consequently, the White supremacy bias in schooling, as well as the prejudice against Blacks, is a matter of the construction of the school's social reality by educational leaders and followers. Therefore, those who think that the color bias in schools was overcome by the Supreme Court and the Civil Rights Acts have not understood the nature of the relationship between educational leaders and followers.

Those who try to address the issue of bias in terms of "minorities" are not viewing bias as a result of a particular construction of the social reality. Simply placing persons who belong to minority groups in positions of leadership may not improve educational leadership in our schools. The term "minority" is a misnomer when thinking about the process of schooling. For one thing, in those places where racial biases are so strong, the number of Black students easily outnumbers the number of White students. For example, in many large inner city school systems the "minority" students (Blacks, Hispanics, etc.) far outnumber the Anglo students in schools, while the teachers, the textbooks, the curriculum, the language accepted, the administrators, and the culture of schooling are Anglo, White, middle-class—with no questions asked.

Physically "integrating" the "minorities" into the White systems did not work in the United States, and is not working in South Africa. The consciousness of White supremacy is the problem, and White educational leadership should not be surprised to hear a Black subculture with a Black consciousness demanding schooling which meets their needs, teaches their values, history, and heroes, and accepts their language and culture.

The issue of the color bias is even broader for educational leaders and learners; what is really at stake is the meaning of human freedom in education. To speak of education within a democracy, as Dewey did, implies that educational leaders and learners have taken seriously freedom as a value which is embraced by all who are involved in the process of education. Dewey's thoughts on freedom in schools are quite relevant to our discussion. Although both leaders and learners in the school tend to identify freedom with an absence of social direction or with a lack of physical restraints on movement, the essence of freedom's demand is the need for conditions which will allow each person to make his or her own unique contribution to a group's interest or need or to participate in freedom's activities in such ways that social guidance is a matter of each person's own mental attitude, and not a mere authoritative dictation of one's acts. Often freedom in schools is thought of as the opposite of discipline or classroom management or proper student behavior. Rather, freedom is essentially the part played by thinking and existing as a person in schooling which involves the intellectual initiative, independence in observation, judicious invention, and foresight of consequences and ingenuity of adaptation to them.[20]

The question of freedom in school is not the absence of restraints or the presence of mere choices. Rather, what do the choices, restraints, and indulgences mean to the students? If the choices are no more than allowing learners to choose which flavor of ice cream, which pencil, or which math problem they are allowed to choose, freedom is not an issue. On the other hand, if obstacles and restraints reduce or destroy the human spirit or stupefy, make insensitive, crush, or diminish self respect and self actualization, they should be leveled to the ground. Yet obstacles and restraints which strengthen, challenge, and enhance the individual's self worth and social development should be encouraged and cultivated by leaders.

Maxine Greene expands a John Dewey Lecture on the theme of freedom in education from a phenomenological perspective which applies to the color bias. She asks if we can "educate for positive freedom." Can we find an authentic public space in which diverse humans of all classes and colors can appear before one another in our highest dignity and happiness? This requires provision of opportunities for the articulation of "multiple perspectives in multiple idioms," out of which a common life can be conceived and developed. It also requires a consciousness of norms and values which support this freedom-- "of what ought to be , from a moral and ethical point of view, and what is in the making, what might be in an always open world."[21]

In contexts where people care for one another there is a place for freedom to appear and to achieved by people searching for themselves. Greene hopes to awaken concern for and belief in a humane framework where people hunger for becoming different, becoming new. She further reminds us what it means to be alive among others, to achieve freedom in dialogue with others for the sake of personal fulfillment and the emergence of a democracy dedicated to life and decency."[22]

Human freedom is the capacity to challenge the inhuman in life and to see alternative modes of being which are more human. Dewey saw freedom in coming to be, in growth, in consequences rather than antecedents, in becoming different from what we have been.[23] However, willing to be free does not mean being able to be free, especially in a world of color biases and prejudices.

The color bias in schools strikes at the very heart of the U.S. Constitution which states that every American citizen has the right to good "life," true "liberty," and the "pursuit of happiness" in a "just" society. Educational leaders who are worthy of the name will strive to identify the White supremacy consciousness with the inhuman, immoral, and miseducative force which it is. In turn, educational leaders should affirm the worth and dignity of every human person, regardless of color, class, or ethnic identity. Educational leaders who learn to recognize and to bracket the color bias are more likely to transform schooling into an educational process which engenders a human, communal consciousness.

Language Biases

What is inside us finds its total expression in and through our language. Thus, language is the objectification of our understanding of our existence; it is the reservoir of our culture and the medium in and through which our world is experienced and interpreted. The way in which we analyze and interpret all data and knowledge is dependent on our language. Both leaders and learners in schools structure their views of reality by means of their language. This means that an educational leaders's attitude toward the language of the learners is critical to the nature of leadership in the school setting. Education is that terrain where meaning, desire, language, and values engage and respond to basic beliefs about the very nature of what it means to be human, to dream, and to opt for a good life in the future.

Language is possible only when a community of individuals agree on the meanings of the language symbols which are socially derived and validated. The meaning of language is socially constructed, a "sedimentation" of constructions of reality which are relevant in a social situation. Words do not have meanings in themselves; we assign the meanings to words on the basis of our common experiences and our common views of reality. Merleau-Ponty tells of a child who picks up his grandmother's spectacles and is sorely disappointed when he cannot read the book from which his grandmother had read stories to him. The child exclaims, "Where are the stories? All I see is black and white." The child understood the "story" as a world which could be magically called up by putting on spectacles and leaning over a book. Merleau-Ponty concludes from this incident that the power which language possesses to bring into existence the thing expressed, of opening up new ways of thinking, new dimensions and new landscapes, is finally as obscure to the adult as to the child.[24]

The bias which is inherent in the sedimentation of meanings in language symbols, grammar, syntax, and literary forms is fundamental to the meaning of leadership in education. Paulo Freire found that leaders in Brazil who wanted to teach peasants to read must enter their world of reality and view the learning process form the peasant's viewpoint, using language patterns out of their own peasant culture.

A similar concern for taking into account the language bias exists when leaders attempt to teach students in a culture where English is a second language. In a growing number of U.S. school systems in the Southwest and West the Anglo language and culture and values are dominant, although the Hispanic student population is clearly dominant.

The result of this situation is that Hispanic students become the "slow learners," the discipline problems, the dropouts, the below average achievers, the functional illiterates. The lament is raised as to why the Hispanic students are not learning. The obvious answer is the bias of the educational leaders toward the English language and the Anglo culture of the schools where Hispanic students are trying to learn.

The importance and prestige of any language are determined by the biases of the persons who use it, the purpose, the audience, and the place where it is used. If educational leaders convey that the language of students is unimportant or unacceptable by reason of its lack of use in school or its use in a begrudging manner, the result will always be negative. Hansen and Johnson found that the self esteem of students is related to dominant evaluations of a student's native language by educational leaders and teachers. If students are encouraged to abandon their native language in favor of English, bilingual education does not get beyond a compensatory level. The biases and attitudes of leaders which are brought into the schools have a direct effect on the instructional program and on the learning processes of the students themselves. [25]

The language gap between leaders and learners also exists among students other than those who speak no English or very limited English. Educational leaders learn a White, English idiom, vocabulary, and culture in public school and teacher and administrator training programs in college. Thus, new teachers and leaders go to schools and try to impose their language on students, correcting them, ridiculing them, and demanding that the students speak and act like the leaders. Many students who do not understand this "school talk" drift into a world of silence, confusion, and reduced self esteem. Thus, teachers cease to become educational leaders.

Dialogical leadership begins with the language level and milieu of the students, not in a condescending manner, but in an idiom and manner as parents would talk to their own children or friends. Most educational leaders do not use academic jargon or school talk to teach their own children. Closing the language gap with students means to use words, metaphors, stories, themes, rate of speech, rhythm, syntax, thought patterns, and views of reality (world views) which the students understand. A good educational leader attempts to take the students into his or her own realm of existence, to show them new possibilities, different beliefs and values, and a "better" life, to open to them a world and a life in which the students want to participate and to incorporate into their own culture and consciousness.

MODES OF EDUCATIONAL LEADERSHIP

An examination of the landscapes of educational leadership questions whether certain modes of behavior or role expectations are common to all educational leaders. What is the nature of the basic mode of being an educational leader? Relationships between educational leaders and followers can be structured according to at least two broad categories: ideal types of persons who are educational leaders and ideal types of behaviors of educational leaders. The constitution of the leadership experience in the education process includes both what the leader and the learners do, believe, and experience and who the constituency is.

Typologies of Educational Leaders

The primary mode of leadership in the educational process is a type of relationship between the leader and the learner (teacher and student). The role structure of an educational system focuses on the interaction between the learner and the learning facilitator. All other role definitions in the educational process are directly related to what happens between the teacher and the student. Was it Mark Hopkins who defined education as "a boy on one end of a log and a teacher on the other end of the log?" Educational organizations are best understood as systems which are structured around the teacher–learner type of relationship, and the primary type of educational leadership is that of teacher–learner.

Students are the focal point of teacher–learner relationship. Without students, the roles, positions, and professional offices of teachers and administrators become meaningless. Wherever the educational process starts and whomever it involves, the student is the one indispensable participant in the interactive relationship which is basic to any type of education. Even the interaction between an educational administrator and a teacher tacitly involves how that interaction relates to the student. Not to include the learner in the consciousness of educational leadership is to assume an "ivory–towerism" and to misunderstand the interactive nature of the relationship between the teacher and learner in the educational process.

The ideal type of educational leadership is that of teacher–learner, and the structure of the social experience of educational leadership is primarily one of face–to–face, I–Thou, being–with–others relationship. Leadership in an educational system must begin with the leader's (teacher) and the learner's awarenesses of the presence of the other and with both the leader and the learner having knowledge of and respect for each other. The leaders and learners may experience education with different degrees of immediacy, intensity, or intimacy, from different points of view, or within different degrees of formal structure. However, educational leaders must recognize the personal nature of the primary role of the teacher–learner relationship.

Teachers assume their roles in educational systems voluntarily on the basis of prior experiences and academic training. However, the role of a teaching leader has become professionalized. To become a teacher one must in principle, if not in fact, complete a teacher training program in an accredited college or university, be licensed, and must demonstrate at least potential expertise in the subject areas to be taught. These credentials for teaching do not take into account the personal nature of the teacher–student relationship, and they create bureaucratic educational organizations which threaten the effectiveness of the entire educational process. Bidwell found evidence of bureaucratization of teacher roles which are defined as "offices" or "positions" within the formal educational organization.[26] When the role of a teacher is determined by professional policies, codes, and norms, the primary social experience, that of teacher–student, of an educational leader is endangered.

The second typification of an educational leader is an administrator. Educational administrators sponsor, manage, provide resources, and facilitate the educational activities and programs in educational systems. Superintendents, principals, board members, state and federal officials, radio and television programmers, publishers, curriculum specialists, and psychologists are categorized as administrators who are engaged in mediating the expectancies of the educational constituencies. Administrative roles of educational leaders are constituted out of their relationship to those in the teacher–learner role. The primary role of administrators consists in face–to–face interaction with those in the teacher–learner roles. The more intimately an educational leader is related to the teacher's role, the stronger the administrative role becomes. The rule–of–thumb is to keep all administrative policies and practices as close to the teacher–learner relationship as is possible.

However, just as marriage is made up of countless separate but integrated events and experiences, the administrative role is constituted by countless integrated activities. The interrelationships between administrators and teachers constitute a complex element of the educational process. What must be kept in mind is that administrative roles grow out of the teacher's role. The policies, procedures, norms, and values of administrators flow naturally from the educational aims and values which support and provide for the teacher–learner interactive relationship. Thus, the practice of developing educational policy and practice at the federal, state, local, or central office level and imposing them on the classroom is antithetical to the primary role of educational leaders and is detrimental to the educational process.

Administrators who design and develop policies and practices for learners without considering the consciousness of the teacher–learner relationship are managers and manipulators more than leaders. Educational managers tend to be power, knowledge, and skills brokers, rather than leaders who share the consciousness of the learners.

A third role which an educational leader typifies includes many people who may not have a direct responsibility in the educational system, but who have a profound influence on what happens in the educational process. Society at large plays a significant role in exerting influence on the determination and the outcome of expectations and goals of the educational system. Parents, voters, taxpayers, legislators, church groups, health providers, professional organizations, and business and industrial groups have strong influences on the aims and policies which shape the educational process. This third typification of an educational leader is no less real than a teacher who works directly with the learner; yet, these general educational leaders are some of the most visible and most readily recognized by the general public.

The influence of these general educational leaders can be gigantic and can be either negative or positive. A person could occupy a national office in government or a professional organization and could promote educational policies and practices which would enhance his or her own political aspirations without really experiencing a consciousness of the teacher–learner situation. In fact, a recent Secretary of Education has been criticized because he seemed to delight in telling major universities how to run their schools without experiencing what was happening at the teacher–learner level. The danger here is for persons to advocate, and sometimes set, policies at levels which are the farthest from the primary typification of an educational leader. Bureaucracy and power wielding in the educational process contribute to a prostitution of this third typification of an educational leader.

Educational leaders impact on the educational process within the complex, interrelated network which involves the total educational constituency. Whether one, in fact, becomes an educational leader is not dependent on the particular role assumed or the typification which is recognized, but on whether the leader actually assumes that role or typification as a part of the educational process. The strength or effectiveness of an educational leader relates to the degree of identity which the leader experiences with the aims, expectations, values, and cultural artifacts of the entire educational constituency and to the degree that typification of the teacher–student is primary in the consciousness of the leader.

Typification of Educational Leader Behaviors

Granted that certain behaviors constitute a mode of educational leadership, but does a common set of behaviors exist for all educational leadership? Behaviorists assume that by observing what educational leaders do which result in desired behavior patterns, one can construct a list of behaviors which are common to all educational leaders. Consequently, by teaching someone to perform this set of behaviors, anyone can be taught to be a leader. The devastating criticism of the behavioristic method of teaching educational leadership is that definitions of success and effectiveness of leader behaviors are predetermined by the observer, and the list which results from observations is incomplete and also dependent on the observer.

Mintzberg has attempted to categorize managerial behavior without using predetermined categories. He uses a method of unstructured observation and develops new content categories during and after the initial observations. Although Mintzberg's list of ten "roles" which he concluded would account for all the managerial activities which he observed is subject to the same criticism which can be directed toward the behavioristic approach, the three "types" of roles which he described are instructive. Three of the ten roles which he described involve interpersonal behaviors (figurehead, leader, and liaison); three others deal with communication behaviors (monitor, disseminator, and spokesman); and four are decision making behaviors (entrepreneur, disturbance handler, resource allocator, and negotiator). All three typifications of behavior can be interpreted in different ways while the manager is engaged in them. Although the roles can be described individually, they cannot be isolated from each other. In fact, Mintzberg says that the ten roles form a "gestalt," "an integrated whole."[27]

Typing the leader behaviors of educators will meet with no more success than attempting to categorize the behavior of business managers. General types of leader behaviors of educators can be classified as valuing, relating, communicating, deciding, knowing, and acting, but the nature and content of specific behaviors of educational leaders is quite relative, depending on the values, aims, and purposes of the entire educational constituency. Thus, to attempt to predict what an educational leader will do or should do is always dependent on what the predetermined expectations and definitions of the observer are.

The behaviors of educational leaders which seem to be typical involve: valuing a view of human life which will contribute to the learner's welfare and happiness; relating dialogically to all elements of the educational constituency as a being–with–others; deciding all issues and options on the basis of the values, goals, and cultural beliefs of the educational constituency; knowing data and principles and ways of thinking which will lead to the "good life"; and acting responsibly and freely to help others to learn what is meaningful and fulfilling in human existence and how to avoid as many failures and unpleasant experiences as is possible. The qualifier, "educational," which describes a leader's behavior, is unique to the extent to which the constituency assigns meaning to what happens in the educational process.

What one discovers when examining typifications of educational leaders is that educational leaders are those humans who are valuing, relating, knowing, deciding, and acting in such a way that the learners voluntarily choose to follow them. There is nothing mystical or other-worldly about being an educational leader; it is a matter of all things working together to the end that purposeful and relevant learning occurs at the primary typification of an educational leader.

INTENTIONALITY OF POLICY PROCESS

Educational aims and purposes find expression in social relationships between educational leaders and the followers (the educational constituency). The process through which these educational values, aims, and purposes are formulated and enacted into regulatory norms and rules is the educational policy process. Educational policies are the operative rules or norms by which the process of education regulates all educational practices.

The phenomenological concept of intentionality is a helpful way of examining the leader's participation in the policy process of education.

Intentionality of the educational process deals with both the structures of theoretical experiences and the nature of educational content and practices.

Intentionality of Theory and Practice

Two major approaches to theory and practice of educational leadership have dominated the literature of leadership theory, yet both approaches are based on Descartes' contention that a thinking subject is separate from the object of thought.

The first approach places heavy emphasis on the theoretical, rational side of leadership. According to this approach, leaders are born with personal traits and capacities to think clearly, judge rationally, and formulate theories of education. Educators who subscribe to this rational approach devise ways to identify those with leadership traits and to bring out their personality traits through rational training exercises in logic, math, history, and study of the great thinkers of the past. Potential leaders are thrust into the educational arena where "the cream rises to the top," i.e., leaders naturally arise if they utilize their natural gifts. Thus, educational leaders are born, not made.

The second approach to educational leadership focuses on the positivistic method which holds that social actions can be explained by the same principles as natural events are explained. The positivist considers the practical, observable side of the theory–practice question and seeks to explain the causes of successful and efficient educational leadership. Leadership behaviors are categorized, and methods are developed to shape the behavior of potential leaders. Thus, the slogan of business schools that "leaders are made" is based on the positivistic claim that leaders are made out of anyone who can learn the techniques and how to apply the methods which result in leadership behaviors.

Do we have to choose between one or the other of these paradigms, or is there a way to bridge the gap between theory or rationality and practice or behavior? The concept of intentionality advocates that theory and practice cannot be separated so easily.

To explain the social phenomena of a leader's relationship to an educational process is to analyze the agent's or actor's constitution of meaning in the leadership situation. How leadership is perceived in education depends on how the leader and the learners interpret what is taking place in the educational setting. The connecting strands among the aims, values, and policies of an educational leader and what actually happens in the lives of the learners and the leader are meanings which the leader and the learners give to educational experiences as a feature of a total life experience. What is experienced in an educational leadership situation becomes the connecting link between the policies and aims of the educational process and the actual classroom learning and school administration. Or as Kurt Lewin would view it, the leadership situation is the totality of the experiences of the policies and practices as a field of forces.

Meaning becomes the link between knowledge, theory, values, aims, and beliefs and practices, actions, and educational techniques. The relationship of ideas, theories, aims, and values of education to the life-world of the leader and learner provides the basis for leadership in the educational situation. Theory and practice cannot be separated. The leader and the learners give meaning to the aims and methods of education according to their perceptions of their being-in-the-world.

What education means and what is meaningful to the followers of an educational leader are read into the educational process by leaders and learners through interpretative and meaningful principles that have come from the leaders and the learners themselves.[28]

Merleau-Ponty's analysis and integration of behaviors and theories avoids the subject-object dualism through a conceptualization of the body-organism analogy as a model of being-in-the-world or belonging-in-the-world through its openness to the world. In a given leadership situation, each leader exhibits a chosen mode of behavior which is not the simple sum of the system's aims and goals or the function dictated by the educational system, but the leader's behavior is determined by the leader's and the learner's general interpretations of the aims and purposes of education in general.[29] The leader modifies his or her milieu in accordance with the operative norms or policies of the educational process. Educational leadership is a unity of meanings in which the leader and the learners are polarities in the educational system.

The body is the primary mode of being-in-the-world, not as a passive agency of sensory perception or as an obstacle to idealistic knowledge, but as a center around which the world of education is given as a setting, condition, or state of the leader's being-in-the-world. The leader can never be detached from his or her body, not even in an attitude of objectivity as the positivists contend. The body of an educational leader is the vantage point of all perception and action in the educational setting.[30]

To a football player the football field is not an object, but is a field of forces, vectors, and openings which call for lines of movement in accord with the play which is called. The player is not a consciousness who surveys the field as a datum; the field is present only as the schema of the player's intentions, and lines of force in it are continuously restructured with the player's moves throughout the game. The player becomes one with the field and feels the direction of the goal as the player experiences the vertical and horizontal plans of his or her own body. Thus, the player "knows" where the goal is in a manner which is "lived" rather than "known."

These lived interpretations which each leader and learner give to what is happening on the educational "field" bridge theory and practice by seeing the situation as a whole, a totality. Not by thinking about leadership theory nor by doing leadership acts, but by contemplating the interpretation of the thinking and the acting is the meaning of educational leadership revealed. Meaning–intending is the relevance system which gives birth to both theory and practice. Meaning in an educational leadership situation is an inward, creative activity, a gift to events, objects, and states of affairs, inscribed with each person's distinctive interpretation. When these leadership events and knowledge are given meaning by educational leaders and learners and are directed toward educational aims and purposes, the meaning is the link between leadership theory and practice. Educational aims, values, and policies will have different meanings for each leader and learner who reflects on them, and each act of educational leadership has a unique meaning for each person contemplating it. The way ideas, facts, values, beliefs, theories, and aims are related to the life–world of the leader and the learner and what these mean to each person become the basis for what the leader and the learner do about the educational leadership situation. Accordingly, the leader and the learner give meaning to both theory and practice as a total experience, not by separating the subject from the object of consciousness.

Intentionality of Educational Content

Educational leaders formulate and enact values, aims, goals, beliefs, and culture into educational policies and practices in the educational process. These policies and practices can be either formal or informal, but educational leaders are vitally and inseparably bound up with the content and curriculum which flows through the policies, which in turn, issue from the aims and values of the leaders and the followers.

The Cartesian method of viewing educational content is to equate it with a body of information which is to be poured from the leader's container of wisdom into the learners' sensory receptacle. This information can emphasize natural phenomena after which humans need to pattern their behavior or the liberal arts which have been transmitted through the works and words of great thinkers. The problem with this view of educational content which is dominant in American education today is that the knower and the known are separated; the mind apprehends data and files it in the brain; the subject studies an object (the content) "out there."

Could we not view educational content as the meaning of the total experience of leaders and learners relating, knowing, valuing, deciding, and recalling in the educational situation? A phenomenology of the educational policy process reveals the interrelatedness, the intentionality, the holistic, the field of forces of the educational programs, curriculum, schooling, administration, and informal learning activities. Giroux, following Freire, suggests that the content of education be thought of as ideology. Ideology in this sense considers education as a process and the content as "meaning-intending" of learners existing in the education situation, i.e., being-in-the-world educationally. [31]

Leaders relate not only to the knowledge and skills of schooling, but the content of education is the distilled meanings in culture, as happenings in families and among friends, as a hidden curriculum in the school. An effective educational leader takes note of the tacit knowledge imbedded in the formal curriculum, the landscapes and horizons of learning which make up the larger learning environment. In other words, the content of education cannot be separated from the media by which learning is communicated, just as McLuhan points out that the medium of communication is the message.

Educational leaders are the subject matter and the content of the schooling process. The content cannot be passed on or communicated to learners in isolation from the landscapes and the larger context outside the learning situation. Teachers and leaders are so full of the subjects they teach that content of the subjects spills out upon the potential learners. Think back when you were in school. You remember data and experiences as bound up with and inseparable from the teachers and the situations of the learning situation. Further, the things which you learned had strings attached to the whole school, the community, and the larger world.

The concept of intentionality allows us to see the interrelatedness of the leaders and the content in the policy process of schooling. Therefore, educational policies which are relevant to a local school setting should not be developed in the central office, the state office, or at the federal level without considering how the leaders themselves (being the content) relate to the learners. Policies and practices, as well as theories, embody the values, the culture, and the visions of the educational leaders and cannot be totally isolated from the lived-world of those participating in the schooling process.

Intentionality of Educational Leader's Actions

The social actions which result from educational practices are linked to the aims and theories of the leaders and the constituents of the educational process through the interpretation of these actions by the leaders, the constituents, and the learners who are participating in the educational process.

The intentional nature of action is widely recognized by social scientists. Searle contends that a more intimate connection exists between actions and intentions than between beliefs and states of affairs because actions contain intentions in action as one of their components:

> An action is a composite entity of which one component is an intention in action. . . . There are no actions, not even unintentional actions, without intentions, because every action has an intention as one of its components. [32]

Schutz helps to clarify the intentionality of action by analyzing the structures of human action in social settings. Every action is "future-directed" toward some goal or aim.

> Every action is carried out according to a project and is oriented to an act fantasied in the future perfect as already executed. The unity of the action is constituted exclusively by this project, whose span may be very different depending on how explicitly it is planned. . . . [33]

The motive which explains the action toward its future goal is the "in-order-to" motive, according to Schutz. If the project which is viewed in the future perfect state is explained in terms of the actor's past experiences, a "because-motive" exists. Meaning-intending of the action is as much a part of the action as is the physical or mental changes which are in process. Thus, Searle explains the process of human action as having four elements: "the prior intention, the intention in action, the bodily movement, and the action."[34] All of these elements are linked in the action-chain which moves from intention to completed act.

In contrast to the intentionality of action, positivism views action in a cause-effect paradigm, whereby the action is clearly separated from its cause. The positivistic researcher studies the causes of behaviors empirically in order to control and modify human action. An identification of the cause of an action allows the positivistic researcher to predict the nature of the future action or the result of that action. Behaviorists, though, make the critical mistake of observing the result of actions and trying to reconstruct the causes of the observed behavior in order to prescribe a technique which will alter or modify future actions.

Phenomenologically, the intentionality of action or practice in educational leadership explains educational actions as a unified process in which the leader is vitally involved at every stage and in every aspect. A leader's value system and educational aims and purposes figure prominently in the leader's actions, by way of the meaning-intending of the actions which cannot be separated from the educational practices. Thus, educational actions of a leader have a basic intuitive dimension in the intending of meaning by the leader.

An educational leader who does not reflect on and clarify his or her own values, cultural beliefs, and hopes and their impact on the meaning-intending of the educational actions may be controlling, exploiting, forcing, manipulating, or changing the behaviors of learners without consciously intending to modify their behavior. However, we should not call this behavior modification "leading." A leader who uses rewards and punishment, behavior modification, or any other means to control or to manipulate learners has not taken seriously the strong position which values, aims, and purposes occupy in the policy process. The intentionality of an educational leader's actions involves the entire process of motives, intentions, meanings, actions, and results as a unity, a totality. The actions which result from educational policy are firmly based on the values and aims of the educational leaders and learners.

The quality and effectiveness of an educational leader's actions are in direct proportion to the quality of his or her educational aims and values. Effectiveness and efficiency of educational leaders are related to the degree of similarity between the aims and values of the educational leader and those of the educational constituency. Leaders whose actions are preferred hold and promote the aims and values of the educational constituents. The intentionality of educational actions is a state of educational existence in which all educational theories, practices, policies, programs, and actions are viewed within the framework of the entire process of education, not as isolated behaviors or motives which can be changed or directed toward the leader's preferred goals, values, and results.

All people, leaders included, do what they believe to be consistent with their view of the world and reality. A friend told me of an acquaintance who lived on the West Coast in California. This person believed that the West Coast was falling into the Pacific Ocean. He left a very successful job, sold his house, and moved to a safer location in Iowa. Only an irrational or mentally disturbed person would deliberately do that which was contrary to his or her view of reality. A much closer tie binds a leader's beliefs and actions than a tie between either knowledge or skills and behavior.

Actions which issue from educational policies are firmly rooted in the beliefs and hopes of the leaders and the learners. Thus, a study of educational policy should analyze the aims and values of both the leaders and the learners in the educational process and should then clarify the interrelatedness of the leader's beliefs and the beliefs and values of the learners. Otherwise, the often–employed study of educational policy is conducted in a context and value system which is totally isolated and foreign to the primary participants in the educational policies. The concept of intentionality links educational actions and policies and leaders and learners into a total inseparable unity. To be a leader of learners is to be situated in a web of actions, beliefs, policies, and values.

EXCELLENCE IN EDUCATIONAL LEADERSHIP

Another component of the landscape in which educational leadership occurs is evaluation of the process of education. Of late, the question of the achievement of excellence in the educational situation involves the phenomena of evaluation and testing to determine whether leaders are effective in the schooling experience. The question for us is how the leader experiences the phenomena of evaluation in an educational system.

Positivistic models of leadership employ empirical data (cause and effect) and quantitative methods to evaluate the effectiveness of educational leadership. This method measures the effectiveness of educational leaders in terms of: (1) test scores of learners, (2) cost-benefit analysis in the school system, (3) numerical grading of the acquisition of knowledge of learners, (4) academic credentials of the leaders, and (5) other quantifications of educational activities, such as the number of high school graduates going to college.

I am presently involved in an accreditation visit from the regional accrediting agency of which my university is a member. The "Institutional Effectiveness" "criteria" which the accrediting agency suggests encourages the use of a method of evaluation of effectiveness which investigates those actions and behaviors which are quantifiable, observable, logical, and attainable. Effectiveness, or excellence, of educational leadership is judged by measurable criteria. All subjective, intuitive, qualitative data are discouraged and considered to be inferior.

In contrast to the positivistic paradigm of evaluation, the phenomenological approach to educational evaluation includes subjective as well as empirical data. Excellence in educational leadership can utilize the criteria of consistency, comprehensiveness, completeness, relevance, morality, clarity, happiness, love, justice, and physical and mental health. The primary tools of qualitative, subjective evaluation are reflection, description, questioning, reporting, discussion, and interpretation. The methods are varied and manifold, not monolithic. New directions in qualitative evaluation offer valuable alternatives to the positivistic approach. The basic thrust of qualitative educational evaluation is global, cultural, and field based. Its goal is to bring together logic, science, faith, and subjective interpretations of the whole picture of educational leadership.[35]

This section will analyze the various aspects of the evaluation process in education to determine the quality of educational leadership. Applying the qualitative research method to the functions which educational leaders are most vitally involved in the educational process will reveal how well leaders are achieving excellence in the process of educating the learners.

Monitoring the Aims of Educational Leaders

Evaluation of educational leadership rests on the values, aims, and beliefs of the educational leaders and learners. Judgments of good and bad, right and wrong, efficient and inefficient, appropriate and inappropriate are based on the values, aims, and beliefs of the entire educational constituency. Effective leadership is ultimately dependent on what good education is, and good education is in turn based on what those involved in the educational process consider valuable and satisfying.

The tools of philosophical reflection and analysis are indispensable for monitoring the quality of excellence in educational leadership. Consequently, good leaders tend to be good philosophers, good thinkers, good analyzers, good synthesizers, good visionaries, good creators, etc. Hodgkinson refers to leadership as "philosophy–in–action" and says that the art of leadership finds its true basis in the humanities. [36]

Educational leaders monitor values by means of value audits, values clarification, and philosophical reflection on the consistency, completeness, relevancy, and moral quality of the educational process. Are the values of teachers consistent with the values of the educational constituency, and are the values of the constituents relevant and moral for the learners?

The educational constituency demands that the educational leaders be accountable for what happens in school systems. Thus, leaders feel pressure to amass considerable documentation to verify that education is indeed occurring among the learners, and leadership is evaluated on the basis of this documentation. However, in the average school the evaluation of data does not speak to what actually occurs in the learning situation. Rather, attendance records, lesson plans, formal credentials of teachers, dollar–to–pupil and teacher–to–pupil ratios, dropouts, discipline problems, and such criteria are used to judge the effectiveness of schools. Is leadership effectiveness to be measured only in these quantifiable terms of scores, buildings, budgets, and noses?

A better measure of quality in educational leaders might be to ask whether leaders promote and embody those values which are central to the life of the educational constituency? A White lady once shared with me her concern about her son being bussed to a school in Nashville, Tennessee which was previously a predominantly Black school. She asked me how the lower academic standards which she falsely assumed existed in the school would affect her son's chances of going to college and succeeding in life. After I engaged her in a lengthy discussion to reassure her about the quality of the school, she sort of confessed, "At least he has a wonderful Black teacher. Maybe he will learn something from her that will help him relate to Blacks later in life." While she expressed concern about grades and test scores, her son was apparently learning one of her own, as well as her educational constituency's, most valued skills, i.e., relating to others in a meaningful way.

Thus, the aims and values of education are basic to evaluation of the quality of leadership in a school system. Good educational leaders will engage in a continuous process of values monitoring and qualitative evaluation and will lead in the clarification, statement, promotion, embodying, and implementation of those values and aims which are central to the educational constituents.

Monitoring Interpersonal Relations

Evaluation of educational leadership also involves reflections on the quality of interpersonal relationships in an educational system. The quality of these relationships is judged on the basis of whether the personal element is pervasive and authentic throughout the educational system. Do leaders engage learners and others as being-with-others in a genuinely and meaningfully dialogical manner? Are the feelings, attitudes, beliefs, needs, and values of the learners considered in the educational policies, programs, and practices?

The translation of personal qualities in an organizational expression is most easily accomplished through consensus, but is also recognized in community and consistency in interpersonal relationships. Averaging in a mathematical sense does not lead to consensus; consensus is achieved through concessions within value-driven and cultural boundaries, but without disturbance of the overall zones of indifference and acceptance. Consensus in educational values involves the processes of compromise, cooperation, trade-off, negotiation, conciliation, and bargaining which occur whenever the educational constituents possess differential power and seek divergent ends.[37] The ends which are reached through consensus must not conflict with the values and aims of the educational constituency or of the leaders and learners. No one may be entirely satisfied with the consensus, but neither is anyone dissatisfied to the point of sabotage, disruption, or withdrawal from the constituency. The consensus operates around the commonly held values, beliefs, and cultural bonds of the educational organization. Whenever consensus dissolves and the zones of acceptance are violated, the organizational process becomes manipulative and coercive.

Much that happens through consensus in educational systems is a tacit working out of agreements about the values and aims of the educational process. Open discussion and sensitivity training help to keep the value issues at the conscious level. Although the quality of the relationships depends on the values within the zone of acceptance of those relating in the educational process, true consensus in educational leadership implies a profound recognition and acceptance of the common stock of values and beliefs which maintain and promote the community of the leaders, the learners, and the constituents. The leader who can achieve true consensus in an educational organization is unusual, but some minimal degree of value consensus is necessary if an educational system is viable.

If consensus is understood as "feeling–with" and "being–with" others, then consensus is appropriate for dialogical leadership and encourages quality and excellence in educational leaders. Monitoring the being–with–others relationships insures that the quality of interpersonal relationships is in harmony with the aims, values, beliefs, and cultural artifacts of the educational constituency.

Monitoring Decision Making

How does a leader achieve quality in decision making in an educational setting? Evaluation of the decision making process of leaders focuses on how decisions are made and not on the quantification of the results of the decisions made. The root of the word "evaluation" is "value," and values cannot be separated from the process of decision making.

A phenomenological description of the decision process of educational leaders reveals a need to focus more attention on the questions rather than on the answers to the questions. By reflecting on questions, the leader obtains a clearer perception of the nature of the questions or problems to be answered. An attempt to see, and to see clearly, the questions to be decided reduces the probability of biases, prejudices, and preconceptions which determine the decisions. Thus, evaluation of the quality of leadership decisions requires a clear description of the questions to be asked, the reasons answers are required, and the meaning of the answers proposed to the leaders and the learners.

In order to get a clear perception of the questions, or problems, which need addressing the leader enlists the views of as many people with as many alternative perspectives as is possible. Antagonistic, complementary, and alternative views are welcomed and encouraged, and no attempt is made to coerce opponents to compromise their positions. The goal is to reformulate and restate the questions in terms of the values and aims of the educational leaders and learners. Selection criteria are almost infinite in number, depending on the values of a particular educational constituency. Without a clarification of educational values and cultural artifacts, an educational leader has no dependable way of making decisions which are of value to the constituency and to the leaders and learners.

Zones of acceptance and zones of indifference which are prominent in educational leadership theory indicate whether the followers identify with and accept the values and aims of the educational leader. As long as the followers value the questions which are being asked and as long as the followers can contribute knowledge or perspectives on the questions, educational leaders should involve every possible learner and constituent in the decision making process. However, participation in decision making may be accomplished by dissemination of information or discussion of the questions and problems, as well as participation in the actual choosing.

Because educational leaders do not react to educational environments as much as they enact and create them, meaningful educational decisions are always in the past tense. Meaningful lived experience can be evaluated only after it has been experienced, not as it is lived nor before it happens. The enacted educational environments are known as meaningful only when they have been completed. Knowing and meaning derive from reflection, from a looking back at the completed experience. A leader can visualize an act of decision as completed in the future perfect tense. The meaning of a lived experience undergoes modifications depending on the particular kind of attention an individual gives to that lived experience.[38] The present interests and values of the educational constituents determine the meaning of the decisions which they are making. Educational leaders who make good decisions focus on the decision process and not on the answers.

The criteria for good decisions of educational leaders are questions of comprehensiveness, consistency, and completeness. More time should be spent on asking questions than in collecting data to support answers. Monitoring the quality of educational decisions involves a conscious attempt to recognize biases, presuppositions, and prior knowledge which will shape the questions, limit the data to be used for evidence, and determine the meaning of the final choice. Such techniques as brainstorming, interviewing, divergent thinking, simulation gaming, fantasizing, and futuristic projecting are ways of encouraging alternatives, options, and possibilities which will result in better decisions. Value audits identify those values, aims, and beliefs which will determine how leaders and followers perceive and judge everything which is considered, as well as that which is decided in an educational setting. Quality educational decisions, finally, are those decisions which promote the welfare and quality of life for the total educational constituency.

Monitoring Commitment and Responsibility

One of the most elusive, yet most crucial, aspects of educational leadership is the commitment and responsibility to become a leader or follower. Behavioral science has operated on the assumption that all humans have a set of basic needs and that knowledge of these needs permits the leader to "motivate" and to control the behavior of followers. A phenomenological description of the dynamics of educational leadership indicates that both leaders and learners are always motivated, but whether persons become leaders is related to values, commitment, and responsibility. One can possess all the personal traits which leaders should have and be trained in the best leadership programs in the world and still not be a leader. The will of a person must be directed toward the values and needs of the potential followers.

Unless both educational leaders and learners are committed to the aims and values of an educational project, policy, or program, nothing short of coercion and force will cause the educational system to achieve its desired aims and goals. Commitment is an affective attachment of the will to the values, aims, goals, and cultural artifacts which are involved in an educational project, program, or policy.[39]

Yukl sees a connection between the successful influence of leaders and the exercise of the charismatic style of leadership.[40] In other words, leadership which is characterized by emotion, myths, symbols, intuition, values, love, and care attracts the commitment, loyalty, trust, and involvement of followers. Commitment is the process of internalization of the values and beliefs which the leader projects. As followers internalize the values of the leader, the leader becomes the ego-ideal, the model, of the potential followers. Thus, dialogical leadership is not possible without the existence of commitment and responsibility between the leaders and the followers.

Monitoring of commitment is a matter of self-examination on the part of leaders and followers. Is the leader committed to the aims and values of the educational constituency, or have the educational aims and values been internalized by the leader? Do the learners perceive the leader as an ego-ideal, a model of the desired life? If control or compliance of the followers is achieved by force, intimidation, threat, coercion, or punishment, then the values and modeling of the leader are undesirable.

The corollary of commitment in educational leadership is responsibility. Leaders and learners who are free to choose what to follow, whom to follow, and who they desire to become are individually responsible for what each becomes, believes, and does. The definition of responsibility for each person in the educational leadership process is dependent on what each constituent values. Responsibility of leaders and learners is measured by the degree of acceptance or internalization of the values of the entire constituency by both the leaders and the learners.

Monitoring commitment involves a consideration of visible signs and symbols of affective attachment to the educational system's aims and values. Educational leaders who strongly influence their educational systems are adept in utilizing myths, symbols, traditions, rituals, and emotive expressions and practices. For instance, a certain Texas high school has a fifty-year unbroken string of superior ratings in the state marching band contests. The values and aims which support this tradition permeate the entire school system: there is a two-hundred piece seventh grade band which is better than most high schools; first-chair trumpet in the high school band is more prestigious than being captain of the varsity basketball team; and spectators go to the high school football games to see the band perform at half-time and leave before the second half of the game begins. The leaders of this band program developed and cultivated values and traditions which their constituency supported. Educational myths, symbols, and rituals which support the educational aims and values of an educational constituency encourage a committed and enthusiastic group of followers. Research needs to be conducted on the power and influence of "school spirit," clubs, and extra-curricular activities on the quality of education throughout a school system.

Educational leaders who monitor the subjective, intuitive, emotional, moral, and cultural expressions of excellence and values of what education really is to the constituency will be more effective, and "better" leaders.

CONCLUSION

A phenomenological description of the landscapes, or horizons, of educational leadership reveals the central position which values, beliefs, and other subjective data play in determining what happens in the educational process. Educational aims, content, methods, policies, organization, and evaluation are built on the values of the educational constituency. All meanings which are assigned to any educational policy, practice, or program are relative to the values of the person who is intending the meaning. Separation of theory and practice is impossible in a phenomenology of educational leadership since what is practiced is incomplete apart from the intention and bestowal of meaning by the leaders, learners, and the constituency.

Being an educational leader is not restricted to the cause–effect behaviors in the classroom or in a school building. The leader is personally bound up with all other persons in the entire educational constituency, as well as being influenced, and influencing, all other aspects of the landscape, larger world of the educational setting.

Educational organizations do not exist except as social realities which are constructed by intended meanings which are assigned to collectives of educators and potential learners. The nature and meaning of educational leadership is studied by examining the "educational" landscapes, the larger world, the "lived world" of the leader, not by observing how leaders behave in business, governmental, military, religious, or political organizations. The basic transaction in an educational moment is a relationship between a teacher and a student, around which all other roles and relationships in an educational organization gravitate. Educational leaders are leaders in schools only to the extent that the desires, hopes, dreams, values, and cultural beliefs are being addressed in the educational process.

Evaluation of the quality of educational leadership is subjective, but can be carried out by philosophical reflection, analysis, projection, and auditing of those values and principles which are prized by the educational constituency. The entire process of education can be examined on the basis of the values of the leaders, learners, and the constituency. Educational leaders who are effective have internalized the values and cultural mores of the educational constituency, and the followers have identified with and accepted the leader as an ego-ideal and personal model of the meaningful and happy life. Quality of educational leadership is judged on the basis of a subjective self-examination by all who are involved in the educational process and by the criteria of consistency, completeness, clarity, comprehensiveness, and consequentialness.

NOTES

1. W.N. Watkins, "Historical Explanations in the Social Sciences," in *Theories of History*, ed. P. Gardiner (Glencoe, Ill.: The Free Press, 1959), 505.

2. A.F. Davies, *Skills, Outlooks, and Passions* (Cambridge: Cambridge University Press, 1980), 69n.

3. Thomas Barr Greenfield, cited by William Foster, *Paradigms and Promises: New Approaches to Educational Administration* (Buffalo: Prometheus Books, 1986), 61.

4. Greenfield, "Leaders and Schools: Willfulness and Nonnatural Order in Organizations," in *Leadership and Organizational Culture*, ed. Thomas J. Sergiovanni and John E. Corbally (Chicago: University of Illinois Press, 1984), 152.

5. Ibid., 154.

6. Alfred Schutz and Thomas Luckmann, *The Structures of the Life-World*, trans. Richard M. Zaner and H. Tristram Engelhardt, Jr. (Evanston: Northwestern University Press, 1973), 16.

7. Paulo Freire, *The Politics of Education: Culture, Power, and Liberation*, trans. Donaldo Macedo (South Hadley, Mass.: Bergin & Garvey Publishers, Inc., 1985), 68.

8. "Johnny Can't Read Because He Never Gets a Chance," *New Haven Register*, 15 September 1985, p. E10.

9. Freire, *Education for Critical Consciousness* (New York: The Seabury Press, 1973), 48ff.

10. John Dewey, *Experience and Education* (New York: Macmillan Publishing Company; "Collier Books," 1938).

11. Maurice Merleau-Ponty, *Phenomenology of Perception*, trans. Colin Smith (London: Routledge & Kegan Paul, 1962), xvi-xvii.

12. Maxine Greene, *Landscapes of Learning* (New York: Teachers College Press, 1978), 214.

13. Bernard M. Bass, *Stogdill's Handbook of Leadership*, revised and expanded edn. (New York: The Free Press, 1981), 494–95.

14. Cf. Donna L. Shavlik and Judith G. Touchton, "Women as Leaders," in *Leaders for a New Era: Strategies for Higher Education*, ed. Madeleine F. Green (New York: Macmillan Publishing Company, 1988), 98–117.

15. Maxine Greene, *The Dialectic of Freedom* (New York: Teachers College Press, 1988), 58–86.

16. Cited by Bass, *Stogdill's Handbook of Leadership*, 508–09.

17. C.T. Vivian, *Black Power and the American Myth* (Philadelphia: Fortress Press, 1970), 5.

18. King E. Davis, "The Status of Black Leadership: Implications for Black Followers in the 1980's," in *Contemporary Issues in Leadership*, ed. William E. Rosenbach and Robert L. Taylor (Boulder: Westview Press, 1984), 192–208.

19. Ibid., 198.

20. John Dewey, *Democracy and Education* (New York: The Free Press, 1916, 1966), 301–02.

21. Greene, *The Dialectic of Freedom*, xi–xii.

22. Ibid.

23. John Dewey, *On Experience, Nature, and Freedom*, ed. R. Bernstein (New York: The Liberal Arts Press, 1928, 1960), 280.

24. Merleau–Ponty, *Phenomenology of Perception*, 401.

25. D.A. Hansen and V.A. Johnson, *The Social Contexts of Learning in Bilingual Classrooms: An Interpretive Review of the Literature on Language Attitudes* (Rosslyn, Va.: National Clearinghouse for Bilingual Education, 1981), 2, 4.

26. Charles E. Bidwell, "The School as a Formal Organization," in *Handbook of Organizations*, ed. J.G. March (Chicago: Rand McNally, 1965), 975.

27. Henry Mintzberg, *The Nature of Managerial Work* (Englewood Cliffs: Prentice–Hall, Inc., 1973), 54–99.

28. Henry A. Giroux, "Ideology and Agency in the Process of Schooling," *Journal of Education* 165, No. 1 (Winter 1983): 30.

29. Cf. John O'Neill, *Perception, Expression, and History: The Social Phenomenology of Maurice Merleau–Ponty* (Evanston: Northwestern University Press, 1970), 11–12.

30. Merleau–Ponty, *The Structure of Behavior*, trans. Alden L. Fisher (Boston: Beacon Press, 1963), 168.

31. Giroux, "Ideology and Agency in the Process of Schooling," 30.

32. John R. Searle, *Intentionality: An Essay in the Philosophy of Mind* (New York: Cambridge University Press, 1983), 107.

33. Alfred Schutz, *The Phenomenology of the Social World*, trans. George Walsh and Frederick Lehnert, with intro. by George Walsh (Evanston: Northwestern University Press, 1967), 87.

34. Searle, *Intentionality*, 92.

35. Cf. David M. Fetterman, ed., *Qualitative Approaches to Evaluation in Education: The Silent Scientific Revolution* (New York: Praeger, 1988).

36. Christopher Hodgkinson, *The Philosophy of Leadership* (New York: St. Martin's Press, 1983), 10. Although Hodgkinson used the word "administration" in the context cited, he clearly equates leadership and administration, e.g., on p. 197 the terms "administration" and "leadership" merge and become synonymous.

37. Ibid., 122.

38. Schutz, *The Phenomenology of the Social World*, 73.

39. Hodgkinson, *The Philosophy of Leadership*, 215.

40.   Gary A. Yukl, *Leadership in Organizations* (Englewood Cliffs: Prentice–Hall, Inc., 1981), 59–61.

Chapter 5

Training Educators to Be Leaders

What are the implications of a phenomenological analysis for the training of educational leaders? Most nations of the world do not have preparation programs for leadership positions in educational institutions. Are the educational leaders in nations which do have leadership training programs for educators (e.g., the United States, Canada, and Australia) any better or stronger than the educational leaders in nations which do not have training programs? An answer to that question is not possible here, but training is an integral aspect of educational leadership in America.

In the United States preparation programs for educational leaders have focused on behavior control, classroom motivation and management, and the acquisition of knowledge and techniques to manage and to manipulate the learners. Management techniques, behavior modification, and empirical research tools (such as cost-benefit analysis) are taught to prospective educational leaders on the assumption that anyone can learn to be an educational leader by acquiring the knowledge and skills which have been found to be "effective" or "excellent" in business management. Training programs for educational leaders in the United States are based primarily on the philosophical premises of logical positivism. Positivistic programs of leadership training can result in an identification of leadership with the power to control the behavior of the students, but these programs do not necessarily result in educational leadership which is defined phenomenologically within the parameters of the nature of education itself.

167

The philosophical assumptions behind most educational leadership training programs in the United States reduce leadership to knowledge and skills which will enable the leader to manage the student's behaviors, to cause the student to obey the leader, and to impose the leader's will and desires upon the students. Even the so-called "human relations" and "organizational development" training programs are directed toward the leader's power to control, to manage, and to manipulate the followers. A phenomenological analysis of educational leadership raises questions about whether either the positivistic or the human relations approaches to leadership training in business organizations is appropriate for educational organizations.

A leadership training program should first clarify the difference between the nature of educational leadership and the use of coercion, behavior modification, manipulation, control, force, or threat to cause compliance of the students by a power-wielding leader. Although the uses of power to control subjects may be appropriate in certain business, medical, military, or law-enforcement situations, educational leaders are those people whom the followers choose voluntarily to accept as their leaders. Thus, educational leadership is a state or condition of a leader who is engaged in the process of education in such a way that the educational constituency wants to follow and to become what the leader is, believes, values, advocates, and practices. The very nature of education encourages the opposite of power-wielding, manipulation, and behavior control of the learners.

Schools of business administration and management are not designed to teach educational leadership, if leadership is understood as a state or condition of being and not a set of behaviors. Mintzberg asks whether management is a profession and whether it can be taught. While there is clear evidence that all managerial jobs require the incumbent to perform a common set of roles, there is remarkably little evidence for the requirement for formal learning in order to perform any of these roles.[1]

Because most contemporary theories of educational leadership are based on positivistic methods of research, leadership training programs consist of empirical research methodologies and behavior modification technologies. Consequently, educational leadership training focuses on the leader's ability and power to cause the "subordinates" to behave in a manner consistent with the leader's desires. Programs of "educational leadership training" in most schools of education are designed to train administrators to control, manipulate, manage, and modify the behavior of the students.

Since leaders are neither "born" nor "made" exclusively, then "being" an educational leader cannot be taught simply by means of behavior modification techniques and the transmission of knowledge; nor can leaders be trained or discovered by compilations of "great person" traits which match the personalities of potential leaders. Just as heroes cannot be trained, in one sense leaders cannot be trained. Hook's description of a hero as an "event–making" person applies to being an educational leader:

> The event–making man is an eventful man whose actions are the consequences of outstanding capacities of intelligence, will, and character rather than accidents of position. . . . A hero is great not merely in virtue of what he does but in virtue of what he is.[2]

Although educational leaders cannot be trained to *be* leaders as we usually think of training, certain educational experiences can support the state or condition of *being* an educational leader. Those experiences which raise the consciousness of leaders and learners in regard to what educational leadership is and to the values and states of being which encourage persons to become educational leaders should be included in training programs for educational leaders. An educator and psychologist, Arthur Combs, issues a warning about counselor training which I think equally applies to educational leaders; he says that training programs should concern themselves more with perception and meaning and less with behavior and methods.[3] Educational leadership training programs should consider the perceptual organization of consciousness and the personal meanings of leadership for both leaders and learners.

This chapter will explore some of the educational experiences which will promote the condition and state of being an educational leader. Granted, this is not a laundry list for training educational leaders, an outline of a seminar on training leaders, nor a one–minute method of educating leaders, but hopefully it suggests ways to increase the chances of teachers, administrators, staffers, and concerned citizens of *being* educational leaders.

LIBERAL ARTS AND EDUCATIONAL LEADERSHIP

On September 3, 1986 a landmark symposium entitled "Corporations at Risk: Liberal Learning and Private Enterprise" was conducted in Cambridge, Massachusetts under the sponsorship of the Corporate Council on the Liberal Arts in association with the American Academy of Arts and Sciences. The Permanent Representatives, or Executive Board, of the Corporate Council on the Liberal Arts include: American Express Company, American Telephone & Telegraph Company, Cabot Corporation, Carter Hawley Hale Stores, Inc., CBS Inc., Exxon Corporation, General Foods Corporation, General Motors Corporation, Honeywell Inc., Johnson & Johnson, Prudential Insurance Company of America, and Union Pacific Corporation. In a brochure introducing the Corporate Council, The Chairman and President of CBS Inc., Thomas H. Wyman, stated:

> The importance of a liberal arts education to leadership within the corporate world has been the subject of occasional and eloquent comment by heads of individual corporations. Yet there has never been a concentrated attempt to analyze this thesis and to apply it with consistency on an institutional basis. It is with this in mind that we are initiating the Corporate Council.

The first paper in the collection prepared for participants for the above symposium at Cambridge was given by David G. Winter and began with these words:

> For over two thousand years, the West has nurtured its future leaders with the ideal of liberal arts. From the "educated gentlemen" who ruled the British Empire of the learned clergy who guided puritan New England down to the "best and brightest" of mid-twentieth century America, those who were to become leaders first became, in Plato's words, "lovers not of part of wisdom only, but of the whole . . . able to distinguish the idea from the objects which participate in the idea. . . . <with> a naturally well proportioned and gracious mind, which will move spontaneously toward the true being of everything" (*Republic*, V, 475-76, 484).[4]

An editorial in the December 1978 issue of the *Saturday Review* lamented the "vocationalization" of higher education at the expense of the liberal arts. This editorial claimed that the liberal arts have much to offer those in a professional or vocational career. The irony of the emphasis being placed on careers is that nothing is more valuable for anyone who has had a professional or vocational education than to be able to deal with abstractions or complexities, or to feel comfortable with subtleties of thought or language, or to think sequentially.

> The humanities would be expendable only if human beings didn't have to make decisions that affect their lives and the lives of others; if the human past never existed or had nothing to tell us about the present; if thought processes were irrelevant to the achievement of purpose; if creativity was beyond the human mind and had nothing to do with the joy of living; if human relationships were random aspects of life; if human beings never had to cope with panic or pain, or if they never had to anticipate the connection between cause and effect; if all the mysteries of mind and nature were fully plumbed; and if no special demands arose from the accident of being born a human being instead of a hen or a hog.[5]

In 1956, AT&T initiated a longitudinal study (which was still continuing in 1983) whose objective was to compare the performance of liberal arts graduates with their counterparts in the Bell System from technical and business backgrounds. The humanities and social science majors achieved the best overall performance and advanced up the corporate ladder higher and faster than did engineering and business graduates.[6] A growing number of chief executive officers of *Fortune 500* companies are issuing strong testimonies about the capabilities and need for liberal arts graduates in business today. Many of these industry leaders are themselves products of liberal arts educations. Dick Munro, CEO of Time, Inc. told a group of career planning professions, "I would personally opt for a liberal arts graduate every time. Almost all of the CEO's I know are liberal arts graduates."[7] Daniel R. DeNicola flatly advocates, "The best preparation for a career in business is a strong liberal arts education. The record supports my assertion."[8] Roger B. Smith, General Motors Chairman, says, "And I think that there is almost no phase of business life that can be successfully conducted without the benefit of humanistic values and insights."[9] A growing number of people in the business world are saying that a humanities background can be a great benefit both to the individual and to the corporation in which he or she works.

Businesses have found that they need people who have learned how to learn. They need people who can read and listen with understanding; who can write and communicate clearly and effectively; who can recognize, define, and analyze problems; who can imagine, investigate, and propose appropriate solutions; who can analyze, synthesize, evaluate, and present results of research. Arthur F. Oppenheimer, President of Oppenheimer Companies, Inc., asserts:

> What is most needed in management today is the ability to think independently and creatively; to function in a imperfect, changing, and ambiguous environment; to make decisions when all the data required to solve the problem are not available; to negotiate and compromise; to be risk-seeking and entrepreneurial, not to rely on quantitative and analytical data; to recognize short and long-term implications; to avoid the obvious and solely subjective; to develop effective working relations with peers; to motivate people and resolve conflicts; and to establish effective informational networks. [10]

Oppenheimer hits the nail on the head when he concludes that all these abilities are fostered by the liberal arts. Two associate deans of the business school of the University of North Carolina proposed in the *Harvard Business Review* that business schools educate managers to take "a broader, more humanistic view of the corporation." They recommend a change in the focus of the faculties and in the focus of the curricula. Students must understand the meaning of the sweep of history, develop a holistic view of the entire world, learn to humanize the corporation, and understand the ethical implications of every management decision they make. [11] The humanities teach leaders to see clearly and completely, to apply reason and creativity to problem solving, to look into the future and to analyze the meaning of the present and the past, and to view problems and opportunities through the eyes, ears, language, and culture of other human beings. [12] The liberal arts are a solid foundation for leadership in general.

But what about educational leadership? Are the liberal arts foundational for training educational leaders? The liberal arts are essential to the kind of leadership advocated in this study, but liberal arts are not a substitute for the study of education itself.

People like William J. Bennett and Alan Bloom, among others, are advocating that we return to a form of idealism as a model for teachers and leaders. They assume that educational leaders are the philosopher–kings who become the examples for all other humans in schools and in society. Leaders are those chosen few who are endowed with the benefits of the great traditions and values of the past and who possess the personal traits needed to transmit this body of knowledge and values. Since the leaders are responsible for transmitting the cultural and scientific heritage to the next generation, the leaders must know their heritage, know their absolute values, know the subject matter they are to pass on, and have the abilities to communicate their knowledge. This idealistic mind–set views the training of educational leaders as substituting liberal learning for behavior modification methods. Thus, a big push in education today is "back to the basics," back to the values and traditions of the past, back to the body of knowledge which is important and reliable, back to the scientific laws and principles on which the future can be built. Most assuredly, this return to Platonic idealism is not what is happening in business today when executives are advocating the value of liberal arts as the foundation for business leadership.

However, many of the benefits of a liberal arts education fit like a glove with what being an educational leader means. The liberal arts broaden one's perspective of the world and one's responsibility in it. The liberal arts teach one to listen to all sides of an issue before making a decision, to stretch the mind and see things in new ways, to develop interpersonal skills and become more sensitive to cultural and ethnic differences, to respect quality and excellence, to communicate effectively, to think holistically, analytically, and reflectively. The parallel between what liberal arts provide and what the nature of educational leadership means is striking. A liberal arts foundation is basic to the training of educational leaders if the nature of educational leadership includes valuing, reflection, analysis, synthesis, deciding, communicating, relating, dreaming, evaluating, planning, caring, creating, persuading, acting, and being.

The choice is not to substitute a liberal arts major for a professional certification program in teacher training programs. Alas, some state education systems are trying to implement such a preposterous proposition. To focus more attention on preparation of specific subject matter fields will simply narrow the focus of potential leaders and will compound the problem of training leaders. The biggest problem in most schools is not an absence of knowledge on the part of the teachers and leaders, but rather a problem of not knowing what education means to the learners.

Study of the liberal arts needs to be applied within, not instead of, professional educational programs. Programs which train educational leaders need to ask questions about the meaning of education itself. Leaders of education need to know more of the history, philosophy, ethics, literature, sociology, psychology, anthropology, art, and science of education itself. A leadership position in the law profession requires that an individual learn about law, what it is, how to interpret it, how to apply it to life, how to evaluate laws, how to be responsible as a lawyer, the history of law, and such subjects. Why not approach the profession of educational leadership as one would approach judicial leadership, medical leadership, military leadership, religious leadership, or business leadership. Not that we train educational leaders by using business, military, or religious training models, but that we provide a learning environment where educational leaders can broaden their visions of education and the good life, evaluate educational policies and practices, communicate what they teach or lead, reflect and analyze their beliefs and values as they relate to the aims and purposes of education, and relate to others in the educational situation in a meaningful manner.

George Peabody College for Teachers, before it was dismantled and merged with Vanderbilt University in 1979, claimed that over 50 of its alumni were then serving as presidents of colleges and universities. This unique institution's purpose as stated in its last catalog of 1979–80 was:

> To elevate the quality of life in the nation by the education of better qualified personnel to serve in administration and in teaching at all levels of schools, colleges, and universities. Special emphasis shall be devoted to the improvement of teaching and learning and to the inspiration of those who will achieve leadership in the field of education (p.2).

This catalog proudly displayed a statement from the 1976 commencement address of Terrell Bell: "Peabody is to education what M.I.T. is to engineering and the Mayo Clinic is to medicine" (p. 8). Prior to its shift away from a teacher training institution and toward a research institution, which began in the fifties and culminated in its merger with Vanderbilt, Peabody provided an academic climate and curriculum which encouraged the development of educational leaders. We can learn a great deal about the training of educational leaders by studying the programs of Peabody during the first half of the twentieth century, not to go back to those days, but to understand what Peabody did to produce educational leaders. Peabody's last catalog stated that all baccalaureate students must take courses in six areas of learning (liberal arts) in order to "insure that Peabody graduates have breadth of knowledge and understanding about the world in which they live" (p. 51). In addition to the liberal arts, all students were required to take a professional education core component which "aimed at developing a basic understanding of education in society and human learning" (p. 55). Peabody's purpose statement even stressed "holding to high ideals, morally, spiritually, and intellectually" while promoting "fields appropriate to the principal purpose of the College" (p.2). Regrettably, the ideals of democratic values, religious sentiments, humanistic attitudes, philosophical inquiries, ethical reflections, and moral concerns of a meaningful society were undermined by the growing emphasis on empirical research and behavioristic methodology in Peabody's last three decades of existence.

The fact that George Peabody College for Teachers produced so many educational leaders was not the result of an accident nor the result of any particular educational leadership training programs. The explanation of Peabody's success was an indefinable quality which permeated the atmosphere on the entire campus. The professional education of leaders was set in the context of a profound appreciation of the liberal arts and sciences with the avowed purpose of elevating the quality of life of all humans who are touched by Peabody graduates.

A liberal education which is the foundation of educational leadership training is not a program in the baccalaureate degree, nor does it end at graduation. Such an education gives educational leaders knowledge, skills, attitudes, experiences, intentions, hopes, values, and perspectives which enable them to be truly free, caring, happy, and effective, to be a generalist who profits from mistakes, applies what has been learned, and can elicit the very best in those whom they lead. The liberal arts education which educational leaders receive needs time, resources, and opportunities to prove its worth and its fundamental position in the training of persons who can *be* educational leaders.

Maybe what we need in leadership training in education is some of what we hire a guru or consultant to tell us *after* we have left school. Managerial skills, technological expertise, and scientific knowledge are essential for educational leaders, but must not be viewed as the sole requirements for being effective leaders. A significant exposure to the humanities is sorely needed to undergird the education of potential educational leaders. Educational leaders should consider what Michael Maccoby says about the training of the business leaders:

> The study of the Bible, comparative religion, ethical philosophy
> and psychology, and great literature leads one to explore the

inner life, particularly the struggle to develop the human heart against ignorance, convention, injustice, disappointment, betrayal, and irrational passion. Such an education prepares one to grapple with his fear, envy, pride, and self–deception. . . . Without it, a would–be leader tends to confuse his or her own character with human nature, guts with courage, worldly success with integrity, the thrill of winning with happiness.[13]

Whereas the status of philosophy in education has suffered immeasurably and is almost extinct in professional educational programs in America, leadership training must provide experiences in asking questions about the meaning, the aims, and the purpose of education. Leaders need to develop insights into human nature in general, to analyze right and wrong ways of thinking and solving problems, to probe character, integrity, honesty, and justice among those who are to be taught in school. In short, those things which a liberal arts education claim to support are many of the things which are fundamental to the nature of educational leadership.

DREAMING DREAMS AND SEEING VISIONS

From the Patriarch Abraham who saw a vision of a civilization based upon Judaic–Christian principles to a Martin Luther King, Jr. who dreamed of racial justice for exploited Blacks, leaders continue to exhibit non–rational peaks of enthusiasm, insight, passion, commitment, intuition, courage, hope, integrity, connectedness, and vision. Call it charismatic, or whatever, but deny it you cannot; leaders tend to possess a world view, a frame of reference, which allows them to put the whole of life in perspective, to envision goals which encompass the needs of the common person, to draw out the best and down–play the worst in followers, to elicit the courage for followers to be the best that they can become, to call forth hidden capacities, to work miracles and wonders in the name of goodness, wisdom, justice, and love. Educational leaders surely can identify with this wisdom of seeing clearly and dreaming boldly for the educational betterment of the masses.

As maintained earlier, this process of envisioning future conditions of existence, of seeing new and different dimensions of a phenomenon as well as grasping its typical ways of being, of perceiving particulars and principles and grasping new patterns of meaning, is not some other-worldly, wild-eyed, out-of-body experience. Edmund Husserl called our attention to the "rules for seeing" clearly and developed a "method" of seeing, i.e., phenomenological analysis.[14] The same rules apply to seeing particulars as to seeing patterns of meaning. To see what love means is in principle analogous to seeing the color red. We either *see* the patterns of experience or do not grasp them at all. Meanings cannot be derived speculatively or inductively. We cannot move from the observation of instances of killing to the knowledge that killing is wrong. We *see* killing is wrong, just as we see that someone is being killed. What things are in themselves, in principle, is unambiguous and certain. A triangle must have three sides because it *is* a triangle, not because we observe three sides.

Phenomenological seeing is generally not a one-shot look or a casual glance. This kind of seeing is looking intently, gazing in awe and wonder, looking and looking again and again, focusing and refocusing, comparing perspectives, seeing as a *process*. You never had to observe an experiment nor have had to attempt to put an inflated basketball in a wine bottle to know that a basketball will not fit into the mouth of a wine bottle. When considering an idea, we often focus on it, move away from it and closer to it, turn it over in our minds, look at it again and again from different perspectives, until its meaning is clear, with no blurred edges, no obscurities, no ambiguities.

This process of seeing clearly is like my experience of trying to spot Halley's Comet with a low-power telescope. First, I had to point the telescope in the general vicinity of known constellations and clusters of stars which I had been told were close to Halley's Comet. Next, I had to focus the telescope and scan the sky until I recognized something I had seen with my naked eye. Then, I moved the telescope around narrowing my vision until I found an unusual mass of light which was not like the stars around it. Finally, I refocused the telescope again and again, trying to sharpen the image of the comet to obtain its peak brilliance.

We can learn to see educational leadership in the same way that we learn that basketballs will not fit in bottles and that Halley's Comet was really up there, even though invisible to the naked eye. Educational leaders need instruction in seeing visions and dreaming dreams. Instruction in seeing clearly enables educational leaders to develop the ability to examine issues and alternatives with the least amount of bias, prejudice, stereotypes, and preconceptions; it allows them to examine natural phenomena, others, and themselves in the fullest freedom.

Educational leaders need the vision to see complexity, to recognize various nuances of expression, to distinguish the subtleties of the slightest difference in sense data, to notice shifts and changes in the social structures, to be aware of the degree and amount of measurement required for the highest quality of evidence which results in the most probably conclusions.

Instruction in seeing means developing the vision to see far into the past, knowing from where we have come, how we developed, what values and traditions have shaped and determined us the most, and to what degree we are indebted and enslaved to our predecessors. It means seeing into the far future, knowing how to analyze trends and forecasts, how to identify scientific and intuitive factors and options which will help to achieve a desired future.

Educational leaders also need to see inside themselves with integrity, humility, and honesty, to know the importance and necessity of self examination, and to know how self analysis is best achieved. Instruction in seeing means seeing out of ourselves, beyond ourselves, to others with whom we come in contact in our daily lives, to other cultures of past and present. The ability to see enables educational leaders to see farther, clearer, and better in the best sense of the word vision. This ability to see clearly is an essential ingredient in the training of potential educational leaders.

But how is this instruction in seeing visions and dreaming dreams conducted? No step–by–step training program is available because no one learns to see all at once. We learn to see by practicing the "art" of seeing. Some of the kinds of things which go into training leaders to see more clearly and more completely require us to break out of our normal ways of seeing. For instance, looking at the world through the wrong end of a telescope often gives a new or different perspective. Viewing the English countryside from the air helped archaeologists discover the Roman Wall across England. Looking up at the landscape, people, and sky from a prone position opens new vistas. Picking up a common object, like a rock, and describing it from every conceivable vantage point is quite instructive. Taking two totally unrelated objects or ideas and trying to relate a third question or idea can help us to see things not expected or anticipated.

Williams College in Massachusetts has a leadership training program for business executives which includes courses in music, drama, literature, art, and political science. The Dartmouth Institute is a summer program to train blue–chip business people in imaginative, long–range thinking. The faculty at Dartmouth are drawn from such fields as religion, astronomy, history, and comparative literature. Washington and

Lee in Virginia has a two–week course for executives which studies the philosophy and literature of Kierkegaard, Melville, and Thoreau. The testimonies of participants in these and similar programs confirm that studying and participating in the arts gives new, better, sharper, broader perspectives on the problems and opportunities in the business world. How much more would studying and practicing the arts give new and dynamic visions to education leaders?

Perhaps Jacob Bronowski's statement that imagination is the common quality in both arts and sciences provides some insight as to why studying the fine arts is important to the development of educational leadership. The use of words and symbols not just to communicate, but to manipulate your own ideas inside your own head sets humans apart from all other animals. This ability to conceive of things which are not present to the senses is crucial to reflection, making analogies, speculating, and drawing conclusions. Only humans can project themselves into the future and imagine what the situation will be in order to alter present plans and actions. Imagination is the human habit of making images in one's head. The metaphorical images work in our minds to shape our thoughts, link the different fields of our experience, and bring out the likenesses between them:

> In this sense, all art is metaphor. It takes one part of your experience, and another part of your experience, and it forces you to look at them together. And by this act of looking at them together, the work of art makes you see each experience afresh and differently. . . . The gift of imagination is that twofold movement by which it both manipulates images in my head and sets them spinning with a kind of communicative force which recreates them in yours, whether I am looking at a work of art, reading a poem, or talking about a theorem. Indeed what is certainly true is that all important human work in the arts and in science consists exactly in fashioning in one's head a hypothetical situation which can overlap the intervening space and be reformed in the head of somebody else.[15]

That quality of symbolic and conceptual thinking of which humans are uniquely capable is made possible by the "gifts" of the eye to get information about the natural world and gifts of the ear to obtain information about people. Unifying images of sight and sound, content and style, image and world is the essence of the visual arts, literature, and the sciences. These abilities of reflection, association, analysis, projection, speculation, induction, and deduction are quite central to the development of educational leadership. Those who advocate a "situational leadership" theory depend on these same integrative and interpretative abilities to assume an appropriate "style" of leadership for a given leadership situation. If exposure to the visual and literary arts and the study of philosophy, religion, and the social sciences encourage these abilities, then educational leadership training must find a way to expose educational leaders to these liberal arts.

DEMYTHOLOGIZING EDUCATIONAL LEADERSHIP

Rudolf Bultmann, a German theologian, developed an approach (in 1941) to biblical texts called "demythologizing" which attempted to strip away the mythical and unhistorical elements to get at the essential meaning which the authors and editors of the New Testament documents intended. In order for the interpreter to rediscover the specific meaning of a human's self-understanding which had been veiled by the myths and time-locked language of the biblical materials, Bultmann used the phenomenological and existentialist categories of Martin Heidegger's philosophy to analyze, or "demythologize," the biblical documents. This program of demythologizing of literary texts is the same as the program of phenomenological reduction or "bracketing" which was outlined in Chapter II. The vast confusion concerning the numberless definitions of leadership, the ambiguity of theories of leadership, and the interchangeable use of leader, manager, supervisor, and administrator are reasons enough to demythologize the word and the concept of educational leadership.

A very real epistemological problem exists in theoretical and practical studies of educational leadership. Common usage of the terms "educational leadership" includes everything from casual influence to dictatorial control, from meeting budgets to meeting global objectives, from friendly persuasion to criminal bribery and inhuman intimidation. The term "leadership" denotes such a wide variety of traits, behaviors, and styles of action that it means very little explicitly. "That which means everything, means nothing." That aphorism certainly applies to the jungle of theory, research, and practice of educational leadership.

Is leadership the power of one person to influence or control the thoughts and behaviors of others? Is it a personal trait or a set of traits in certain individuals that attracts followers? Or is leadership a type or style of behavior which results in the achievement of goals? Is leadership in a person, in behavior, or in a circumstance? Does leadership reside in the power to cause others to obey the leader, or is it the personal, legal, or official authority of a leader to control, coerce, intimidate, entice, seduce, convince, threaten, or manipulate others? These descriptions of leadership can all be found in contemporary studies of educational leadership. Progress in the training of educational leaders must take seriously the problem of confusion and ambiguity of the meaning of "educational leadership."

The concept, "educational leadership," needs to be demythologized of the biases and presuppositions which have attached themselves to it over the many years of common usage. We need to look back at beginnings, essences, gestalts, foundations, consciousness, meanings, and "pure" experiences of educational leadership.

One persistent tendency in current educational leadership studies is to relate (at times equate) power and behavior control (management of learners) with educational leadership. Using force, threat, coercion, and manipulative techniques to get the followers to do the bidding of the power wielder greatly distorts the history of the use of the word "leader," if we assume that "leader" refers to a voluntary experience of a person following the one leading. Granted that behavior control may be appropriate in certain educational situations, just as directive behavior or task orientation is appropriate for certain business, military, or law enforcement settings. But training programs of educational leaders should not use the terms "educational leadership" to refer to the exercise of power or the management of the learner's behavior. The voluntary nature of the experience of being lead is essential to the "pure" meaning of the concepts of educational leadership.

Demythologizing is an attempt to bring out into the open the presuppositions, assumptions, biases, and preunderstandings of the concept of educational leadership. Thus, the contemporary meanings of the terms "educational leadership" should be bracketed and set aside in order to focus on what educational leadership means to the ones who are experiencing it. Once the prejudices and preconceptions at work behind the uses and interpretations of the meaning of educational leadership are detected and labeled, the educational leadership trainee must re-experience what "pure" educational leadership is. Heidegger believed that we are living in an age of counterfeit language, unauthentic speech, where the language of Western culture has degenerated into the corruptible, objectifying language of a technological society which turns humans into objects to be controlled and manipulated like other objects. The exercise of bracketing is an attempt to get beyond the fixed definitions which have accumulated around the concept of educational leadership. We will understand educational leadership much better if we acknowledge our philosophical, scientific, empirical, positivistic, idealistic, academic, grant-inspired, common usage, cultural baggage which is hidden in the concept of "educational leadership."

A training program must help students of educational leadership to raise questions about the nature of educational leadership itself. The myths, prejudices, and common understandings of educational leadership must be set aside temporarily and nullified as far as is possible. Then, the question must be asked again and again as to what educational leadership is and what it means to those who are experiencing it.

An exercise which might be helpful or consciousness-raising for students of educational leadership is to require those who are training to be leaders to answer the same question ten or twelve times during a specified period of time, preferably during one class period, but repeated several times during a semester in the same course: What is educational leadership? The more times the question is asked, the more difficult it becomes, but the deeper the answers penetrate the layers of meaning which have been placed on the concept by earlier users. Yet, progress in the training of educational leaders depends to some extent on peeling away the countless definitions and meanings which have rendered the concept of educational leadership so confusing and so hopelessly ambiguous.

Getting back to the authentic foundations of educational leadership will take us away from other disciplines and back to education itself. The nature of education is so unlike the nature of business, military, religious, or political organizations that imposing on educational leadership the principles of leadership which have been derived from other fields of endeavor and other disciplines contributes to the misunderstanding and confusion of the real nature of educational leadership. Whereas business essentially is product and profit oriented, the military is goal, action, and competition oriented, religion is deity and faith oriented, and politics is party oriented, education is learning and life-quality oriented. Educational leaders are dealing with a quality, or condition, of bringing out the best of which the learners are capable. Therefore, the one place to begin the study of training educational leadership is to take apart, piece by piece, the concept of educational leadership in the context and in the real-life (lived-world) situations of the education of learners.

The tools required to perform this phenomenological analysis on educational leadership are some of the tools which philosophy, anthropology, sociology, the fine arts, languages, history, literature, athletics, and psychology provide; these tools are in addition to the empirical and logical techniques which are dominant in present–day educational leadership training programs. Educational leaders need to learn how to ask the right questions; how to reflect on meanings, as well as causes and results; how to judge what is right and good and meaningful, as well as collect and quantify data; how to appreciate and feel subtle differences and changes, as well as measure them; and how to interpret meaning within fields, horizons, and world–views, as well as measure degrees of correspondence to natural phenomena. Liberal arts education provides many of these tools to probe the depths and meanings of the nature of educational leadership, but liberal arts are not substitutes for empirical and pragmatic examinations of the experiences of educational leadership.

But you are saying that all this is so general and non–quantifiable, that demythologizing sounds so esoteric and other–worldly. The point is that educational leadership needs to be brought back to its beginnings, its core meanings, its essential nature, its is–ness. Educational leadership needs very badly to be demystified and stripped of all the confusing and ambiguous encrustations and biases. Although starting all over is beyond our reasonable expectations, something like demythologizing and bracketing the current usages of the concepts of educational leadership is a step in the right direction.

BEING–WITH–SELF IN EDUCATION

Chester Barnard states near the beginning of his now classic work on the functions of an executive:

> I have found it impossible to go far in the study of organizations or of the behavior of people in relation to them without being confronted with a few questions . . . 'What is an individual?' 'What do we mean by a person?' 'To what extent do people have a power of choice or free will?'[16]

Perhaps the most misunderstood principle in any kind of leadership is the fact that leaders do not *change* other people, nor do they *cause* others to follow them. All a leader can do is to change his or her own attitudes, values, perceptions, and actions so that others will *desire* and will *choose* voluntarily to follow him or her. That principle is almost impossible for us to accept practically, even though we may give intellectual assent to it. But, can we not find out what people need and either withhold or provide those needs and cause others to do what we desire them to do? Yes, but only to the extent that those who are being "led," manipulated, or threatened allow us to "cause" them to follow us. If you take a stick and threaten to beat others or use a gun to threaten their very lives, they have the freedom to choose to accept the punishment, or even die, rather than "follow" your so-called leadership. How many times do we find those who believe in basic human rights and freedoms to reject any and all attempts to be "led?" How true is the old adage which declares that you can lead a horse to water, but you cannot make it drink water. Educational leaders have somehow overlooked the internal nature of leadership.

Those who train educational leaders must recognize that the process of leadership begins internally and works itself outward, rather than being something out there which works itself into a person. Failures in educational leadership training programs are not really the result of bad teachers, poor programs, inept institutions, a lack of resources, or flawed systems of education. The real obstacle to training educational leaders is the failure of the individual to actualize (*to be*) his or her potential to become a leader. And that is not intended to be double-talk or other-worldly idealizing. The fact is that understanding who you are as a person, what your strengths and weaknesses are, and what you are seeking in life is essential to becoming an effective educational leader.

Know Thyself!

The admonition to "know thyself" is as important in the training of effective educational leaders as is any suggestion or program which can be offered. Knowing who you are as a person is indispensable for an effective and authentic educational leader.

What makes one an educational leader and not something else is one's consciousness of self, the world as he or she knows it, the sum of one's experiences and of one's feelings about those experiences. Self identity is realized by choosing, by trying things out, by finding out through experience what one's values and needs are, what one can and cannot do physically, and what images of self are reflected by others. By valuing, choosing, relating, and acting, educational leaders develop their identities. "Self-consciousness, as the term is ordinarily used, implies two things: an awareness of oneself by oneself, and an awareness of oneself as an object of someone else's observation." [17]

The very fact that one chooses the educational profession reveals something about how a person views herself or himself. Phenomenological psychology emphasizes the way in which individuals perceive their environment and themselves. A person structures his or her environment by projecting herself or himself into the environment. Here the emphasis is not on behaviors in a personalistic or sociometric trait psychology, but on the individual's perceptions, concepts, and consciousness of self.

Thus, projective and reflective tests of all sorts are some of the most profitable training exercises educational leaders can attempt. An entire graduate-type course in leadership training should be devoted to taking and analyzing dozens of tests which reveal personal strengths and weaknesses, attitudes and values, interpersonal needs and styles of relating to others, personality inventories, maturity scales, and management style inventories.

We could learn something about the training of educational leaders by studying the way some hospitals train psychiatrists. Harry Stack Sullivan, a neo-Freudian psychiatrist who leaned toward a view similar to phenomenology, related how psychiatrists were trained in his hospital. Psychiatric training offered opportunities for students to learn about themselves, their strengths and deficiencies. They had to undergo the same types of therapeutic techniques and analysis which they would practice on their patients. This exercise prevented perpetuation of their own "blind" spots which distorted their views of the problems of their patients; further, it prevented them from being unconsciously influenced by their supervisors or by other significant persons in their practice of psychiatry. Through a long process of apprenticeship these young psychiatrists slowly expanded their conscious awareness of themselves as they related to the neuroses and problems of their patients. The purpose of this apprenticeship program amounts to "a vast augmentation of alertness." [18]

Those who are training educational leaders might consider the value of "self analysis" as seriously as do those who train psychiatrists. A rather old technique which was developed by Karen Horney, if demythologized of its Freudian biases, offers a valuable exercise for training educational leaders. Self analysis involves expressing oneself completely and honestly through free association, becoming aware of one's unconscious motives and their influence on behaviors, and on developing capacities to change attitudes and feelings which disturb relations with oneself and others.[19] Self expression through free association prepares the way for insights into one's strengths and weaknesses, and insights bring about or prepare for changes in one's attitudes, values, and behaviors. Shakespeare realized the value of self understanding as it relates to leading others when he said, "To thine own self be true, and it must follow, as the night the day, thou canst not then be false to any man" (*Hamlet*, Act I, Scene 3).

Is it coincidental or accidental that most of the great leaders in history have kept personal journals and diaries? Certainly not. Remembering the events of a day or experience, reflecting on their personal impact and significance, and recording them in a journal or diary is an invaluable, but greatly neglected, tool for educational leaders to understand their own strengths and weaknesses. By writing down one's alternate successes and failures in the educational arena, one comes to understand attitudes, values, biases, needs, and dreams which shape decisions, relationships, goals, etc. in an educational context. Further, by going back over one's journal after a given period of time the leader can evaluate decisions, communication skills, interpersonal relationships, planning, and goal setting as they relate to educational leadership. While changes may not be obvious from one day to the next, the long term perspective can reveal subtle, yet definite, shifts in perspective. Hidden biases, unseen obstacles, and confused thinking sometimes almost jump off the page when reviewed in a different frame of mind, in another time frame, and in a new set of circumstances.

Educational leaders can learn by reading their own journals or by having a trusted professional to read them and to dialogue about their contents. Also, not to be overlooked are the journals of the great educational leaders of history or of leaders in general. Beyond the personal value to the journal keeper the written record is for others to read in the future. Keeping journals not only preserves the leader's perspectives for the journalist, but it provides a record for the training of future educational leaders.

The object of reading the journals of others is not to learn about "great men" in order to become like them, but to learn more about oneself by comparing perceptions others have of themselves with one's own perceptions. Leaders who feel good about themselves and know about themselves are more likely to view others as worthwhile, capable, trustworthy, and deserving of happiness in life. Thus, leaders who are comfortable with themselves are able to give themselves to others and to open themselves to others and to receive others into their own world views.

Loving Oneself

The greatest separation which humans can experience is the separation of self from self, a feeling of total alienation of self from that to which each person knows he or she belongs; in like manner, the acceptance of oneself is that which unites life meaningfully for the individual. Loving oneself is not an egocentric selfishness nor a psychotic preoccupation with one's own desires and comforts; rather, loving oneself is to look at oneself honestly, to respect the personal assets one has, and to seek actively to fulfill one's highest potential.

Loving and respecting oneself frees leaders from that awful fear that others are out to get them, to tear them down, to make them powerless, to dominate and destroy them. Thus, educational leaders who love and respect themselves in a healthy manner are those who can affirm the strengths of others, can forgive mistakes and help to overcome weaknesses in others, can trust the words and capacities of others, and can rejoice in the successes and the happiness of others.

Leo Buscaglia's comments about love are good advice for the training of educational leaders, even though his books are too otherworldly to be of much practical or realistic use. Loving oneself is prerequisite to loving others. Giving to others presupposes that one possesses something to give. How can you give love when you do not possess it? Love is not lost when it is given to others. It is possible to offer love to lots of people and retain the same love which you gave away. Love is like knowledge in that wise person can teach all that he or she knows and still know everything which he or she knew originally. One can share love or knowledge, but one cannot share what one does not possess.[20]

The anthropologist Ashley Montagu goes so far as to say that the need to be loved and the need to love others is a unitary need. He declares that wanting to be loved without wanting to love others is impossible. The infant's need for love is not adequately satisfied unless it receives adequate stimulations for the development of its capacity to love.[21] The self concept develops only when it receives the opportunity to exercise its capacity to love. George Chapman (1559–1634) says this

so clearly in his play *All Fools*, Act I, Scene I, lines 97–110, where
Valerio addresses Rynaldo:

> I tell thee, Love is Nature's second sun
> Causing a spring of virtues where he shines;
> And as without the Sun, the World's great eye,
> All colours, beauties, both of art and Nature,
> Are given in vain to men; so without love
> All beauties bred in women are vain,
> All virtues born in men lie buried;
> For love informs them as the Sun doth colours;
> Against the earth, begets all fruits and flowers;
> So love, fair shining in the inward man,
> Brings forth in him the honourable fruits
> Of valour, wit, virtue, and haughty thoughts,
> Brave resolution, and divine discourse.

Almost all educational leaders possess a very strong, healthy feeling
of self–worth or self–esteem. What happens inside leaders and between
leaders and others is determined by the degree of self worth each person
possesses. Integrity, honesty, responsibility, compassion, love,
friendship, trust, and happiness are the natural descendants of the leader
whose self–worth is high. Leaders who feel that they really matter will
also feel that the world is a better place because they are here. Leaders
have faith in their own competence; they are able to ask others for help,
but believe that they can make their own decisions and are their own
best resource. Appreciating their own worth, they are ready to see and
respect the worth of others. They radiate trust, hope, and love. They do
not have inflexible rules about how they feel or how others feel. They
accept themselves as truly human with capacities to learn, to change, to
love, to relate, to grow, to know, to hope, to create, to be.

Like all leaders, educational leaders feel that they are unique;
everything which comes from them is authentically theirs; they have
freely chosen who they are. They own every word, facial expression,
gesture, action, feeling which they in any way reveal to others. They
own their dreams and hopes, fear and illusions, triumphs and successes,
failures and mistakes, strengths and achievements, weaknesses and
limitations. They can discard that which is bad, keep that which is good,
and invent something new to replace that which is discarded. They have
the resources to survive, to be close to others, to be productive, and to
make sense and to relate meaningfully to the world of people and things
outside themselves.

Those educational leaders who have such feelings of self-worth are free to lead others. They create an atmosphere where individual differences are appreciated, mistakes are accepted for what they are, communication is open and honest, rules are flexible and centered in the learners, decisions are poly-option focused, relationships are dialogical, planning is reality-based and futuristic, and goals are value-laden, with the happiness and well-being of the followers always considered.

No educational leader will always have a strong concept of self, nor will he or she always be able to relate to followers meaningfully. However, educational leaders who have strong self-concepts will be better leaders than those who have a consistently low self image.

And the good news about the development of self-esteem is that it is primarily learned. No one has ever found a gene for self-esteem. If self-worth is learned, then one of the important facets of a training program for educational leaders must include exercises in self exploration and self understanding.

BEING-WITH-OTHERS IN EDUCATION

One of the fundamental conclusions drawn from a phenomenological analysis of educational leadership is that what happens inside a leader cannot be separated from how the leader relates to the learners, or followers. What you believe about yourself, how you feel about your worth, determines how you relate to other persons. If you feel that you are a person of worth and responsible for all your thoughts and actions, it follows that you believe that other persons are worthy of respect and dignity and are capable of responsibility and creativity. Any discrepancy between your beliefs and feelings about yourself and about other persons frustrates effective leadership in education. Feeling that you are responsible while all others are irresponsible undermines meaningful relationships with other persons and totally frustrates leadership. Believing that others (either followers or leaders) have something worth saying is a prerequisite to listening and responding in a leader-learner relationship. You have to feel that people are trustworthy, honest, capable, and caring in order to trust them and share in a responsible relationship of leadership.

The human relations movement in business management as represented in the works of Maslow, McGregor, Follet, Likert, Herzberg, and others has demonstrated what love, respect, and cooperation mean in human organizations. Educational leaders who can love themselves and others will be more successful than those leaders who are selfish, cold, and detached. Schools, beyond all other organizations, must be places of education in the art and science of developing persons and in training in human relations.

Further, any time someone is in the presence of another person for a prolonged period of time, as in the case of a teacher in a classroom of students for a semester or even a year, the teacher will have a profound effect on those in the room in many different ways, as well as those in the room affecting the teacher. Everything, from body odors, touching, perfume, breath, sound of voice, glint of eye, gestures, posture, clothes and how worn, rate of speech, length of sentences, and vocabulary, can excite, arouse, depress, oppress, threaten, calm, confuse, and encourage students in ways which neither the teacher nor the learners are fully aware. Both conscious and unconscious, verbal and non–verbal messages are being exchanged all the time. Anyone who would endeavor to train educational leaders must take account of the complex, yet profound, nature of how humans relate in the context of educational leadership.

Educational leadership has profited from a wealth of significant research literature and successful applications in the field referred to as "human relations," "organizational development," "human resource training," etc. Hardly anyone will dispute the contribution which the human relations emphasis has made, as it relates to interpersonal communication, conflict management, team building, cooperation, group morale, listening, sharing responsibility, decision making, and evaluation in schools and educational systems. University schools of education are doing an excellent job in training educational leaders in the area of human relationship skills. Excellent courses exist in organizational dynamics, human processes, conflict management, organizational communications, and planning for change in training programs for educational leaders.

What is needed is greater sensitivity to the complexity of the human relationships in educational leadership and an awareness of the dialogical nature of these relationships. The mistake which the human relations movement in educational leadership made is two–fold. First, emphasis on human relationships excluded some dimensions of the leadership situation. This person–centered approach assume that educational leadership could be equated with good relationships in groups and in classrooms, without proper concern for the relationships, as well as the beliefs and goals, of the educational constituents in general. Second, the bias of behaviorism from which many human relations people worked allowed the meanings of leadership and power to be confused. Leaders were thought to be those who could "cause" others to do what the leaders wanted them to do. Training educational leaders to be–with–others must go beyond the human relations approach, although not overlooking the fact that this approach has been very helpful in training educational leaders.

The following suggestions are offered as complements to human relations exercises in educational leadership training. Being–with–others in educational settings takes seriously the unity of the subject–object phenomenon (intentionality) in educational leadership.

Training in Dialogue

A careful analysis of the relationship of being–with–others in education at any level in or outside the school reveals its fundamentally dialogical character. This relationship involves a leader who is bound up inseparably with the lives of the learners. The leader and the learners through dialogue become jointly responsible for the process in which all who participate learn. Leaders and learners are co–investigators in the process of education. Dialogue is the encounter of a Subject with another Subject, not a Subject with an Object. In dialogical leadership the leader views the world and the life of the learner as a constituent of a common life shared by both leader and learner. Based upon love, humility, faith, hope and critical thinking, dialogue results in a horizontal relationship of mutual trust between leaders and learners. Education is not practiced *on* learners, but is a social reality which is constructed in the consciousness of the leaders and the learners in a joint venture of dialogical life–sharing. How then can we train leaders in dialogue?

First, exercises in sensitizing leaders to others and in conflict resolution open up the parties in the leadership situation to each other. Under controlled supervision, individuals become sensitive to who the "other" really is. These sensitivity sessions do not need to be clinical experiences, and sharing of pathological symptoms should be discouraged and handled accordingly. Each person in a leadership training situation could practice sharing backgrounds, dreams, needs, beliefs, values, preferences in colors, cars, music, art, sports events, travel experiences, places to live, or any number of other things which get "life" out in the open where sharing in world views begin to happen.

Another valuable technique in training educational leaders would be the use of a "verbatim" report of an encounter between a leader and a potential learner. This exercise requires that the trainee record literally every word that is exchanged in a conversation with learners. The object is to allow a group of colleagues to analyze the transactions which occur between the leader and the learner. Do others interpret the words of the leader in the same way as the leader intended them? Not only does the leader learn to improve communication with the learners, but a group of leader trainees can learn to analyze the quality of the dialogue which transpires in this context. The dynamics of interpersonal relationships in groups could be video-taped and then analyzed in a group setting. Teachers would learn a lot if an average day could be video-taped and teacher and students had an opportunity to view how the teacher and students related to each other.

Other case-study exercises could be employed by using incidents from leadership situations and having the leadership trainees and experienced leaders to examine the dialogical phenomena in these incidents.

Trust Enhancement

The building of trust is a presupposition of the experience of being-with-others in an educational leadership situation. Leadership involves a high degree of trust of the leader by the learners, as well as the leader's trust of the learners.

Several years ago I had the opportunity to talk with a group of individuals from Wolfcreek Wilderness, a training camp in the North Georgia mountains. This group provided students and business executives with training experiences over a twenty-one day period. The purpose of this training experience was to enhance feelings of the participants' self esteem, team building, decision making, etc. They did several things to build the trust level among group members. For instance, a person would lower another person by rope a hundred feet or more down a steep cliff. The person being lowered learned to trust someone else with their very lives. On another occasion they took the group several miles into an unfamiliar area of woods and gave one person a map. The person with the map was required to get the group back to camp safely. The group had to trust the person with the map and cooperate with his or her efforts or spend a day or even night without finding their way back to camp. This group also engaged in cave exploration near Chattanooga, Tennessee, during which members were linked together with nylon ropes and depended on each other to navigate the caverns. These and more exercises were expertly supervised to avoid possible danger to participants, but the reports which these experiences generated concerning developing self confidence and trust were startling.

Similar trust enhancement exercises could be designed for laboratory settings using money, articles of value, information, personal comfort, or personal acceptance. Extreme care must be exercised in such circumstances to insure that no harm come to any participant and that no article is damaged or lost.

Human Synergistics of Plymouth, Michigan is representative of training groups who design materials to train individuals in human relations. Two of their exercises deal with survival problems in the desert and the arctic and focus on decision making processes. Such materials could be adapted to emphasize trust among team members. Such materials are valuable exercises in teaching educational leaders to trust their followers and to elicit trust from them.

Experiencing Communion

Being-with-others in education implies that the leader experiences a sense of community with the learners. Group facilitators often use "ice breakers" to elicit a sense of community in a group. The facilitator may request that all members inflate balloons or paper bags to experience being a part of the group.

Certain religious communities have an ordinance which they call Communion. The purpose of Communion is to develop a sense of unity among the members of the church body. The ritual of Communion in churches involves members eating unleavened bread and drinking wine to experience a deeply religious sense of communion within the membership of the church group. During the Communion service the members experience a union with the life which they believe they have received from God.

Being-with-others in education means viewing the learners as Subjects, not simply Objects. Freire developed what he called "culture circles" as a basis for a literacy program. The culture circles shared a consciousness of life where literacy is a way of self-transformation. Thus, Freire offered participants instruments to teach themselves to read and write. His method was based on the existence of communion in the culture circles. Freire described the relationship between the literacy leader and the learners as empathy among those engaged in a joint search for a meaningful life. When the leader and the learners are linked by "love, hope, and mutual trust" in a common search for self-transformation, learning content is identified with the learning process.[22] In this way educational leaders and learners experience communion in the process of education.

If inflating paper bags or blowing up balloons is not one's style, extra-curricular activities might provide ways of experiencing communion with learners. Educational leaders are passing up a golden opportunity to be-with learners when they do not actively participate in the extra-curricular events of schools.

William Purkey and John Novak make a list of ways to "invite school success." Among their two hundred suggestions are several things which will encourage togetherness and communion. One was to encourage the class to select a name, emblem, motto, and colors for the class as a whole. Another urged teachers to use first-person plural pronouns to include students in the class unity. Keeping up with what high school students are reading, listening to, viewing, and doing outside class and using images and language in class from their culture will develop closeness and communion in the class, even though the teacher does not have to agree with everything in the youth culture. Purkey and Novak also believe that students should be allowed to plan and change the room arrangements and other aspects of the physical environment.[23]

Ceremonies and rituals could be designed to offer possibilities of communion in educational settings. Communion exercises might involve sharing chocolate "kisses," cookies, pencils, note pads, etc. in a ritual to represent the common sharing of life in the educational process. The important thing to note is that the exercises dramatize symbolically the communion between the leader and the learners in the experience of learning.

Learning to Listen

A very simple phenomenon of the experience of being–with–others in education is a consciousness of listening to each person in this communion of learning. Listening does not just happen in the process of communication within the learning group, and neglect of this important state of being in an educational setting sabotages the authenticity of the experiences of learning. Notice that listening in this context is a *state* of listening and not simply an act of hearing sounds. Learning to listen is first a recognition that listening is an attitude of openness, respect, and concern which is inseparable from the physiological experience of the ear receiving sound waves which are transmitted to the auditory cells of the brain and recognized as hearing. Listening with one's heart is a way of looking at this state of existence in which listening is viewed as a state of being.

Carl Rogers developed a therapeutic approach to listening called "non–evaluative" or "active" listening.[24] One of the rules developed by Rogers at the Center for Studies of the Person at La Jolla, California required that each person be allowed to speak up only *after* he or she has first restated the ideas and feelings of the previous speaker accurately to enable the previous speaker to either confirm or correct the message. This simple technique can be employed in any leader training group; its importance resides in the fact that before presenting one's own point of view, he or she must enter the other person's frame of reference––to understand the other person's thoughts and feelings so well that the listener can summarize them to the speaker's satisfaction.

Another example of being–with–others by listening is what psychiatrist, Harry Stack Sullivan, called "participant observation," (which he claimed could be used outside the medical field as well as in a psychiatric interview).[25] Sullivan maintained that the listener (psychiatrist) has an inescapable, inextricable involvement in everything that goes on in a psychiatric interview. The psychiatrist listens to every statement critically, notices intonation of words, vocabulary, and words avoided. Even the slightest gesture is full of meaning to a listener who is intimately involved in what the client is experiencing. Sullivan's process of interviewing requires an endless series of questions during the interview sessions, not because Sullivan disbelieved the client, but because Sullivan wanted to find out about the client's anxieties, self concept, and interpersonal relationships. In other words, Sullivan wanted to get to know the client, to be personally involved in the way the client viewed and experienced things.

One of the best examples of an educational leader listening to learners in a school setting is the Personalized Reading program of Walter Barbe.[26] This program is not to be confused with so-called individualized instruction or other programs. The key to this program is that the teacher is "involved" in the learning process "with" the learners; the curriculum is flexible and tailored to each student's abilities, interests, and limitations. Barbe states that personalized reading is not a single method with predetermined procedures to be followed in a certain sequence. Rather, personalized refers to the style, attitude, creativity, perceptions, interpersonal relations, and values of the leader–teacher.

Educational leaders and learners who are in a state of listening to each other are optimizing what education really is. Listening to the learners is an art, a skill, and a state of being which requires a listening heart, respect for the learners, intent to understand, and personal involvement in the learning process. Training leaders to listen is to develop a sensitivity to others, an art which is not developed overnight, but is learned and acquired over a long period of time. However, good educational leaders must learn to listen at all levels, to all followers, as a state of being an educator whom students and learners want to follow.

Living–with Learners

While taking a teaching methods course in college some thirty years ago, I recall a young lady asking what could be done in a class when children came to school without adequate food, clothing, and supplies. The instructor told the student that she could not get involved in the personal affairs of her students; it would depress her and "drive her crazy." Let the social welfare people handle that part of schooling. She was supposed to stick to the subject matter. I wanted to shout, but did not, "But what about the kids? Don't we care about the kids?" I realize that the instructor may have been trying to say that the personal problems of the learners made teaching and learning challenging, but on the other hand, I got the message that schooling was somehow separate from the lives of the students.

Those training for the helping professions, which includes educational leaders, need direct experience in the lives of the learners. Educational leaders need more than just academic knowledge about the hopes, needs, beliefs, abilities, and backgrounds of learners. They should be exposed to the everyday problems and joys which the learners are experiencing.

A few years ago students in the Divinity School at Vanderbilt University were required to spend an entire weekend alone on the streets of downtown Nashville, Tennessee, with something like two dollars in their pockets. The object of this experience was to allow the future ministers to learn how it feels to be destitute, hungry, alone, exploited, and desperate.

Every educational leader trainee or teacher should be required to spend some time in the homes of learners, not just observe a classroom or practice teach in a nice, orderly, clean school building. Educational leaders need to know what it feels like to be hungry, cold, oddly dressed, alone, homeless, unloved, abused, sexually molested, etc., while a teacher is trying to "motivate" you to learn about the Civil War. Being–with–others in education means to live with others, to share some of their hurts, joys, hopes, disappointments, abilities, and limitations.

BEING–IN–THE–WORLD OF EDUCATION

Heidegger says that being–in–the–world is concrete existence ("existence precedes essence"), that being a human person precedes an interpretation of human actions. Further, the meaning of human existence cannot be separated from an interpretation of that existence from within a human body which experiences feelings, holds beliefs, has needs and goals, and is bound up with a world of other humans and other things. Thus, the meaning of educational leadership must take into consideration the leader's being–in–the–world of education. Being an educational leader means to be involved with the whole world of the process of education.

However, training educational leaders to experience the meaning of being–in–the–world of education is primarily a matter of perception and consciousness raising about the intentionality of the lived–world of the educator. An analysis of the lived–world of educational leaders who are being trained includes an examination of the mode of existence of educational leaders.

Epistemology of Schooling

Since epistemology is a philosophical question concerned with the origins and nature of knowledge in general, an epistemology of schooling involves ways of looking at the knowledge of being an educational leader in the world of education. Training educational leaders is a very serious exercise in looking at modes of relating to the world of schooling. Educational leadership does imply necessarily someone who is leading in the world of education. Being–in–the–world of education as leaders means to go beyond the empirical facts of acting as an educator in the world and beyond the mind's constitution of meaning in the world through pure reflection; the goal of leadership training is to enable educational leaders to rediscover their situation in the educational world in a way that makes the world of education and the leaders in that world more accessible to our understanding. In other words, the basic training of an educational leader is to ask questions about the nature and meaning of experiences of education and schooling from various perspectives.

One of the best sources of curriculum for such leadership training would be to dig up some of the studies and experiments which came out of the Alternative Schooling, or the Radical Reform, movement of the 1960's and 1970's. The radical answers of the reformers need not be accepted, but educational leaders need to consider the alternative ways of thinking about the world of education. Educational leaders must never quit asking questions like Ivan Illich, John Holt, Jonathan Kozol, A. S. Neill, Charles Silberman, Neil Postman, Charles Weingartner, James Herndon, Herbert Kohl, Sylvia Ashton–Warner, Paul Goodman, George Dennison, and others were asking. Knowledge about the world of schooling and education must not become frozen, but must be addressed within an epistemology which will be open to evidence and insight from any and all sources.

Is schooling the best way to educate? If children can learn to read, write, count, etc. by watching television, should we consider some other forms of schooling or consider ways to supplement schooling through the use of television, computers, and other high tech in commercial settings? Is there an alternative to the preposterous practice of age–grouping or intelligence grouping? Does all schooling need to take place in a school building, or could more of it occur in the home during periods of time when the parents are home? What do students really need to know and to experience to function successfully in society? Is there an alternative to the school as a "baby–sitting" institution in our society for working mothers? What about using churches, retirees, or women's clubs for help in this area? Since the strongest correlation between success in life and anything that happens in schools has been found with those who participate in extra curricular activities, should we not consider how to integrate schooling and extra curricular activities more closely? Educational leaders need to consider how band, basketball, and clubs can enhance the teaching of math, communication skills, cultural awareness, and basic living skills.

In order to encourage educational leaders to consider new ways of thinking about schooling and education, leader trainees should be placed in real life experiences where alternative schooling principles and practices must be considered. Moreover, the trainees should participate in simulation games which provide the opportunity to consider new ways of doing schooling and education. For instance, there is a game called Ghetto which requires the players to make decisions about all sorts of social problems by pretending you are actually experiencing these problems. The same kind of gaming and simulation exercises in educational problems could provide valuable training for educational leaders.

The whole world of schooling and education must be open to educational leaders, and leaders must be sensitive to the ways the world is open to them. Being–in–the–world of educational leaders is seeing that the individual leader is inseparably related to all those who participate in that world, as well as the horizon, the context, the lived–world where the leader exists. Educational leaders must learn to view "school" and "education" as a mode of existence in the world, as an interrelated complex of leader–teacher–learner transactions, not simply as organizations which have a life separate from the leader–teacher–learner interaction situation. Leaders do not relate to organizations or schools; leaders relate to individual persons within the grouping of individuals called "schools."

Professionalization of Teaching–Learning

The primary way of being–in–the–world as an educational leader is participating in the teaching–learning process. Two modern trends in education today need to be examined under the rubric of being–in–the–world: the unionization of teachers and the separation of teaching from learning. Both of these concerns have to do with the professionalization of those participating in the teaching-learning process.

The inadequate and embarrassingly low salary schedules and oppressive working conditions in so many school systems in the United States have pushed teachers into the role of collective bargainers who are trying to bring about changes in this unfortunate and deplorable situation. However, when arbitration cases have been placed before the National Labor Relations Board, a need to clarify the definition of a "teacher" has emerged. Is a teacher a "laborer" or a "manager"? Disregarding the question of whether collective bargaining is good, lawful, or beneficial to teachers, bargaining with public officials has tended to change the definition of a teacher. If a teacher is an employee, a laborer, as is a production worker on an assembly line, then the teacher as an artist, public servant, and certified professional is eclipsed. Further, treating teachers like laborers in a sweat shop is an utter disgrace and contributes to the national illiteracy which we are now witnessing in America.

Pouring more money into educational leadership training programs will not automatically produce the kind of educational leaders who are "in sync" with the real world of teaching-learning. What is needed in educational leadership training programs in our universities is not rearranging the furniture, giving new names to the same old courses, requiring more hours in methods courses or courses in the teaching-area content, or changing the certification and licensing of educational leaders. A new perceptual base for looking at educational leadership is needed. A new perceptual tool is needed which can translate the "lived world" of the teacher and learner into attitudes, skills, knowledge, and values which educational leaders can use.

The training of these educational teacher-leaders is a process of becoming a person whom learners and constituents of the educational system choose to follow, imitate, respect, identify, share life with, hope and dream, laugh and cry, love with, grow, search and find, think, analyze, synthesize, speculate, reflect, and problem-solve. This kind of training calls for the deepest involvement of teachers and leaders in every aspect of their professional training and the use of their own experiences, knowledge of the experiences of others, and feedback from other professional teachers as a laboratory for reflection on the meaning of educational leadership in the teacher-learner situation.

Teachers need to ask throughout the training experience what really makes a good teacher. Is there one set of criteria for all good teachers? Are the competencies which are necessary for good teaching a particular set of behaviors, attitudes, knowledge, skills, styles of management, intelligence quotients, physical or mental attributes, some combination of these, a blend of all or them, or something different? I am convinced that whether persons become effective educational leader–teachers depends on how the leaders perceive themselves, how they view the students, other educational leaders, and the other educational constituents, and how they view the larger world in which the educational process is situated. Thus, a good training program for professional educators should include an examination of their self perceptions, the nature of learners, the meaning of being–with–others in education, and the meaning of the lived–world of education.

A research project at the University of Florida a few years ago found several major areas which are crucial in the perceptual organization of good teachers. Among the perceptions which good teacher have are: they have a rich, extensive, and available field of perceptions about their subject matter; they have accurate perceptions about students and their behavior; they incorporate a good self concept in their programs; they perceive that society's purpose of education is to help all students become the best they can become; and they are committed to finding methods which are suited to the individual students, as well as methods which are suited to each teacher. [27]

Effective teachers provide the basic conditions for personal and meaningful learning to occur in students. First, these conditions include the creation of the need to learn from the perspective of the learner. Students are not "motivated" by teachers; rather, students are helped to see how problems and knowledge relate to their perceived needs and goals. Second, an atmosphere which promotes personal learning includes fun, fantasy, wide choices, self–confidence, cooperation, feelings of belonging, feelings of uniqueness and integrity, open communication, problem solving, flexibility, individuality, and experimentation. The third condition for personal learning is the assistance and encouragement of active exploration and discovery of personal learning. Effective teachers are autonomous, self–directed, and responsible themselves and encourage the same in the learning environment. Differences are valued and encouraged, wide options are offered, personal decisions are respected and admired. In a personal learning atmosphere both teachers and students perceive the classroom as a laboratory for trying, failing, adjusting, trying again, failing again, reflecting, trying over–and–over again until something meaningful happens or until the project seems hopeless.

Thus, the professionalization of teaching–learning is the development of an attitude, a consciousness, of the teaching–learning process, as well as the acquisition of skills, methods and knowledge of subject matter.

The primary role of the educational leader is to be–with–teaching–learning (the hyphens hold the conception together) as a vital aspect of the education process. Whatever the educational leader thinks or does, the teaching–learning consciousness is central and cannot be disassociated it. Educational leaders gain the right to become professionals through training and certification, but a professional educational leader is a complex of roles which emerges out of the consciousness of being in the teaching–learning world; it is a life style as well as a life profession.

"Externships" for Educational Leaders

The dictionary defines an "extern" as a person who is connected with an institution, but who does not live or board in it; specifically, an extern is a nonresident doctor or medical student at a hospital. Thus, an "externship," as applied here, is a state or condition of a person who is connected with an institution (such as a school), but who also exists in a state or condition outside the school. An externship for educational leaders recognizes that the learning which occurs inside the school cannot be separated from the landscapes of learning in the world outside the school. In fact, more learning occurs outside the classroom in higher education than occurs in the classroom. Training educational leaders through externship experiences takes seriously the intentionality of the relationship between the leader and the world ("lived–world").

Externships can be approached from the perspective of the present learning context of the classroom. An externship in a classroom would seek to bring a living–world into the classroom experience of the leaders and the learners. I know of a teacher who prides himself in bringing forty or fifty different resource people into his classroom each semester. The assumption behind bringing so many "outside" people into the learning situation is that the learners feel that what they are learning is "real," dealing with real people and real problems and issues, not just "book" knowledge.

Some medical schools train medical students from this perspective. They try to expose medical students to knowledge of as many diseases and physical disorders as is possible in a clinical–academic–laboratory setting. The doctors are not expected to become experts in every imaginable disease and disorder, but are expected to relate what they learned in med–school to what they observe in their medical practice.

When a particular symptom is observed of which the practicing physician is only casually knowledgeable, the physician goes back to the medical journals, books, laboratories, and data retrieval systems to determine what to prescribe for the patient or to refer the patient to another physician who is knowledgeable concerning the particular symptoms. The learning in medical training is co-extensive and continued in the actual practice of the medical profession. The world of the classroom and the world of practicing physicians are viewed as a "lived-world," an intentionality in a phenomenological sense.

The other side of an externship is to consider the world as a dynamic learning situation which is an extension of, and inseparable from, what happens in a classroom. Thus, the classroom is carried into the world where educational leaders are exposed to problems, issues, ideas, possibilities, values, phenomena, resources, and persons within horizons and landscapes of the process of education. The difference in an externship as here conceived and an apprenticeship or internship as universities presently utilize them is that the externship minimizes the distinction between what is learned in the classroom and what is learned outside the classroom. Externs are more likely than interns to recognize problems and personal needs in the real world, to bring them back to the classroom, library, laboratory, or clinical setting, and to continue the learning which originated in the "outside" world. On the other hand, field work, practice teaching (what does this concept teach?), observation, data analysis, and subject matter learning often are viewed from a classroom perspective and in isolation from the real world. A real temptation exists in the training of educational leaders to assume that learning begins and often ends in isolated, unreal, content-based, university classrooms.

If that which turns off students to learning is to enter a classroom (and many students will claim this to be the case), learning could be greatly enhanced by getting the students out of classrooms and into a live, problem-filled, resourceful world. The university-without-walls phenomenon of a few years ago failed because universities tried to take the "classroom" into the world instead of extending the learning environment to include the world. The school-without-walls is still a viable option to train educational leaders and to enhance learning in subject-matter disciplines. Externships for educational leaders endeavors to view learning as a lived-world phenomenon, the intentionality of the process of education.

CONSCIOUSNESS-RAISING IN LEADERSHIP TRAINING

A phenomenological analysis of educational leadership shows that existence precedes consciousness and meaning of existence, but consciousness and knowledge precede decisions, and decisions precede changes in attitudes, relationships, and actions. Thus, consciousness-raising becomes a major objective in training programs for educational leaders. Consciousness-raising elicits in the educational leader a state of awareness of those conditions and states of existence which lead to the achievement of decisions which, in turn, lead to changes which result in achievement of educational aims and purposes.

Most attitudes, interpretations, decisions, and behaviors of educational leaders are based on the manner in which individual leaders construct their consciousness of the world and reality. These constructions of reality may not be the same for any two individual leaders, but one's perception of a meaningful life and the values, attitudes, and actions which promote that world view is the basis of all educational leadership. The way an individual leader constructs the perceptions and images of self, others, and the world and the relationships which exist within this lived-world is an internal gyroscope which keeps the leader on the course toward the goals of the educational process.

The failure to obtain authentic and meaningful constructions of reality results in anxieties concerning a personal interpretation of life in general. Thus, feelings of aloneness, disconnectedness, guilt, impotence, failure, and incompleteness lead toward incapacity and ineffectiveness of the individual educational leader.

Consciousness-raising is an attempt to raise in bold relief the need to become aware of the conditions under which world views and perceptions of reality stabilize or change. Schutz claims that a change from one province of meaning to another can only happen by means of a Kierkegaardian "leap," the exchange of one style of lived experience for another.[28] The lived-world does not change as long as our experiences participate in the same cognitive style. And only when we are motivated by our life-plan to accept another attitude, or when we are disturbed by a shocking contradiction to our perceptions of our experiences, must we transfer the accent of reality to another realm of meaning.[29] The issue then in educational leadership training is one of establishing conditions and experiences which are most likely to raise our awareness of the phenomenological nature of the change of consciousness of perceptions of self, others, and the larger world.

Kurt Lewin and his associates found that individuals learned best when the learner participated egoistically. Group participation and experiential learning utilizes the dynamic of ego–involvement. When learners participate in discussion, reflection, analysis, problem–solving, planning, interpreting, evaluating, and reformulating theories, the resulting experiences are highly personal with implications for development and stability of one's self-image.[30] Personal involvement is a key in the consideration of the consciousness–raising of educational leaders.

A second consideration in encouraging consciousness–raising is that the individual be given feedback concerning how he or she is perceived in the leadership situation. The more open, honest, and accurate the feedback is, the greater is the degree of "wide–awakeness" and awareness of one's involvement in the leadership experience and its meaning.

The third important factor in consciousness–raising is the reflection and reconstruction of the experiences of educational leadership to the end that some personal meaning is assigned to the lived–world in which the educational process is operating. Training future leaders involves a process of questioning, wondering, reflection, experimenting, analyzing, reconstructing, and interpreting the lived–world of educational leadership.

Many of the techniques of organizational development and human relations training utilize the dynamics of consciousness–raising. The works of Lewin, Sherif, McGregor, Maslow, Herzberg, Likert, Blake and Mouton, and Rogers have demonstrated how ego involvement and awareness impacts the effectiveness of leaders in educational and other settings. Those types of experiences which many universities are already providing in organizational dynamics and human relations training provide valuable opportunities for consciousness–raising in both leaders and learners. What tends to happen is not exactly that which is planned by the instructors. The expected outcome of organizational dynamics courses is that students learn behavioral skills and knowledge to "manage" the group situation. But, what often takes place is a transformation in consciousness or heightened awareness of the totality of the experience of leadership in education.

COURAGE TO BE AN EDUCATIONAL LEADER

That which transforms a person with traits, skills, knowledge, and opportunities into an educational leader is the courage to engage one's will to become an educational leader, in spite of all the forces, actions, attitudes, and obstacles which prevent it. Genuinely effective educational leaders in the long run do not become leaders by accident, nor by being placed in a powerful position, nor by being born with certain traits, nor by knowing about leaders and leadership, nor by manipulating or managing the behavior of others. The bottom line of what an educational leader really is involves a commitment of heart and soul, the courage to be a leader "in spite of" everything which tends to prevent a person from becoming a leader. Great leaders do not become great without the courage to be, to act, and to dream of a better life for those who are being lead. Martin Luther stands on the threshold of a new era, the Reformation, and declares, "Here I stand! I can do no other." That courage to stand against the odds, to chart a new course, to dare to be different, to care for the welfare of the whole at the risk of one's own welfare, is possible only by drawing on the soul-power (the ability to will one thing--Kierkegaard) "to be" a leader. Educational leaders are those who possess the courage to be a leader in spite of the bureaucracy, the lack of resources, the indifference of learners, or any other obstacle.

The problem with the Great-Man theory (unfortunately women were not considered by early theorists) of leadership is the assumption that leaders have inherited unique traits, qualities, and abilities that capture the imagination and following of the masses and that leaders emerge once the opportunity is presented. Thus, the adage, "cream rises to the top." However, to remove the princes, heroes, and miracle-workers from the roll-call of history's leaders is to distort history itself. Nietzsche contended that a sudden decision by a great man could redetermine history (e.g., Truman's decision on the atom bomb). Society and culture are altered by great persons. Great leaders initiate revolutions and calm warring nations; they inspire greatness in others and light the path toward duty, loyalty, love, and service. Although great genes do not make great leaders, those who create values instead of conforming to established rules, who are dedicated to remaking the world in terms of the needs and requirements of the masses, and who call the lowly and the "little" people to greater heights of respect and dignity are the "movers–and–shakers" of any society. Great leaders are great people whom the followers want to follow.

The sad thing about heroes and miracle–workers is that they can lead the masses in the wrong direction as well as in the way of "life, liberty, and the pursuit of happiness." The key to determine whether to follow heroes and miracle–workers is to ask questions about their values and goals. Watch their hands instead of their heads and listen to their hearts instead of their lips. Leaders who are manipulating, exploiting, and managing the behaviors of others with evil intent are the despots, charlatans, Hitlers, Stalins, Elmer Gantrys, and Ayatollah Khomeinis of our world. Nevertheless, the heroes and miracle–workers cannot be disregarded in the consideration of educational leadership.

Exposure to the heroes and miracle–workers of education is an essential ingredient in the training of educational leaders. Training should not be just a historical survey of the great persons who have developed and shaped education, but an examination of the values, aims, goals, methods, and foundations of education's great people. The training of all educational leaders should include the study of great teachers and the reading of biographies and autobiographies of great teachers.

In the final analysis, the great people are those who have the courage to be a person who can lead others out from the bondage of not–knowing into the realm of knowing (the Latin root of "educate" is *e–ducare*, "to lead out"). The consideration of courage, commitment, beliefs, values, goals, and purposes which are consistent with the better things of life and the pursuit of happiness are indispensable in the training of educational leaders.

Meaning–Creating Educational Leaders

Alfred Schutz maintains that lived experiences have subjective meaning only when they are represented in actuality, when they are examined as regards their constitution in our consciousness, and when they are explicated in regard to their position in a frame of reference at hand.[31] Those attitudes and actions which are intended toward educational leadership are "meaning–endowing experiences" of consciousness.

The meaning of experiences of educational leadership is that frame of reference which sees the experiences as meaningful in the process of education. Nothing is really meaningful until one has related it to his or her own view of the world, reality, and that which is valuable and desirable. Thus, meaning–creating experiences of educational leadership must be "ego–acts" or some modification of such acts. Instead of being, as if being is apart from being some–thing, consciousness has to make itself, create itself, choose itself, and invent itself. To be is to act, and to act is to be. Being an educational leader means becoming something of that toward which the individual projects himself or herself as an educational future. Humans are beings who come to themselves on the basis of the future, who define themselves by their goals, and the goals revert backwards to the present situation to clarify and transform it. Meaning–creating for educational leaders is a process of being, seeing, choosing, doing, changing, and having that which is most basic in education.

Structures of Leader–Values

Training in the phenomenon of meaning–creating for educational leaders is, for one thing, an examination of those values and goals toward which the leader is projecting himself or herself. Hermann Hesse's "Journey to the East" is a story of a group of people on a mythical journey to the East. Leo, the central character, is a servant who provides for the group's needs not only through menial service but by his character, guiding spirit, authenticity, and nobility. Then, Leo disappears and the journey is abandoned because of the lack of Leo's leadership. The storyteller who is on the journey years later finds Leo and discovers that Leo, whom he had known as a servant, was really the leader, the head, of the Order which sponsored the journey to the East in the first place. Leo was the leader of the group journeying to the East all the time, but he was first seen as a servant because that was what he was deep within himself. What Leo was in the first part of the story was central to his being a leader throughout the story.

An examination of the structuring and construing of those values which contribute most to being an educational leader is not to be confused with the practice of values clarification. To clarify the values of a leader is important, but one may find out that a Hitler is being trained by the values which are exposed by the clarification process. On the other hand, a study of the structure of the consciousness of educational leaders whose values help learners become stronger, more knowledgeable, wiser, freer, kinder, nobler, healthier, more creative, happier, and richer is fundamental to meaning–creating in educational leadership. The intentional nature of values is a recognition of the fact that valuing always assumes "a thing or a principle is valued." An educational leader who values freedom cannot think or behave without being influenced in some way by the value of freedom.

Meaning for educational leaders is created within the intentionality of their educational values, and values are structured within the framework of one's consciousness on the basis of a hierarchy of personal needs not unlike Maslow's hierarchy of psychological motives. Thus, the values of educational leaders are not so much imposed from without, prescribed by external authorities, nor developed out of biological needs alone; values are created within the totality of the leader's world view and in interaction with the entire body of lived experiences. Therefore, some values are created out of the common experiences of being a human being, i.e., everyday human existence; certain values for human life are not matters of opinion but are biologically and socially (e.g., cooperation and love) created out of basic requirements for survival of human existence. Other values are created in the context of a socially determined existence which is meaningful for participants. In 1945, Franklin D. Roosevelt stated in a speech which he never delivered that if civilization survives, all of us must "cultivate the science of human relationships," i.e., the ability of all humans to live together and work together in the same world at peace.[32]

Educational leaders are not in the business of creating and prescribing values for others in the educational process, but educational leaders whose own values are cheap, selfish, dishonest, cowardly, unjust, destructive, and, alas, inhuman are not worthy of being followed in the educational process. Creating–meaning for educational leaders begins with the presupposition that values must be measured by whether they contribute to the happiness, welfare, and creativity of human beings living in community and accomplishing the goals shared by their own community and by the larger world.

Leaders as Event–Making Persons

Training educational leaders in creating–meaning acknowledges the intentionality of the theory–praxis phenomenon. An educational leader is not someone who merely has ideas and dreams about education and who can discuss theories, methods, aims, and values of education; rather, an educational leader is involved, acting, living out the ideas and values, practicing the theories and aims. Thus, creating–meaning for educational leaders is making things happen, making events; not reacting, but pro–acting.

Event–making leaders are those who believe great things and say, "Come, follow, be something great yourselves!" Moses was an event–making leader who called a group of nomadic slaves who had escaped from Egyptian bondage to follow him into nation–hood in a Promised Land. Columbus invited the world to follow him across unknown and treacherous waters to found a new world. Einstein gazed into the abysmal depths of time and space and beckoned us to follow him into new dimensions of relativity and atomic energy. John F. Kennedy was told about rockets which could defy earth's gravitational barrier and called on America to send a man to the moon. A meaningful story in American history is that of a man named John Henry, "the Steel-Driving Man." He was pitted against the best machine a railroad industry could muster, and those who believed that machines threatened their jobs said that John Henry drove more spikes than the machine did. The legendary John Henry epitomizes the event–making leader.

Educational leaders who are event–making persons are those who are doing education and inviting their peers and their learners to follow. Former Secretary of Education, William Bennett, was criticized by Harvard President, Derek Bok, as talking a good game of education, but not doing anything himself. Educational leaders are needed who will roll up their sleeves and plunge into the world of ignorance, confusion, mystery, and unhappiness and who will lead others toward knowledge, newness, practicality, and happiness through the educational process.

Somewhere in the training of educational leaders is a place for the recognition and affirmation of event–making people who participate in creating–meaning in the educational situation. The event–making educational leader will fuse theory and practice from a lived–world, intentional, holistic, meaning–creating frame of reference.

CONCLUSION

An analysis of the training of educational leaders from a phenomenological perspective will not result in a neat, step–by–step set of principles and practices. However, this does not mean that believing, valuing, and doing certain things will not encourage the development of leadership in educators. Quite the contrary. The training of educational leaders is training in a new perception of self, others, and the world; it is being the kind of educator whom learners desire to follow.

The foundations of training educational leaders reside in a liberal arts context, an environment in which "artists" of educational leadership can thrive. Educational leaders must envision what the practice of education means in the lives of the learners before they are going to have much of a following. In order to see clearly and holistically the visions with which the followers can identify, the training process needs to focus on leadership within the field of education itself. A process of demythologization of the definitions and interpretations of educational leadership will make possible a clear understanding of the terms and the meaning of that which we refer to as educational leadership.

The concept of intentionality (connectedness?) as used in this study opens up new perspectives of the nature of educational leadership. Educational leadership is meaningful to a leader and to learners only as the meaning is constructed in the consciousness of both the leader and the learner. This process involves the perception of self, others, and the world from the frame of reference, or view of reality, of those participating in the educational process. Thus, we see how fundamental are values, beliefs, attitudes, hopes, dreams,and desires in the interpretation of what is meaningful in educational leadership. What a leader values is probably more determinative in training educational leaders than is the knowledge and skills which are offered. The intentional perspective requires that we view the process as a totality.

Perhaps no other point is more important in the training of educational leaders than is viewing educational leadership as a dialogical phenomenon. Decision making, communication, planning, and practice in educational leadership requires a leader to assume a being–with–others perspective of everything which occurs in the teaching–learning and leading–following experiences. A dialogical style of leadership is neither authoritarian nor non–directed; it asks the leader to put himself or herself in the place of the person who is being lead. That relationship of caring for the welfare and happiness of the learners is as important as it is to know what content to offer in a school. Dialogical leadership will create higher learner readiness and will result in more meaningful learning. But, make no mistake. Dialogical leadership does not happen in educators by accident or by birth. Training in dialogical leadership involves constant reflection, clarification, commitment, responsibility, and a strong faith in, and respect for, the worth and dignity of those being lead.

Finally, the kind of training advocated above involves consciousness–raising as a life style in the educational leaders and as an ideal in the constituency. Along with the empirical research and the rational thinking, an awareness of the nature and meaning of education, teaching, learning, and thinking in a real lived–world is indispensable. The meaning for educational leaders is created, constructed, and sustained in the consciousness of the educational leader.

NOTES

1. Henry Mintzberg, *The Nature of Managerial Work* (Englewood Cliffs: Prentice–Hall, Inc., 1973), 186–87.

2. Sidney Hook, *The Hero in History* (Boston: Beacon Press, 1943), 154.

3. Arthur W. Combs, "The Perceptual Approach to the Helping Professions," *Journal of the Association for the Study of Perception* 5, No. 11 (Fall 1970): 7.

4. David G. Winter, "Framework for the Analysis of Liberal Arts Education and Corporate Leadership," a paper prepared for the Corporate Council on the Liberal Arts Symposium, "Corporations at Risk: Liberal Learning and Private Enterprise,," Cambridge, Mass., September 3, 1986.

5. "Editorial: How to Make People Smaller Than They Are," *The Saturday Review* (December 1978); 15.

6. E.M. Block, in a speech to the Texas Independent College Fund, 1983 Annual Meeting and Symposium, Lakeway Conference Center, Austin, Texas, April 11, 1983.

7. Emanuel (Skip) Struman, "Do Corporations Really Want Liberal Arts Grads?" *Management Review* 75 (September 1987): 57.

8. Daniel R. DeNicola, "Liberal Arts and Business," *Nation's Business* 76 (December 1986): 4.

9. Roger B. Smith, "Humanities & Business: The Twain Shall Meet–– But How?" *Management Review* (April 1985): 36.

10. Cited by Emanuel Struman, "Do Corporations Really Want Liberal Arts Grads?" 57–58.

11. J.I. Behrman and R.I. Levin, "Are Business Schools Doing Their Job?" *Harvard Business Review* 62, No. 2 (1984): 142.

12. Kenneth R.R. Gros Louis, "Why the Humanities Are More Important Than Ever," *Business Horizons* 24 (January/February 1981): 19.

13. Michael Maccoby, *The Leader* (New York: Simon and Schuster 1981), 232.

14. Edmund Husserl, *Ideas: General Introduction to Pure Phenomenology*, trans. W.R. Boyce Gibson (London: Macmillan Publishers, 1931; Collier, 1962), 175–84.

15. Jacob Bronowski, *The Visionary Eye: Essays in the Arts, Literature, and Science*, ed. by Piero E. Ariotti (Cambridge: The MIT Press, 1978), 16, 83–84.

16. Chester I. Barnard, *The Functions of the Executive* (Cambridge: Harvard University Press, 1938, 8.

17. R.D. Laing, *The Divided Self* (Baltimore: Penguin Books, Inc., 1959, 1969), 106.

18. Harry Stack Sullivan, "Psychiatric Training as a Prerequisite to Psychoanalytic Practice," in *Schizophrenia as a Human Process* (New York: W.W. Norton & Company, Inc., 1962), 317.

19. Karen Horney, *Self Analysis* (New York: W.W. Norton & Company, Inc., 1972), 101–22.

20. Leo Buscaglia, *Love* (New York: Ballentine Books, a Division of Random House, Inc., 1972), 135.

21. Ashley Montagu, *On Being Human* (New York: Hawthorn Books, 1950, 1966), 93–95.

22. Paulo Freire, *Education for Critical Consciousness* (New York: The Seabury Press, 1973), 41–49.

23. William Watson Purkey and John M. Novak, *Inviting School Success: A Self–Concept Approach to Teaching and Learning*, 2nd edn. (Belmont, Calf.: Wadsworth Publishing Company, 1984), 102–29.

24. Carl Rogers, *On Becoming a Person* (Boston: Houghton Mifflin Company; Sentry Edition, 1961), 331–37.

25. Harry Stack Sullivan, *The Psychiatric Interview* (New York: W.W. Norton & Company, Inc., 1954).

26. Walter B. Barbe, *Educator's Guide to Personalized Reading Instruction* (Englewood Cliffs: Prentice–Hall, Inc., 1961).

27. Arthur W. Combs, et. al., *The Professional Education of Teachers: A Humanistic Approach to Teacher Preparation*, Second Edn. (Boston: Allyn and Bacon, Inc., 1974), 21–27.

28. Alfred Schutz and Thomas Luckmann, *The Structures of the Life–World*, trans. Richard M. Zaner and H. Tristram Engelhardt, Jr. (Evanston: Northwestern University Press, 1973), 24.

29. Ibid., 16.

30. Kurt Lewin, "Frontiers in Group Dynamics (1947)," in *Field Theory in Social Science: Selected Theoretical Papers*, ed. Dorwin Cartwright (Chicago: The University of Chicago Press, 1951; Midway Reprint, 1976), 188–237.

31. Schutz, *The Phenomenology of the Social World*, trans. George Walsh and Frederick Lehnert (Evanston: Northwestern University Press, 1967), 54.

32. Cited by Ashley Montagu, *On Being Human*, 110.

Chapter 6

Re–Inventing Educational Leadership

A conclusion for a phenomenological analysis of educational leadership is not appropriate if the term "conclusion" is identified with the "conclusions" deduced from empirical data of scientific studies of educational leadership. Maurice Natanson begins the concluding chapter of his study of Husserl's phenomenology with the following pertinent words:

> It is inappropriate to bring a discussion of phenomenology to an end by artificially trying to tie together stray bits of critical thread. Neither expository recapitulation nor interpretative summation will heighten what we have written or bring into balance the assortment of analysis which has been presented. If phenomenology is a search for beginnings, so should this conclusion continue that search.[1]

Similarly, Richard Zaner begins the final chapter to his study of phenomenology with the following epigraph:

> `We shall not cease from exploration
> And the end of all our exploring
> Will be to arrive where we started
> And know the place for the first time.'
>   T.S. Eliot,
>   Little Gidding (Four Quartets)[2]

Zaner notes that Husserl conceived of all of his publications in one way or another as "introductions" to phenomenology. Thus, the concluding chapter to a phenomenological analysis of educational leadership will continue to ask questions about the nature and meaning of educational leadership as it is re-invented in the context of current educational principles, programs, and practices.

No attempt will be made in this chapter to develop a new theory of educational leadership from the preceding presentation of research. Neither will we attempt to set forth a final or definitive word on educational leadership. This study has been about re-visioning educational leadership, about foundations, interpretations, and re-inventions of educational leadership. In the previous chapters we have pulled apart the concept of educational leadership from various perspectives, trying to isolate the biases and to see the real nature of educational leadership. The task remains to put the concept of educational leadership back together in light of the phenomenological analysis. What would it look like in a given educational setting? What are the challenges and admonitions for today's educational leaders and followers?

Those who do not understand Husserl's method of phenomenology and those who have not read the preceding chapters carefully are cautioned about drawing certain conclusions. For one thing, this approach to the study of educational leadership does not pretend to be the only way to view the subject. Hopefully, for as long as there is interest or need, educational researchers will continue to ask questions about the nature of educational leadership, to analyze the meanings of educational leadership, and to interpret how the experience of educational leadership is structured and interpreted in an educational leader's consciousness. A different set of questions could be asked about the nature of educational leadership in each unique setting of the educational process, and different results will be expected. What educational leadership means will depend on the values, landscapes, and interrelationships of the leader and the educational constituency. An ongoing need will exist to clarify the meaning of the terms leadership, educational, and a combination of those two terms.

Although the emphasis of this study has been the application of the phenomenological method and a criticism of the positivistic and idealistic biases of an analysis of educational leadership, empirical research and idealistic speculation are not to be excluded from our analysis. In fact, empirical studies are needed to compare dialogical leadership with leadership traits and leader behaviors. In the minds of some phenomenologists, concern for an accurate perception of all evidence in phenomenological analysis is a "radical empiricism."

Further, no attempt has been made here to produce a theory of educational leadership which will work in all kinds of settings. What educational leadership means in Cadiz, Kentucky will not be the same as it is in Atlanta or San Francisco or Boston. However, conducting research on the nature and meaning of educational leadership within the context of education itself is the first step in discouraging biased and confused meanings of educational leadership which have been imported from other disciplines.

RECLAIMING EDUCATIONAL LEADERSHIP

What would the results of this study look like if it were applied to the educational leaders of a local school? Although that question does not properly belong to a phenomenological analysis of educational leadership, it is a fair question and deserves some response. Perhaps we can provoke others to apply some of the observations and admonitions presented here. Keeping in mind that "theory" is a way of looking at something, viewing educational leadership in some new ways may lead us to re-invent the concept of educational leadership. One may look at three dimensions of educational leadership: what a person is subjectively and objectively; the interrelationship between a leader and his or her followers; and the educational setting, which in our culture is primarily the school.[3] Yet, the reader is reminded that these dimensions should not be thought of apart from the whole experience of leadership in education.

Rediscovering Educational Leadership

All behavior of every educational leader and every follower is completely determined by the perceptions which each person has of the phenomenal field at the precise moment of leading.[4] Educational leaders and followers do things and say things according to how they see themselves, others, and the world in which they are involved. Further, past, present, and future events are shaped and interpreted by how they perceive reality. In fact, the dreams, visions, values, beliefs, attitudes, hopes, and illusions of educational leaders and followers are determined by their self concept, who they are and how they fit in the educational world in which they are living.

To rediscover educational leadership is to get to know oneself. Although the self of each leader is unique and different, being an educational leader is not unlike a person living happily and effectively in a family situation. Virginia Satir, a family counselor, shows us what she has found to be important in the development of happy families:

> Over the years I have developed a picture of what the human being living humanly is like. He is a person who understands, values, and develops his body, finding it beautiful and useful; a person who is real and honest to and about himself and others; a person who is willing to take risks, to be creative, to manifest competence, to change when the situation calls for it, and to find ways to accommodate to what is new and different, keeping that part of the old that is still useful and discarding what is not.
>
> When you add all this up, you have a physically healthy, mentally alert, feeling, loving, playful, authentic, creative, productive human being; one who can stand on his own two feet, who can love deeply and fight fairly and effectively, who can be on equally good terms with both his tenderness and his toughness, know the difference between them, and therefore struggle effectively to achieve his goals.[5]

Compare Satir's description of a family leader with Arthur W. Combs' description of effective teachers: (1) Good teachers feel identified with, rather than apart from others, seeing themselves as a part of all mankind. (2) Good teachers feel basically adequate rather than inadequate. (3) Good teachers feel trustworthy and not untrustworthy. (4) Good teachers see themselves as wanted rather than unwanted. (5) Good teachers see themselves as worthy of respect rather than unworthy.[6] Each of Combs' characteristics of an effective teacher involves perception. Since all the important ingredients of educational leadership are perceptions which can be learned, changed, and corrected, there is always hope that a leader can change and can learn new things. The crucial thing in what happens both inside and between leaders and followers is the picture of self worth of each member of the educational community. Integrity, honesty, and responsibility, love, and compassion flow from a good educational leader. Educational leaders who count have a high sense of self worth. Again, to quote from Satir:

> He feels that he matters, that the world is a better place because he is here. He has faith in his own competence. He is able to ask others for help, but he believes he can make his own decisions and is his own best resource. Appreciating his own worth, he is ready to see and respect the worth of others. He radiates trust and hope. He doesn't have rules against things he feels. He accepts all of himself as human.[7]

Knowing that change is possible and wanting to learn to be different are first steps in re-inventing educational leadership. After finding out what one needs to learn about self and others, the leader must find a way to learn it. If leadership depends on how one views self and others in an educational setting, the most effective way to re-invent educational leadership is to change one view, change one's perception. A young lady who had unknowingly suffered from near-sightedness (myopia) all her life was amazed when she put on corrective glasses and noticed for the first time that trees had leaves on them. Thus, the first step in re-inventing educational leadership is to change one's view of one's self and of the followers in an educational setting.

The one thing which a leader can change is to change his or her own view of self and others. Leaders cannot change followers very much without their consent and cooperation, nor the world in which they live; they cannot change their inherited traits, who the potential followers are in schools, nor the parents and constituency without moving to another location. But leaders can change themselves; they can change their views, their perceptions, their constructions of reality. Thus, the admonition to educational leaders is to get to know themselves intimately and to be willing to change their views of themselves, others, and their world.

Leaders Can Make a Difference

Since leadership is a quality, condition, or state of existence and not exclusively an inherited trait or a set or learned behaviors, what part does an individual have in determining whether he or she is an educational leader? We have advocated in this book that the individual has everything to do with being a leader. The final determinant of being an educational leader is a consciousness which includes beliefs, values, choices, commitments, goals, and visions of an educational situation of life in which learners or followers desire to participate. Thus, whether a person is an educational leader is determined finally by the affirmation of a self concept which is constructed on the foundation of educational values, goals, and actions with which the educational constituency can identify.

Human existence in a leader mode is the immediate result of the exercise of a leader's free will and under the direct control of the individual leader. And, even though a person's heredity is not self–chosen, choices can be made that overcome a lack of some of those traits which have been associated with successful leaders. Values, beliefs, attitudes, goals, dreams, hopes, and actions which attract the attention of followers are chosen by educational leaders themselves. Becoming an educational leader is not the result of the mechanical enactment of a given set of principles and behaviors; neither does educational leadership automatically happen by possessing certain knowledge or by believing in certain ideals of present or past leaders. Being an educational leader is integrating a self concept around a believable, meaningful, freely–chosen view of education in which an educational constituency identifies and desires to become a part.

Just as Peter Vaill says that all management is people management, one could say that all educational leadership is people leadership. The reason for this is that there is nothing that a manager or a leader can do that does not depend for its effectiveness on the meaning that other people attach to it. How and why people attach meanings to things, how and why these meanings change, and how and why people's meanings and people's actions are interconnected are the subjects about which educational leaders should be concerned.[8] All too often leaders are not concerned with perceptions, but are preoccupied with behaviors and styles of leadership.

In order to make a difference in the world of education, leaders first must believe that they can make a difference and desire to make a difference. One of the most difficult tasks facing those who are leading is to help others see that what they believe, value, and do can make a difference in the lives of the potential followers. Until the followers see themselves as a part of the desirable future which the leader envisions, they cannot see the value or meaning of following. In one sense, all of us who are in the world of education are educational leaders to some extent. The questions are: how influential is our leadership; what is the character of the values and goals of our leadership; what really happens in the lives of the followers; how many followers can identify with the mode of human existence which we are exemplifying; and does our leadership really make a difference in the their world of education?

Living on the precipice of indecision consigns would-be leaders to their hell. Albert Camus has vividly portrayed this phenomenon in his novel *The Fall*. The plot revolves around an incident on a particular November night, about an hour after midnight. It is drizzling rain. A man leaves a bar and starts across the bridge toward home. He comes upon a young woman, dressed in black, leaning over the railing, staring at the river. After a moment's hesitation, he walks on. Then in Camus' own words:

> I had already gone some fifty yards when I heard the sound-- which, despite the distance, seemed dreadfully loud in the midnight silence-- of a body striking the water. I stopped short, but without turning around. Almost at once I heard a cry, repeated several times, which was going downstream; then it suddenly ceased. The silence that followed, as the night suddenly stood still, seemed interminable. I wanted to run and yet didn't stir. I was trembling, I believe from cold and shock. I told myself that I had to be quick and I felt an irresistible weakness steal over me. I have forgotten what I thought then. "Too late, too far. . ." or something of the sort. I was still listening as I stood motionless. Then, slowly under the rain, I went away. I informed no one.[9]

Herein resides the basic difference between an educational leader and a non-leader. The leader hears the bodies striking the water and either summons help or jumps into the water. The non-leader is confused, hesitant, afraid, uncaring, and detached and does nothing-- neither killing nor saving, just being passive. The leader is a pro-active person whereas the non-leader is reactive. Educational leaders believe that learners are of worth in themselves; they believe the learners are both willing and desirous of learning things which are meaningful to them; and they believe a way can be found to involve learners in the experiences of learning.

Educational leaders do not have control over the total landscape of learning. You cannot change the government overnight; you cannot change the state board and the educational guidelines and criteria; you cannot change the school system very much; you cannot requisition a new educational constituency; you cannot easily fire all the teachers, principals, and staffs in a system; in public schools you cannot choose the students; nor can you get new parents for the students. You cannot change external forces in most cases. But leaders do have control over themselves; they can make their own choices and be responsible for the choices they make.

All educational leaders have choices about everything they believe, value, hope for, and do. They can walk into a room with a smile or a frown. They can address others in a confident, pleasant voice or in an angry, anxious voice. They can choose to help or hurt others. They can complain about people and conditions in the system or can decide what they can do to make the system better. They can blame others or can take responsibility for making a difference. Instead of expecting changes to occur in others, educational leaders must first look inward to see what changes need to occur inside. Educational leaders need to examine their own values, aims, purposes, dreams, ideals, and actions in the context of the broader nature, needs, values, and desires of humans existing meaningfully in a world of promises and problems.

An educational consultant and friend, Bill Page, of Nashville, Tennessee, is fond of saying to teachers, "Today is the first day of the rest of your life." Not being able to alter the past or control the future, Page says that teachers can choose to make a difference in their classrooms today regardless of the circumstances. Educational leaders can also make a difference in the lives of their learners, their systems, and their constituencies. Today is the first day for re-visioning educational leadership in the lives of leaders, learners, followers, and in the educational process. The decisions leaders have the courage to make, the things they are willing to do, and the responsibilities they are willing to take-- can make a difference in educational leadership. Being a leader is the courage to choose to be the kind of person whom other educators, learners, and constituents choose to follow.

MODELING EDUCATIONAL LEADERSHIP

In education today we see individuals who have changed the schools in which they served and some who seem to have changed education itself. Their successes are sometimes attributed to their "great learning," their position in government, their personality, or an intangible called "charisma." However, taking a look at some of these educational leaders convinces me that the explanation for the success of each leader is somewhat unique. Each individual leader's perspective is personal, and each leader's lived-world is unique. We certainly can learn something by studying the visions and lived-worlds of some of our educational leaders. The leaders I have selected to mention are simply some of the educational leaders whose work I know and whose lives are models of re-visioning education in the context of a lived-world.

Bill Page: Leader in Basics

Many readers will not be familiar with the work of Bill Page of Nashville, Tennessee. He proudly affirms that he does not have a Master's Degree, "and doesn't intend to get one." He is not a published researcher either.[10] Yet he speaks to upwards of a hundred thousand teachers and other educators each year in Canada and the United States, preaching eloquently his gospel of the basics of teaching, much of which he learned from his own experiences and his own research while teaching all grade levels in all kinds of schools. And his converts are many. I have personally observed radical changes in the classrooms of teachers who went to one of his workshops or who simply heard him speak during an in-service training day.

Typically, Page begins with this promise: I want to give you some specific, practical, concrete, down-to-earth ideas you can use in your classroom tomorrow, and to him, something is not practical unless it can be used by any teacher, in any classroom, at any grade level-- with any kind of kids, with any number of kids, with any subject matter-- without any special materials, special facilities, special training, changes in school policy, permission of the principal or the school board, or of the teacher next door.

Page proceeds to outline "101 Ways" to deal with classroom problems, testing, motivation, individualization, student involvement, learning centers, student responsibility, self-discipline, and self-motivation. Yet, those "101 Ways" are merely a vehicle to communicate some basic beliefs about kids, teachers, and education: kids will choose to learn and succeed if given a meaningful option; teachers should teach 100% of the schooling essentials at 100% proficiency; slow learning simply is not having the prerequisites to perform a task; the learner must be active in the learning process;

learning goals must be mutually established by teacher and child; the educative process is perceptual, and meanings lie inside the learner and cannot be directly manipulated by teachers; students are always motivated to do something; and students want to do "real" things which are meaningful to them.

These basic beliefs have produced some startling results in school systems where Page has worked or where people have applied his approach. Page took a group of the lowest achievers in the University City school system in St. Louis and saw the students quickly begin to work, develop socially, enjoy school, rate their teachers higher, advance more than a year's grade level in academic progress, and begin to accept responsibility for their own learning.

Page is one of the best models of an educational leader I have known. He does what he does because of what he believes. What he calls the "basics" are really the fundamentals of learning which extend far beyond formal education. His basics have to do with the requirements of a meaningful life in general, i.e, learning what makes for life and what does not, going from not knowing to knowing, moving from not having skills to having them. His idea of education is life occurring in a learning situation.

The main concern of educational leaders, according to Page, is to make sure teachers teach and students learn. Simplistic? Somewhat. However, when Page speaks and acts, things happen, and educators follow him. They follow him because of who he is, what he communicates about his beliefs, hopes, values, and experiences, and what he does about how he feels and believes. He lives out his philosophy in the world of education from the perspective of his consciousness of education. His consciousness revolves around being–with–students and being–with–teachers in a world of promise and problems. And his being–with–others in education is characterized by caring and supporting and affirming and helping and accepting. Page's basics make him an educational leader.

Although I doubt that Page would ever allow himself to be called a phenomenologist, his approach to teaching, learning, and education closely parallels the approach outlined in this book. He has re-visioned education from a most basic, down-to-earth, realistic, lived-world frame of reference and has attracted a sizable following of educators. The condition or quality of his existence is first, last, and always a consciousness of education. Those who follow him do so because of his consciousness of education, not because of a business, political, military, religious, or medical consciousness. Page leads educators within the landscapes of education in a lived-world of teaching and learning. He is an excellent model of an educational leader.

Paulo Freire: Dialogical Leader

Numerous references have already been made to Paulo Freire in this book as representing the best application of a phenomenological examination of education available in written form.[11] However, Freire has not written extensively in English, and what he has written is restricted to concerns with Third World literacy and politics. Those who have tried to abstract a universal method of education from his works have sometimes misrepresented and distorted his work. Further, Freire has not concerned himself with educational leadership per se, except as it relates to his passion for literacy. Thus, his value for our study of educational leadership is not in his literacy programs or views of political freedom; rather, he is an example of dialogical leadership.

Freire, as few others have done, has brought together theory and praxis in education. A neutral educational process does not exist; education is always learning to do some thing or explain some thing. Set in a thoroughly historical context (lived-world), Freire advocates reflection and action upon the world in order to transform it, but reflection cannot be separated from action any more than a Subject can be separated from an object. By the same token, Freire cannot think of educational leadership without a dialogical relationship between the teacher and the learner. Leaders must practice "co-intentional" education; leaders and learners are co-intent on reality. Both teachers and students are Subjects unveiling and recreating knowledge of the real world (constructing reality), but both are participating in the same reality. Through dialogue, teacher and student become co-investigators, co-knowers, co-actors in the process of education in which all grow.

However, dialogue cannot exist without "an intense faith in man" and "a profound love" for the world and human beings in it. Thus, dialogue is a horizontal relationship which is based on humility, mutual trust, love, faith, hope, and critical thinking in a partnership of transforming the world into a better place for all.

The practice of educational leadership for Freire is based on this dialogical understanding of human existence. Communication in education is not just speaking to the students, but is living with them. If the students do not understand the teacher, the teacher is obligated to get "into" (be-with) their language, create meanings based on symbols and language they understand. Freire believed in living in communion with the illiterate, obtaining their confidence, and learning to become literate, beginning with the frame-of-reference, world view, and consciousness of the students. Together, the teacher and learner name the world and make it a joint venture in human existence.

Decisions, aims, values, and actions in Freire's view of the educational process are anchored in the depths of dialogue. The illiterate become aware of their humanness, their dignity, their potential to learn what others know, their hope for a better life, and their power to transform their world. Thus, educational leaders do not merely transmit information to the educational constituency; they participate in a process of knowing, interpreting, and acting for the emergence of consciousness and critical intervention in reality for both leaders and learners.

Students of educational leadership need not agree with the political agenda of Freire in order to accept his dialogical approach to educational leadership. The manner in which he has brought together theory and practice is worthy of the most serious consideration in educational leadership in our educational systems. Therefore, Freire is an educational leader who has modeled being-with-others.

John Dewey: Experiencing Educational Leadership

The appearance of Dewey's name as an educational leader in a phenomenological study may surprise some readers, but I have introduced his name for two reasons. First, a phenomenological analysis includes data from every source, including empirical data, even Dewey's experimentalism. A more important reason is Dewey's view of "education as experience." Who would question the impact which that principle has had on American education during this century? I have maintained that educational leadership is a construction of the meanings of those experiences which result in educators and students following an educator.

What Dewey did as an educational leader is more important than what he said in his numerous publications.[12] To try to reduce his comprehensive philosophy to a few summarizing statements is impossible, but a few of the tenets of his philosophy of education will help us see why he is a model of an educational leader. First, education is life, not just a preparation for life. Second, education is growth, a day-to-day development. Third, education is a continuous reconstruction of experience; new experiences are added to the old, thus becoming the basis of new experiences. Fourth, education is a social process, and schools are democratic communities. Peirce's maxim of determining the meaning of an idea by observing the consequences of putting it into practice became the keystone to Dewey's approach to epistemology and education.

Dewey's theory of education as experience in a very real sense bridges the gap between theory and practice. His return to experience, no less than Husserl's, is a turning from the abstract and derived categories of scientific constructions to the life-world in which they are rooted. If educational leadership is a state or condition of the existence of people who are leading educators and students, the meaning of educational leadership is constructed in the lived-world of those who are experiencing it. Thus, an analysis of the meaning and nature of educational leadership is based on the practice of educational leadership itself. Dewey's examination of the action resulting from an idea simply stopped short of admitting that reflection and interpretation of the results of an idea is very much a part of the action.

Interestingly, Dewey's theory of education constantly struggles with the place of instrumental and intrinsic values in the educational process. Ultimately, the question of values and a standard of values in Dewey's educational theory is the moral question of how the interests of life are organized.[13] Is not the organization of life values the result of an individual's organization of consciousness into some meaningful construction? Thus, the meaning of educational leadership for Dewey depends on the values, or life interests, which the leader and the followers embrace and act out as instrumental values. Values and valuing are indispensable considerations of Dewey's educational leaders. Consequently, an analysis of the meaning of educational leadership in the United States needs to consider John Dewey as a model of educational leadership. In fact, educational leadership theory probably would be more advanced had it pursued the theory of the later Dewey, rather than shifting its foundations to positivistic philosophy in the fifties.

PRACTICING THE ART OF LEADERSHIP

Earlier we discussed the nature of educational leadership as an "art". An appeal to practice this art of educational leadership is a fitting way to end this book. However, I must clarify what I have in mind by referring to leadership as an art, since two or three recent books on business management have used the word "art" in their titles.[14] When I am thinking of practicing an art, I am not thinking of simply playing on an instrument expertly, playing a role on a stage mechanically, or drawing an outline of a building. Practicing the art of educational leadership is not just playing an instrument, but rather is like practicing the art of medicine, being a musician, an actor, an architect, a painter, or a trout fisherman. The art of educational leadership is a delicate combination of perceptions, knowledge, skills, subjective and physiological experiences, timing, logic, analysis, and synthesis, aesthetic awareness, values, creativity, sensitivity, commitment, and the practice of education in a world that needs and desires the kind of education which is being represented by the leader.

The art of educational leadership is not learned by reading one book (even this one), going to a quick–fix workshop, taking a university course under a recently published guru, adopting the latest educational fads or leadership games, or by copying what Japanese car makers or Washington politicians are doing. All of the intangibles of educational leadership which are not easily detected or empirically verifiable are just as real as the forces of light, heat, gravity, and sound; in fact, love, justice, honesty, loyalty, freedom, and the pursuit of goodness and happiness in the daily affairs of humankind are basic to the success of an educational leader.

However, practicing the art of educational leadership is not like practicing magic, witchcraft, hypnotism, or transcendental meditation. The image of educational leadership which has been re–visioned in this book is not so ethereal, amorphous, and elusive that it cannot be described in common–sense terms. The following considerations of the practice of the art of educational leadership are intended to be scientific, philosophical, and practical. The picture presented does not pretend to be complete, nor does it imply that every educational leader must practice the art in the manner so described. Keep in mind that the following picture is of a "quality or state of an existing person" and not simply a list of personal traits or a group of behaviors. The following observations and admonitions are intended to show what the ideas heretofore presented will mean if educational leaders apply them during the coming decades.

Seeing Clearly

The first element in practicing the art of educational leadership is "seeing clearly". One of the primary realities of educational leadership is that it is a perceptual process. Time and again we have seen that leadership depends on both the leader's and the followers' perceptions of self, others, and the world in general. And since these perceptions are value-driven, culturally based, and ego centered, educational leadership is not easily learned or quickly changed.

In order to move from a state of not leading to being a leader, two things are necessary. First, an individual's perceptions of self, others, and the world must change in such a way that others need and desire to identify with and participate in his or her frame of reference for viewing life. A leader can change self, but cannot easily or effectively change others or the world in which events occur. Therefore, the greatest opportunity a leader has is to monitor, reflect on, and alter self in accordance with the common values, needs, desires, and cultural heritage of the educational constituency.

The second thing necessary to move from a non-leader to a leader is for others to change their views of the non-leader to a view of a person whom they want to follow. Again, these perceptions of the potential leader are not easily changed. Consequently, the best a leader can hope is to determine what the values, needs, desires, and culture of the constituency are and to relate authentically to the frame of reference of the followers. Being open, genuine, caring, accurate, and comprehensive in sharing with others increases the likelihood of a change in the views of educational followers.

If clarity of vision is so crucial, a leader must cultivate the skills of seeing clearly. We have noted the value of bracketing (holding in abeyance or setting aside temporarily) presuppositions, prejudices, theories, and other cultural baggage in order to see the way educational principles, policies, and practices are constructed in the constructed in the consciousness of both leaders and followers. Leaders must pull apart, separate, label, and analyze accepted pictures, or views, of education in order to obtain the core meanings of the experiences of leading the educational constituency. Is it not time for educational leaders to take a long, hard, critical look at the "taken–for–granted world" within whose horizon and landscape the ordinary practices of education are conducted?

Educational leaders must also see things which others at first do not see. By climbing mountain peaks educational leaders see more and farther into the world of education than do others. Reaching down into the depths of the experiences and culture of learners, educational leaders bring to light dreams and visions of a future which others have never considered. Reading what others have overlooked, listening while others are talking, and using tools and laboratory techniques which others neglect or disdain, educational leaders see as possible that which others consider to be improbable or impossible.

Jesus of Nazareth once told his disciples that the eye is that which enlightens the body and if the vision is singular, the whole body will be full of light (Matthew 6:22–23). This Teacher implied that sight and perception are shaped and determined by beliefs and values. Thus, the educational leader who is aware of his or her own values and valuing process is more likely to see the desirable future which will attract the following of others.

Those authors who are beginning to emphasize the importance of visions in business leaders act as if they have discovered something new. Leaders have always been persons who seem to see clearer, better, and farther into the future than their followers. However, the very nature of leadership is a perceptual process, a way of seeing human existence. And seeing is an inseparable aspect of every dimension of practicing the art of educational leadership.

Personal Knowledge

Practicing educational leadership as an art recognizes that all knowledge is personal. Just as an artist becomes a part of the work which he or she paints, in a similar way the educational leader is very much a part of the educational process which he or she is leading. Therefore, all the feelings, biases, values, illusions, and ideals of the leader and the followers are as much a part of the educational leadership situation as are the curricula, classrooms, state guidelines, teachers, students, and behavioral objectives.

Having a sure grip on the facts, knowledge, understanding, wisdom, philosophy, and technical skills of the process of education is indispensable to the practice of educational leadership as an art. Educational leadership does not happen in a vacuum, by accident, nor magically. Leaders must know what is going on in themselves, in others, and in the world around them. Therefore, a good liberal arts foundation is a necessary prerequisite for effective educational leaders. In fact, the broader the leader's scope of knowledge and experiences is, the more capable the leader is to respond to the needs, desires, and problems of the educational constituency. While state certification agencies are debating whether subject area content or methods are more important, the real issue of the place of the liberal arts in educational leadership is being side-tracked.

Further, educational leadership which is practiced as an art demands a thorough grounding in the philosophical issues in education itself. How can leaders be educational if they do not understand the nature, structures, theories, and problems of education? The decline in the requirements of philosophical studies in the training of educational leaders has resulted in the manipulation of the behaviors of students, the acquisition of irrelevant subject matter data by students, the successful ascent of career ladder rungs by teachers, and the adherence to mandated state and local guidelines by central office administrators, but educational leadership is less effective. An appalling ignorance of what education is and what educators are trying to do in schooling hangs over public education like a dark, tornadic cloud.

By and large educational leaders who have made a lasting contribution have addressed the nature of the learner, knowledge, world views, values, consciousness, acting, communication, society, government, and meaningful human existence. As never before in the history of these United States, we need leaders who can ask, discuss, and evaluate questions about the nature and meaning of educational ideas and practices. And only as leaders are able to delve into the depths of education as an art and science will educational leaders be able to practice educational leadership as an art.

Embodiment of Common Values

Whether a person practices the art of educational leadership is largely dependent on the extent to which that leader can embody the goals, beliefs, purposes, values, and social needs of the educational constituency. Values are not properties of objects or ideas, nor are values "in the world." Values are perceptions of objects, ideas, or other people. A thousand–dollar bill is just so much paper to someone who does not recognize the "value" which has been assigned to it by a representative of the treasury in which all have confidence. Art objects are worth as much as someone is willing to pay for them; if no buyers are willing to bid on a painting, its monetary value is questionable, and value must be assigned on some other basis.

Similarly, educational ideas, events, acts, objects, goals, curricula, courses, and essential elements are worthless or of great value, depending on the value which is assigned to them by the educational constituency. However, the valuing process in education is founded on those values which the constituency holds in common. Further, the values which matter to all constituents have to do with being a human person in a common environment. Thus, such things as life, liberty, happiness, justice, honesty, respect for others and their property, love, responsibility, social security, and personal actualization are the kind of values on which educational aims and purposes are built. Values in education are not just fluff which can be ignored or relegated to some other institution in society. Educational leaders must traffic in those values which are common to the educational constituency.

The days are passing when educational leaders feel a need to apologize for advocating that values are fundamental in practicing the art of educational leadership. Following the cues of business, educational leaders need to examine the ways in which values shape the state of the existence of educational leaders. Business has demonstrated pragmatically that the promotion of certain values which are common to its constituents "is good business." Such values as love, truth, health, dependability, justice, forgiveness, patience, respect, goodness, loyalty, courage, honor, integrity, joy, hope, excellence, community, and wisdom will "work" in any organization, and especially are these values central to educational leadership. The day has come for educational leaders openly and enthusiastically to promote those values which are common to the fulfillment of the goals of the educational process.

Further, why do we need to look to the Far East for our philosophy, beliefs and values in business or education? Taoism, Buddhism, and Hinduism are foundations for the value systems of the Chinese, Japanese, and Indians. Alas, some contemporary business management gurus are telling us that value systems which are derived from Far Eastern religions and mysticism should be applied to business management theory and practice in the United States. Just because Buddhism is the philosophical orientation of the value system of the successful businesses of the Japanese is no reason to think Japanese values are appropriate for American business or education. Although looking to the Far East for criticism, clarification, and correction of American religions, beliefs, values, and culture is in keeping with the phenomenological method, American educational leaders would do well to look at American values which are resident in the American processes of education.

Leadership studies present two extreme positions of values. The prevailing view of researchers today is to separate values and leadership. The assumption behind this view is that leadership is a science of knowledge and skills, while values are emotive, irrational, and unscientific. One is hard put, according to this view, to deny that Adolph Hitler was a good leader. Hitler certainly caused others to do what he wanted them to do; he had a profound understanding of the needs and wants of the German masses and was a skilled manager of his followers. However, when the issue of common values is introduced, Hitler's status as a leader is repulsive. He was a despot, a manipulator, manager, selfish demagogue, murderer, callous fiend, but not a good leader. Hitler disdained the welfare of the masses; he was unable to sustain meaningful relationships with hardly anyone; he communicated in only one direction; his decisions were based on his own personal whims and greed; he recruited others on false pretenses and lies; his goals were always in terms of a selfish craze for power and rule over others.

The other extreme view of values in leadership is that some superior, elitist, self-righteous person or group decides what others should value; these self-appointed leaders feel a need to impose their ideals and values on the masses. The assumption on which this view is based is that a select few will know what is valuable for others. A contemporary example would be a Jim Jones, who lured hundreds to Guyana and decided every move his people made, even their death. Do not mistake the hype, the psychological manipulation, and religious hypnotism for the authoritarian value system from which he operated. Less bizarre examples of this authoritarian view of values abound in business, education, religion, politics, and the military.

Between these two extreme views is the recognition that commonly held values are the foundation of educational leadership. Who would deny that an the embodiment of honesty, integrity, compassion, respect, responsibility, freedom, justice, wisdom, knowledge, joy, happiness, health, friendship, hope, and other such values is central to the practice of the art of educational leadership? The "good" educational leader embodies those values which enhance the process of education and contribute to the life and destiny of the educational constituency as a whole. The list of values will not be the same in every case, but will emerge out of the desirable state of affairs of the educational constituency. Give us more educational leaders who genuinely love students, want the very best for them, and are responsible and authentic in their dealings with students, colleagues, and others.

Poly-Option Decision Making

An essential consideration in the practice of any art is the way decisions are made. We have advocated that the selection of criteria, options, answers, actions, and solutions in the practice of the art of educational leadership be broad-based, factual, follower-involved, open, poly-optioned, future-directed, and life enhancing. Poly-option decision making is a process, rather than a step-by-step answer-seeking sequence. Looking at educational leadership as an art focuses attention on the meaning of decisions, rather than simply obtaining right answers. A poly-option style of decision making seems much more appropriate for educational leaders than a decision science approach.

The poly-option process demands that educational leaders learn how to ask questions about the questions which are asked. Instead of confining a decision to the question at hand, why not ask whether the question is worthy of being answered, whether the question is the correct one to ask, and to imagine what an answer will mean to the educational constituency. Thus, a broad knowledge of the fields of education, learning, and the liberal arts will enhance the quality of decisions of educational leaders.

Educational leaders who make good decisions must envision a future state of affairs of their constituency which is desirable, meaningful, and in the best interests of all concerned. Educational leaders ought to know where they are going and what it will mean if they get there. Thus, the context of the educational aims and goals is a future state of educational affairs, as well as the present lived-world. Educational leaders are not merely reaching for goals and objectives which have been handed down by the central office or a state agency. Goals are set for a desirable future and examined in the context of other values and vital needs of the constituency.

Better decisions are made if leaders have more options from which to select answers and actions. Free choices require that real options are available. Options promote feelings of openness, honesty, and connectedness in followers. Followers who are encouraged to "talk through" and examine as many options and alternatives as is feasible are more likely to support decisions than if decisions are made arbitrarily. When the focus is not on one right answer, new ideas and a higher quality of research is likely to result.

The intention of purposes and aims of educational decisions generally is predicting or understanding. Is a decision intended to predict the outcome of a behavior or chain of events, or is the decision concerned with understanding what the question means? Poly-option decisions lean in the direction of understanding. Not that prediction is undesirable, but that understanding decisions concerning the process of education will mean more in the long run than predicting the effect of a single choice. Looking at the landscapes and contexts of leadership decisions in education exposes the broader meanings of a decision.

The most effective educational leader is one who raises the educational constituency's problems and needs to the highest level of commonly held values in the shortest period of time. A good decision concerning whether to remove a small child who has wandered into a busy street is a decision which addresses the safety and welfare of the child in the shortest amount of time; an educational leader makes good decisions on the basis of the most meaningful and most appropriate learning for the followers. The hierarchy of educational values is built on the vital needs of every individual learner in an educational system.

When timing, options, available knowledge, and other factors are exhausted, educational leaders must cut off debate, deliberation, and research and decide (*de-cido* in Latin means "to cut off"). Little wonder that good leaders are characterized by "decisiveness." Choosing one thing means that you cut off other things; educational leaders must be confident enough to weigh alternatives and decide a course of action on the basis of the commonly held values of the educational constituency.

Making decisions with the above considerations in mind is truly the practice of a delicate art. Options are not always clear or available, mistakes abound, and no step-by-step techniques exist for making decisions in all situations. Just as a work of art is created out of countless variables, endless trials and errors, unique contexts, and unpredictable personal twists, the decision making of educational leaders requires holistic, unbiased, critical, scientific, creative, and personal choices which are based on the highest level of educational values.

Hermeneutics of Educational Leadership

Modern impressionistic art emphasizes the phenomenon of an artist bestowing meaning upon an object. In a very real sense educational leaders bestow meanings on the process of education. Meaning–giving is a basic function of the practice of the art of educational leadership. Educational leaders are at their best when they are reflecting upon and interpreting the meanings of educational aims, curriculum, methods, administration, and evaluation in the context of the needs, values, and desires of the educational constituency.

One of the major responsibilities of educational leaders is to develop this art of interpreting, hermeneutics, in order to understand better the scripts and structures of the educational process. A leader learns to interpret the nature of education by bracketing the biases and focusing on the consciousness of the educational process. Only by studying, analyzing, reflecting, discussing, and being–with–others in the educational process does a leader understand and interpret the meanings of education.

Setting aside the biases and presuppositions of educational aims and purposes allows leaders to examine what the aims and purposes mean in the consciousness of the leader. The phenomenological bracketing, or reduction, opens up the raw experiences of each educational aim and how it is framed and structured in each leader's consciousness. Values, prior experiences, and a host of tacit assumptions shape the construing of meaning by the individual leader. A careful reflective interpretation requires that each element of the educational process be pulled apart, examined, analyzed, and reflectively interpreted for what it is in itself. Applying hermeneutics to educational leadership also demands that the intentionality of the experiences of educational leaders be noted. For instance, the aims of education cannot be interpreted apart from the context, or a lived–world, in which the aims of education are situated. Intentionality is a recognition that the totality of the educational leadership phenomenon is interpreted holistically.

Some of what theorists refer to as "situational leadership" is what we have referred to as "intentionality." Briefly, situational leadership is knowing which style of leadership is appropriate for a given set of goals with a given group of followers. However, hermeneutics goes far beyond situational leadership to examine the totality of the situation and to get a feel for the right thing to do in order to be an effective leader.

A good educational leader is one who has bracketed educational presuppositions, has reflectively interpreted what the experiences of education mean to each person participating in the educational process, and has put things back together in a meaningful lived–world for the leader and the educational constituency. Hermeneutics is an essential exercise in the practice of the art of educational leadership; it reduces bias, examines the total leadership experience, and interprets educational leadership as it is experienced by each individual.

Dialogue with Followers

One of the differences between practicing educational leadership as an art and as a science is the existence of a dialogical relationship between leaders and followers. Dialogue is a two–way relationship between the followers and the leader. Manipulating, exploiting, controlling, and coercing others to do what the leader desires is not to be equated with dialogue nor with leadership.

Dialogue assumes that an educational leader is looking at both sides of the total state of affairs in the educational process. Thus, the leader sees things from the viewpoint of the followers, as well as from his or her own viewpoint. Part of the success of the human relations approach to management can be attributed to seeing how the followers really feel, what they want, and what they value.

Leaders who are in dialogue with followers also listen to what is being said on the other side. Educational leaders are betraying the very nature of education if they are unwilling to listen to what the learners and the educational constituency are saying both verbally and non–verbally. Dialogical listening is hearing with the ear, with the emotions, with logic, and with a caring heart.

Relating to others as dialogue means that the leader is relating to the whole person, every dimension of the follower. Observers of Japanese management have commented on how the Japanese seem to be interested in the whole person, rather than just the labor potential, productivity, and service of an employee. To lose sight of the value of the total person in the educational process is to narrow the focus of education to a state of educational practices which is less than worthy of the name of education.

A dialogical relationship with followers involves basic values such as love, integrity, honesty, responsibility, friendship, cooperation, and community. Those leaders who are practicing educational leadership as an art feel compassion for and desire the best for their followers. The need for a dialogical relationship in educational leaders is more critical than most any other aspect of the educational leadership in today's educational principles and practices. To lose sight of the value of the total person in the educational process is to narrow the focus of education to a state of educational practices which is less than worthy of the name of education.

The result of a dialogical relationship between leader and followers is an interdependence which feeds and empowers the entire educational organization. Observers often comment that the leader and followers "fit" together when the relationship is dialogical. Some anthropologists feel that this need for one another, a sense of cooperation and community, is basic to being a human. What other organism is as dependent on others as the human infant? Educational leaders who practice the art of leadership in a dialogical manner will be more effective as educators than those who manipulate, manage, deceive, and trick their followers.

Subjective Communication

Both art and educational leadership are vitally dependent on communication. All leadership theorists recognize the critical role which communication plays in the practice of leadership, but few seem to realize how subjective, how personal, the nature of that communication is. Viewing communication as an art helps us to see just how subjective the communication process is.

The creation of language itself is a communal project and cannot be divorced from the personal relationships which must exist among humans in order for alphabetical, grammatical, and syntactical constructions to be assigned meanings. Words and sentences have no meanings inherent in themselves apart from that which is assigned to them by a cooperative group who have agreed to use the same language characters and structures. If all knowledge is personal, all communication is intensely personal and subjective.

The very nature of education is bound up with developing skills in communication and being able to understand communication more effectively. Most learning presupposes that a personal relationship exists between the teacher and the learner, and communication is necessary for learning to take place. For education to be what it claims to be means that educational leaders take seriously the subjective nature of communication in the lived-world of the educational process. Education offers a setting in which leaders and learners can struggle with value dilemmas and relationship problems which are central to a meaningful life. Leaders need to develop ways to integrate the learners' feelings, attitudes, values, and relationships with the regular process of education. The key to developing personal communication is learning listening skills, improving interpersonal relationships, and increasing understanding of self and others.

Educational leaders need to feel that it is acceptable to express feelings of concern and compassion for students and others in an educational setting. Communication is not so much a skill as it is a way of existing, and effective communication implies that a personal relationship exists between leader and learner. The practice of educational leadership as an art necessitates that leaders recognize the subjective dimensions of communication.

Intentionality and Holistic Thinking

Several carpenters who were working on a building were asked what they were doing. The first man who was asked said that he was driving nails with a hammer. A second man said he was making ten dollars an hour. A third man said he was building a cathedral. The third man saw his work as part of a work of art. Educational leaders are able to put things together into meaningful wholes. Holistic thinking and seeing characterize the practice of educational leadership as an art.

What might be called balance, level-headedness, etc. is really a result of holistic thinking. Educational leaders seem to realize where that golden mean is located; they know what magic ingredients will produce the right blend; they can take various factions and interests and integrate them into teams and systems. Philosophers refer to this type of thinking as synthetic, i.e., relating to the combination of parts to make a whole. Synthetic thinking is basic to effective educational leaders.

Holistic thinking also results in patience and endurance in leaders. Those who can see the end of the school year do not find it necessary to get everything done the first day. Seeing the whole project helps the effective leader stick to the job until the goal is reached. Effective educational leaders do not allow short-sightedness, impatience, and failures to obscure the real object of education, learning and growth.

Educational leaders who are thinking synthetically often produce a state of educational synergy, working together in a way which produces a learning situation which is greater than the sum of the parts. Synergy explains one reason why leaders seem to get thing done which others find difficult or impossible. Educational leaders see and think in holistic terms.

Synthetic thinking does not allow a total disregard for analytical, scientific, and deductive thinking. All types of data, even the irrational, are eligible for consideration in synthetic research and interpretation. In contrast to educational leadership theorists who claim that only empirical data and leadership behaviors are germane to educational leadership studies, a holistic approach is concerned with getting the whole picture and seeing educational leadership subjectively as well as objectively and scientifically.

Phenomenology is an exercise which allows us to look at the nature and meaning of the consciousness and the experiences of educational leadership in the immediate setting of schooling and in the larger lived-world of the educational process. Thus, that sometimes indefinable, but real, blend, balance, fit, and integration, "that putting it all together," which educational leaders seem to feel and achieve in the educational setting is vital to the effectiveness of the practice of educational leadership.

Knowing and Being Leaders

Educational leaders without knowledge and technical skills of educational leadership are like artists who know nothing about paints, media, painting, or subjects to be painted. Just to address the often-leveled charge that phenomenology is subjective and unreal, it is necessary to point out that educational leaders must know a great deal about many aspects of education and about people, not the least about themselves.

Consequently, a liberal arts foundation is indispensable to an educational leader. Educational leaders cannot be expected to know every detail about everything in an educational system, but the leader had better have a broad, factual understanding of human life as lived in an educational setting. Medical doctors are not trained by teaching them every thing about every disease they will ever encounter; pre-med students are exposed to as much about the entire field of medicine as is possible and are taught where to go to find additional help when needed in the actual practice of the art of medicine. Those educators who are presently clamoring for teachers who know their subject areas without awareness of the art of teaching are as mistaken as those who think education is behavior modification. Being an educational leader is more than just possessing technical skills or knowing academic content. Someone has wisely remarked that experts need to be on tap and not on top. A liberal arts foundation for the profession of educational leadership provides the "big picture" perspective of the teaching subject area, the field of education, the students to be taught, and the methods to use which are most effective.

Although leadership trait theorists have found inconclusive correlation between intelligence and effective leaders, intelligence which is balanced with wisdom, compassion, skills, patience, vision, and values will surely be an asset to the educational leader. Those exercises of the mind which are usually measured by intelligence tests are not guarantee of success in themselves, but intelligence which results in knowing the right things of education in absolutely necessary for educational leaders.

What some educators forget is that knowing about education and subject areas and being an educational leader are both
aspects of the one phenomenon of educational leadership. Knowing cannot be separated from being in the experience of educational leadership. Yet, knowing something about education and about what is to be taught is an absolute prerequisite of an educational leader.

Catherine Twomey Fosnot points out that the problems of higher education today are too complex for the discipline of education to try to train future educational leaders. She advocates interdisciplinary thought to encourage educators to consider new perspectives on some of the old problems.[15] For instance, the hard and social sciences are firmly based in the "real" world that educators cannot afford to overlook what they have to say. A more specific example would be the fairly recent interest of anthropologists in the problems of education, or the interest of educators in the work of anthropologists. More interdisciplinary research is needed in the re-visioning of educational leadership.

Charisma of Leaders

Rarely do you see an artist who is not committed heart and soul to the results of the practice of his or her art form. The artist's identity is bound up with the production of the work of art in such a way that the work of art is really an extension of the person of the artist. Even so, the educational leader is bound up with the ones being educated. Therefore, the voluntary and conscious commitment of the leader to the welfare of the followers is essential to the practice of educational leadership as an art.

A wide gap exists between knowing what is best and how to do it for followers and actually doing it. That critical difference between knowing how to be a leader and being a leader is a free, conscious decision to act and to be something in education which others want to follow and with which followers want to identify. In the final analysis, an educational leader is someone who has committed himself or herself to the process of educating a given constituency. While pseudo-leaders are content to manipulate, modify, "motivate," and even deceive others to do what they desire of them, genuine educational leaders are bound up in the realm of the existence of the educational constituency through the voluntary commitment of heart and soul.

Phenomenological intentionality recognizes the inseparability of being and doing educational leadership. The cement which holds being and doing together is commitment, the engagement of personal will. One reason why a person can complete the very best leadership training program in the finest university and still not become a leader is this factor of will, commitment to the goals and the general welfare of the educational constituency.

The integration of the will and the values of a leader in one basic direction, in the context of the lived-world of education, involves the phenomenon of charismatic leadership. Kierkegaard, the nineteenth-century Danish philosopher, referred to the ability to will one thing as "purity of heart." The current revival of interest in charismatic leadership is the result of both an inability to understand the nature of human beings and an unwillingness to acknowledge that non-empirical factors play such a significant role in leadership. One major publisher rejected this manuscript with the explanation that they only publish empirical studies on leadership. However, what many researchers designate as charismatic leadership involves what we have noted as the commitment of heart and soul.

Max Weber's attempt to describe authority naturalistically in terms of statistical laws was unsuccessful as the principal source of social change, which he classified as "charismatic authority" (the attachment to the person of a powerful, individual leader).[16] Thus, charismatic leadership became that which could not be explained rationally or scientifically; this probably explains why Weber chose the term "charismatic," which he borrowed from the ecstatic, mystery religions of Early Christianity. Charismatic, thereupon, took on a very undesirable connotation in fields other than religion.

To observe how present-day leadership studies skirt the use of the term "charismatic" is quite fascinating. The very heart of Theory Z is the integration of subjective factors, which have been given names borrowed from Far Eastern religious thought. One recent study of management tries to avoid the term charismatic by referring to these subjective factors, "the deeper experience," of leadership as "spiritual leadership." The author tries hard to distance his concept of spirit from a religious connotation, while quoting theologians (Tillich) supportively and connecting "the seven deadly sins" with the "cheap thrill process" (charismatic?) in organizations.[17] Discussions of the need for visionary leaders include factors which properly belong to charismatic leadership, an approach which is employed in a recent study of charismatic leadership.[18] Bennis and Nanus categorize charismatic leadership as one of their "myths" about leadership.[19] These and other studies mention such things as inspiration, enthusiasm, spiritual work, envisioning a future, faith, super-ordinate goals (transcendental?), etc. as having something to do with leadership, but they shy away from even a hint of charismatic terminology.

One of the pioneers in American leadership theory, Ordway Tead, in 1934 seemed to have been aware of neither Weber nor charismatic leadership, but his treatment of the subjective engagement of the will is still worth reading. He talks about the need for "faith" in a good leader. For Tead, faith connotes an active effort to produce something good which is based on the confirming experience that such activity is good and produces good. Faith is a willingness to respond to an appeal to find one's selfhood in realizing those aims and values which lead toward the fulfillment of that which makes human life meaningful. Tead believes that this faith has always been realized by the great leaders and that it is a demand even in ventures where the immediate goals are seen as completely material.[20]

For educational leaders the integration of attitudes, values, and will in the one direction of the general welfare of the educational constituency is demanded, whatever that state of existing may be called.

Many of the so-called charismatic qualities are demanded of educational leaders. For instance, enthusiasm and excitement about the possibilities of students learning how to have a better life are indispensable to educational leadership. Nothing seems to substitute for the spirit of zeal for the goals of education, that sense of confidence and know-how in teaching, that feeling that the leader has been where the followers now are, that knowledge which communicates integrity and responsibility, that awareness that the leader really cares and wants the best for the followers.

Thus, educational leaders who have both charisma and commitment to the process of education are more likely to be effective in doing education than are those who simply possess knowledge and/or skills. Today's educational leaders need this integration of knowing, acting, and being if they expect to be successful in the complex process of education in schooling and in the larger society. Educational leadership which brings together all the aspects of the practice of the art of educating is indeed a great challenge for generations to come. These educational leaders will make a difference in the educational settings where they are existing as educators whom students, colleagues, and the educational constituency want to follow.

CONCLUSION:
RE-VISIONING EDUCATIONAL LEADERSHIP

In this book we have noticed three major outcomes of a phenomenological analysis of educational leadership. These three outcomes seem to surface as a calling for educational leaders to take a serious look at who they are, what their leadership means to themselves and to others, and what they can do to become an effective educational leader.

First, a critical need exists to re-vision educational leadership from within the experience of education itself. Although re-visioning educational leadership does not change the reality of the leadership situation, the focus of what educational leadership means is shifted from character traits and behaviors to perceptions of self, others, and the world within which the experiences of educational leadership take place. By bracketing the biases and presuppositions of what is normally defined as educational leadership, a leader begins to see how attitudes, dreams, values, and cultural beliefs shape one's perceptions of the nature and meanings of educational leadership. Focusing on the consciousness of what being an educational leader is within the process of education itself reveals the root of educational leadership which leads to the very nature of education itself. Thus, educational leadership is unlike all other leadership because the true nature of educational leadership is inseparably bound up with the process of education. Therefore, educational leaders first need to reflect on their own perceptions, their own responsibilities, their own feelings, their own values and beliefs about education and about those who are experiencing education in a given educational situation.

Second, the aims, behaviors, values, contents, methods, and administration of the process of education which a phenomenological examination have strewn on the floor of the educational arena must be reconstructed into a personally meaningful interpretation within the educational community of which the leader is a part. Education means knowing, growing, reflecting, changing, strategizing, committing, and acting on behalf of the commonly held values which lead to a personally satisfying present and toward a desirable future state of living. Thus, the meanings of the experiences of educational leadership are based on the intentionality of the consciousness of being an educational leader; the basic nature of educational leadership is a dialogical relationship between an educational leader and an educational constituency. The experience of education cannot be divided between theory and practice, between subject and object, between subject matter and experimentation, nor between teacher and learner. Educational leadership which is meaningful is a consciousness of the totality of experiences, interpretations, commitments, and actions in a real world of problems and promises of a better life for all.

The third outcome of a phenomenological analysis of educational leadership is the possibility of a re-invention of educational leadership. Educational leaders need not stay the way they are. The history of educational leadership and the study of present and past educational leaders should demonstrate that educational leaders are usually the creative thinkers, those willing to try alternatives, those who work outside standard rules and guidelines. Educational leaders are those who really care about the community of which they are a part; they are not afraid to love and be loved, to risk, to be confident, to forgive, to be open and honest, to get excited, to be sober, to believe, to hope, to laugh, to cry; educational leaders must be human in the fulfillment of the true nature of education. There is a place in our world for those who want to be educational leaders in the context of an educational process which seeks to move both leader and learners toward a more humane and more fulfilling life. Educational leadership is being the kind of person whom an educational constituency desires to follow because the leader is teaching them a better way to be fully human.

NOTES

1. Maurice Natanson, *Edmund Husserl: Philosopher of Infinite Tasks* (Evanston: Northwestern University Press, 1973), 190.

2. Richard M. Zaner, *The Way of Phenomenology: Criticism as a Philosophical Discipline* (Indianapolis: The Bobbs–Merrill Company, Inc., 1970), 205.

3. Cf. Daniel Katz and Robert L. Kahn, *The Social Psychology of Organizations*, 2nd edn. (New York: John Wiley & Sons, 1978), 527, who state that leadership appears in social science literature as an "attribute of a position, as the characteristic of a person, and as a category of behavior."

4. Arthur W. Combs, Anne Cohen Richards, and Fred Richards, *Perceptual Psychology: A Humanistic Approach to the Study of Persons* (New York: Harper & Row, Publishers, Inc., 1949, 1959, 1976), 18. Originally published under the title, *Individual Behavior: A New Frame of Reference for Psychology* in 1949 by Donald Snygg and Arthur W. Combs; revised by Arthur W. Combs and Donald Snygg in 1959 under the title *Individual Behavior: A Perceptual Approach to Behavior.*

5. Virginia Satir, *Peoplemaking* (Palo Alto, Calf.: Science and Behavior Books, Inc., 1972), 3–4.

6. Arthur W. Combs, et. al., *The Professional Education of Teachers: A Humanistic Approach to Teacher Preparation*, 2nd edn. (Boston: Allyn and Bacon, Inc., 1965, 1974), 83–84.

7. Satir, *Peoplemaking*, 21–22.

8. Peter B. Vaill, *Managing as a Performing Art* (San Francisco: Jossey–Bass Publishers, 1989), 126.

9. Albert Camus, *The Fall*, trans. Justin O'Brien (New York: Alfred A. Knopf, Inc., 1956), 69–70.

10. My knowledge of Bill (William R.) Page comes from working as a colleague in Education Corporation of America (EDCOA), Nashville, Tennessee, for four years. To refresh my memory I reviewed some mimeographed materials which Bill used in the numerous workshops he conducted throughout the United States and Canada. Bill contributed notes and edited the *Raspberry Report Card,* a fortnightly "nuts and bolts" aid for teachers, during the academic years of 1973 and 1974. He has contributed two short chapters in a book by Edward Polak, *Teacher's Aid*, revised, expanded edn. (Montreal: Quebec Association for Children and Adults with Learning Disabilities <QACLD>, 1983).

11. Although Paulo Freire has more than six books to his own credit and others which he has jointly authored, his method of dialogue in education is stated in *Pedagogy of the Oppressed*, trans. Myra Bergman Ramos (New York: The Seabury Press, 1968, 1974). Freire's later works have not gone much beyond his first book; certainly this applies to educational leadership.

12. Of the countless books which John Dewey wrote, only two are considered here. *Democracy and Education* (New York: The Free Press, 1916, 1944); and *Experience and Education* (New York: Macmillan Publishing Company; "Collier Books," 1938).

13. Dewey, *Democracy and Education*, 248.

14. Cf. Vaill, *Managing as a Performing Art*. Also see Lin Bothwell, *The Art of Leadership* (New York: Prentice Hall Press, 1983). Richard Tanner Pascale and Anthony G. Athos, *The Art of Japanese Management* (New York: Warner Books, Inc., 1981).

15. Catherine Twomey Fosnot, *Enquiring Teachers, Enquiring Learners: A Constructivist Approach for Teaching* (New York: Teachers College Press, 1989), 119–25.

16. Max Weber, *The Theory of Social and Economic Organization*, trans. A.M. Henderson and Talcott Parsons, ed. with intro. by Talcott Parsons (New York: The Free Press, 1947, 1964), 324–92.

17. Peter B. Vaill, *Managing as a Performing Art*, 211–24.

18. Jay Conger, Rabindra N. Kanungo, and Associates, *Charismatic Leadership: The Elusive Factor in Organization Effectiveness* (San Francisco: Jossey–Bass Publishers, 1989). James M. Kouzes and Barry E. Posner, *The Leadership Challenge* (San Francisco: Jossey–Bass Publishers, 1985), 79–130.

19. Warren Bennis and Burt Nanus, *Leaders: The Strategies for Taking Charge* (New York: Harper & Row, Publishers, 1985), 223–24.

20. Ordway Tead, *The Art of Leadership* (New York: McGraw–Hill Book Company, Inc., 1935), 257–66.

Appendix

A Phenomenology of Educational Leadership

Phenomenology does not designate a clearly defined body of knowledge or a unified system of thought, and phenomenologists themselves often differ radically as to how to do phenomenology. Using the philosophical approach of phenomenology to study educational leadership necessitates a brief description of the phenomenological method and a clarification as to how it is to be employed.

Note that phenomenology is not a technique which can be learned and applied to data as one uses the scientific method. Phenomenology is more a method of study, a way of viewing, a perspective, a stance, a manner of thinking, a mode or style of enquiry. Yet, the phenomenological method is not really a method in the strict sense, it is not a set of techniques to be applied to an object to be studied. Phenomenology is a way of viewing a subject, and its basic tool is "seeing" and "interpreting" what is seen.

Etymologically, the word "theory" is rooted in the Greek word, *theoria*, which means "a looking at, viewing, beholding, gazing at, mostly with the sense of wondering." "Theatre," a place for viewing drama, comes from the same root. This definition is in sharp contrast to the positivistic definition of Feigl and others who equate theory with "science." Hoy and Miskel depart from the etymological meaning of theory when they say that theory is not philosophy, common sense, speculation, values, or ideals.[1] If theory is a viewing, or a perspective on a topic as the etymology of the word clearly indicates, a phenomenological approach is a theory and a way of viewing educational leadership. The phenomenological method is a way to get beyond the empirical assumptions and biases about nature to enable the researcher to study the nature of educational leadership itself. Phenomenology also sets aside the metaphysical assumptions and biases of the idealistic models of leadership in order to focus on the lived-experience of leadership in education. However, phenomenology is not to be viewed as the final answer to educational leadership theory; nor does it discount the contribution which other approaches have made. This study was undertaken with the hope that the phenomenological method can provide some additional insights concerning the nature and meaning of educational leadership.

DEFINING PHENOMENOLOGY

Anyone who attempts to survey the literature in the field of phenomenology will readily recognize the difficulty and confusion surrounding a definition of phenomenology. Researchers from various disciplines have either referred to their own approaches as phenomenological, or others have placed them in the phenomenological camp, sometimes in spite of their own objections to being called phenomenologists. Consequently, everyone who is doing research in education under the rubric of phenomenology is not utilizing the same approach.

Edmund Husserl's phenomenological method is the foundation of the preceding study of educational leadership; not much evidence exists that educational leadership researchers have taken the time or effort to investigate Husserl's method carefully. Husserl spent his entire life developing, revising, and refining his method and left some 45,000 pages of German shorthand manuscripts, the bulk of which remains unedited and untranslated. The chronological interests of Husserl's thought shed some light on the nature of his method.

At the heart of Husserl's entire work is a two-fold preoccupation: on the one hand is a search for an absolute certainty in science and in all knowledge, an interest he shared with Descartes, although not sharing his Cartesian method of solving the problem; on the other hand is a refutation of the excessive claims of positivism and psychologism. Beginning with an examination of the foundations of mathematics

(*Philosophie der Arithmetik*, 1891), Husserl proceeded to study the foundations of science, logic, epistemology, ontology, and history and concluded that the ultimate foundation of all knowledge is in human consciousness. Therefore all knowledge is fundamentally, but not exclusively, subjective.

Positivism claims that scientific principles can be applied to all forms of knowledge, even in social studies. Consequently, the whole world operates by invariate physical laws, and everything can be explained by employing the empirical method. Then, all statements must be either empirical, analytical, or irrelevant, and philosophy is reduced to the practice of logic, language analysis, and scientific verification.

In contrast to positivism, Husserl's method is an attempt to establish philosophy as independent of empirical science. Husserl argues that all questions about human life cannot be answered by the scientific method. Even mathematics and the concept of number are based on the creative intuition and abstraction of human intelligence. Scientific theories are based on models of nature, models of reality, and world views which can never be more than probably true because the models themselves cannot be scientifically verified. Husserl went directly to human consciousness where objectivity (certainty) is purest. For this reason, all knowledge is valid evidence: sense data, dreams, illusions, wishes, values, and fantasies. Thus, Husserl even bases science on the non−empirical foundation of human consciousness. Phenomenological statements are true if they describe the phenomena accurately. The aim of phenomenology is to describe accurately, to analyze the phenomena which are presented directly to the consciousness, and to reflect on the intuitive meaning of the contents of consciousness.

Immanuel Kant distinguished appearance ("phenomenon") from reality ("thing−in−itself"). For Kant, a phenomenon becomes an object only when interpreted through the categories of substance and cause. Husserl goes back "to the things themselves" and retains the unity of the objective world. Husserl's appeal to phenomena does not presuppose a special class of things called "phenomena." The watchword of Husserl, "*Zu den Sachen Selbst*" ("to the things themselves"), directs attention back to the phenomena by describing, examining, and reflecting on anything which presents itself to the consciousness. Thus, phenomena are not limited to those things which are known by sense experience, but include all forms of knowledge which enter consciousness: sense data, mathematical concepts, attitudes, values, intentions, melodies, moods, dreams, fantasies, feelings, illusions, wishes, and motives. For Husserl phenomena include:

All modes in which things are given to consciousness and include, the whole realm of consciousness with all the ways of being conscious of something and all the constituents that can be shown immanently to belong to them. [Phenomena include] as well every sort of feeling, desiring, and willing with [their] immanent 'comportment' (*Verhalten*). [2]

Phenomenology is a subjective, intuitive, reflective, philosophical analysis of the ways by which we become aware of the phenomena which are presented to our consciousness and of the interpretations of the nature and meaning of that consciousness. Consciousness for Husserl involves both the act of intending and the intended object of that act of intending. The ultimately real is not "how things are but how they appear to each individual and to each individual's awareness of them. What survives universal doubt is consciousness." [3]

The phenomenological method incorporates a world view as well as a way of viewing the world, just as the "scientific method" is a way of conceptualizing, or modeling, meaning within the physical world as a whole. Phenomenology is not a way to present either empirical or logical evidence to deduce truths or induce generalizations and predictions. Rather, phenomenology is a way of getting at the "is–ness," the kernel of meaning, of the phenomena being examined.

According to Husserl's method the phenomena of educational leadership would include the lived–experience of a leader of education in the context of a situation in which students are being educated. In contrast to those studies which seek to identify genetic traits of educational leaders or which collect data about behaviors which have been observed to be effective in given circumstances, a phenomenology of educational leadership examines the phenomena of educational leadership themselves. Whereas other studies of educational leadership are based on evidence gathered from business, the military, religion, or politics, a phenomenological study begins with educational leaders themselves in their experiences of educating. The phenomena of leadership are unique to education; the consciousness of an educational leader is unlike a leader of business or politics. Therefore, researchers should examine the phenomena of educational leadership in order to get a better understanding of the nature and meaning of educational leadership.

The subject matter of a phenomenology of educational leadership includes the biases of researchers, the beliefs, values, and attitudes which educational leaders experience, the intentional nature of consciousness of educational leaders, and the lived–world of educational leaders. A phenomenology of educational leadership will attempt to expose, explain, and interpret the nature and meaning of what it means to be a leader of education. The goal of a phenomenological study of educational leadership is to consider the experiences and meanings of educational leadership as a whole. Since most of the studies of educational leadership are either psychological investigations of personality traits or empirical interpretations of data from business and politics, the phenomenological method is a welcome tool for researchers who are studying educational leadership.

Many psychologists who were contemporaries of Husserl insisted that thinking is a mental act which can be studied as any other psychological activity and that logic involves correct and incorrect thinking. Thus, thinking is based on psychological principles and is dependent on empirical observations. These psychologists tried to show that logical and mathematical statements are as empirically grounded as are physical laws. Husserl, following Gottlob Frege, wrote a two-volume refutation of this "psychologism," a psychological view of logic. Husserl argued that both empirical and non-empirical statements are possible because they differ in kind. Psychological statements are factual, empirical, probable, inductive, and either true or false, depending on their correspondence to physical laws. Phenomenological statements, on the other hand, are non-empirical and are true or false, depending on how accurately they describe the phenomena. Thus, the achievement of a pure, direct, unbiased description of the phenomena is the primary task of phenomenology.

With a minimum of prior assumptions, premises, biases, and prejudices, all phenomena are examined over and over until their meanings, their essence, begins to emerge. The phenomenological method turns inward in pure reflection, seeking a change of perspective of the phenomena as they are in themselves. Philosophical priority is given to an analysis of the phenomena from the point of view of the one who is conscious of the phenomena. The phenomenologist is inextricably involved in the perceiving and describing of the phenomena. This shifting of focus away from sense data toward a vigorous science of intuitive analysis of consciousness permits the philosophical examination of virtually any experience, e.g., educational leadership.[4]

The phenomenological method is an attempt to analyze the structures, content, and meaning of consciousness. In order to get at the consciousness as it is directly given, all biases, prejudices, presuppositions, and frames of reference must be held in abeyance, bracketed, so that the essence of consciousness will unfold. Awareness of the world through common sense or sensory experience must be set aside, along with scientific, psychological, philosophical, historical, and other theoretical points of view. Husserl recognized that phenomenology is a world view and tried to bracket the phenomenological perspective. The result of his attempt is a "transcendental ego," which critics correctly identify with a tendency toward solipsism. However, the impossibility of completing the phenomenological reduction to the point of bracketing the ego does not void the need for bracketing and its valuable results when the placement of the ego is examined in the structure of the consciousness of any perspective. The phenomenological method is a process of pulling apart and examining the structure of consciousness, only to piece it back together again into a unity of meaning.

A phenomenology of educational leadership is a way to study educational leadership from a radically different perspective. The phenomenological method provides what is really needed in the field of educational leadership theory, i.e., the development of a view of educational leadership which is based on leadership within education itself, from the perspective of the leaders themselves. Although the phenomenological method cannot be expected to provide a final understanding of educational leadership, the desirability of nullifying the influences of biases and presuppositions of other studies is reason enough to search for a new and different method of study. Further, the phenomenological method presents an opportunity to consider a wealth of subjective evidence which other methods have either ruled out or overlooked.

THE PHENOMENOLOGICAL REDUCTION

One of the primary tools of the phenomenological method is "reduction." In fact, Eugen Fink, a leading authority on Husserl's philosophy, says that "phenomenological reduction" alone is the basic method of Husserl's phenomenological philosophy.[5] The various writings of Husserl describe reduction in ways which have prompted commentators to try to delineate different kinds or levels of reduction, an exercise which goes far beyond the scope of the phenomenology of educational leadership which is attempted here.

Husserl's "phenomenological reduction" must not be confused with "reductionism," a philosophical attempt to "reduce" the number of things that can be said about the world to the fewest possible propositions. Reductionism often results in the idealization of nature or the denial of everything but the material. Reductionism's procedure of selecting a representative sample to stand for a group or class or of generalizing a category of law from individual action is fruitful when it is not oversimplified. However, naive reductionism in both physical and social sciences is a major target of Husserl's criticism.

Reduction for Husserl is a method of pulling apart the phenomena of consciousness in order to describe and analyze the content and structure of consciousness, but the various aspects of consciousness are not considered as totally separate entities. The procedure of reduction can be thought of as raising the shades in a dark room to reveal the contents and arrangement of the room. Reduction exposes the phenomena of consciousness as one raises the hood of a car while the engine is running to see what is going on inside the engine. In contrast, a scientific approach looks as gauges, exhaust emissions, electrical circuits, fuel mixtures, etc. The scientific method would compare the complaints and symptoms of a stomach pain with the symptoms in other persons, but the phenomenological method would become involved with the pain to the point of exploratory surgery to see what the pain "is." Thus, reduction is a process of uncovering the "is-ness" of the phenomena of consciousness. The kinds, levels, or steps which some critics identify in phenomenological reduction are related to the variety of biases or "obstructions" which prevent the uncovering of the phenomena of consciousness which must be recognized and acknowledged if reliable, "certain" knowledge is obtained from research. Husserl's search for certainty leads him to describe the reduction in several modes as he deals with prejudices and biases of science, logic, psychology, and philosophy. Thus, to view the different performances of reduction as a sequence of steps, levels, or kinds is a blatant distortion of Husserl's method.

In order to shift one's focus radically, to wipe the slate clean, to dissolve biases, to begin one's research "presuppositionless," the Cartesian method of radical doubt is recommended. However, the doubting "I" cannot be separated from the act of doubting, as Descartes held. The kind of doubting which Husserl uses in phenomenological reduction is a "bracketing" (as in mathematics), a setting aside temporarily, a holding in abeyance, a suspension of judgment until the evidence from all sources is presented. The object of reduction is to get back to the way phenomena are in themselves.

All frames of reference must be reduced if the phenomena of consciousness are allowed to present themselves directly to the individual consciousness. Reduction does not deny that a real, concrete world exists, but the particular view of reality which is claimed for that world is "tagged" and set aside in order to focus on the *Dasein*, "the being present to the self," of the world, i.e., the "is-ness" of the world. Bracketing the natural attitude shifts attention away from the factuality, particularity, reality, and truth of the world and focuses attention on essentials, universals, beginnings, connections, structures, and meanings of phenomena of consciousness.

For instance, the frames of reference on which the "born" and "made" leader models are based not only determine what educational leadership is but also distort new knowledge about the nature and meaning of educational leadership. All views which focus on leader behaviors consider the causes and effects of leader behaviors, how to control and modify behaviors in leaders and followers, and what behavior is appropriate to obtain a chosen outcome in a given leadership situation. On the other hand, trait theories try to identify those who are destined to become leaders. Holding to these two frames of reference exclusively has prevented educational leadership theory from developing new paradigms. Little wonder then that researchers are lamenting the fact that educational leadership research seems to be going nowhere. The biases of old views need to be set aside, bracketed, reduced.

Phenomenological Description

The success of the process of reduction depends on a phenomenological description of the phenomena. The first movement in the shifting of focus away from the empirical evidence toward the phenomenological reduction is to examine what has been, or is being, reduced. This examination takes the form of a descriptive inventory of the phenomena of consciousness. Again and again the phenomena are examined in order to see clearly and to grasp their meaning. The phenomena are viewed from one perspective, and note is taken of that perspective; then the phenomena, in one sense, are picked up, turned over, and viewed from an entirely different perspective, and that perspective is "tagged"; again the phenomena are turned, pulled apart, and examined again; on and on the "seeing" and labeling continues from various perspectives.

The psychiatric interview as developed by Harry Stack Sullivan is a useful example of phenomenological description. The psychiatrist takes note of the intuitive, subjective, personal, insignificant, and unscientific, as well as the empirical, data of the interview situation. Sullivan observes both verbal and nonverbal aspects of the interview: tone of voice, patterning of speech, facial expressions, bodily gestures. This description requires a high alertness to the field of signs, looking, listening, questioning, restating, recapitulating the situation, trying to see and grasp what is really happening in the interview situation.[6]

Data for the phenomenological description are the phenomena which are presented directly and immediately to the consciousness. The phenomena are the point of the discussion, the subject matter, the contents of the consciousness. Nothing that is ever said, written, or printed can mean anything in itself; only a person who constructs the symbols and interprets them can construct meaning. Phenomenological description requires that the describer return again and again to the phenomena in order to see clearly, to perceive directly with a minimum of biases, and to grasp the meaning of what is viewed. Neither empirical observation nor logical reasoning is necessary to determine whether one is angry, in love, or confident; the raw data are presented directly and immediately to consciousness.

Therefore, knowledge is based on the direct and objective evidence presented to consciousness. "To know is to see." "Immediate seeing" is not merely the sensory experience of seeing, but seeing in general as primordinally given, a givenness of consciousness of any kind whatsoever; this kind of seeing is the ultimate source of justification for all rational statements.[7] This exercise of intuitive seeing is central to phenomenological description which includes all forms of knowledge, even irrational knowledge. By returning again and again to the phenomena, the phenomenological method seeks to describe both the contents and the structure of consciousness of educational leadership.

A phenomenology of educational leadership includes a description of the acts, beliefs, intentions, feelings, choices, hopes, dreams, and world views which make up the total experience of leadership in the world of education. The phenomenological description tries to describe what is really happening in the educational leadership situation. Using the field method, interviewing, case studies, projective tests, personal journals, biographies and autobiographies, psychological games, group dynamics, self reflective exercises, meditative exercises, and other such techniques, the describer becomes involved in the process of perceiving and describing educational leadership as a participant observer.

The Natural Attitude

One of the first tasks of the phenomenological method is the radical criticism of human experience at the level where everyone has faith in the reality of the world, i.e., the "natural attitude." The "natural attitude" begins from the standpoint of everyday life, from the world as it confronts us, from consciousness as it presents itself in psychological experience, and lays bare the presuppositions and biases essential to this viewpoint.[8] The natural attitude is the unreflective, naive, common sense, natural frame of reference, everyday view of the world. This attitude of everyday life allows someone like a farmer to live without raising questions about the nature of reality and knowledge. The world is assumed to be real and logical without question, wonder, or doubt. Alas, some people in the educational world are not able to transcend the natural attitude. The natural attitude is the tacit faith ordinary people have in the reality of their world, the assumption that the shared world of everyday life is indeed the same for all normal individuals.[9]

The thesis of the natural attitude includes an individual's first perspective upon life, imagining, judging, feeling, willing from the natural attitude. Husserl describes the natural attitude as being aware of a world which is "spread out in space endlessly, and in time becoming and become, without end." Being aware of it means first of all that one discovers the world immediately, intuitively, holistically, i.e., one experiences it. Through sight, touch, hearing, tasting, and smelling corporeal things which are somehow spatially distributed are "simply there" in different ways of the sensory perception. Things are present to consciousness in different ways because of the verbal or figurative construction of reality from a natural attitude, regardless of whether one pays them special attention by busying oneself with considering, thinking, feeling, and willing things about them. From the natural attitude Husserl considers real objects to be present, definite, more or less familiar, and agreeing with that which is actually perceived without being themselves perceived or even intuitively and subjectively present.[10]

The natural attitude has been compared to the light of day which is unseen and yet apparent in all shapes and colors which it illuminates. As light determines everything which the eye sees, so the natural attitude colors everything the individual perceives, binding all perceptions into one common experience of the world. All knowledge of self, others, and the world is colored by the "natural attitude" glasses which are fitted by self perception and worn in the realm of consciousness. The natural attitude includes images and conceptions of the world which are so familiar that they are "natural" to the individual. One slips into the natural attitude "naturally," without being aware of it because the attitude is so ingrained in life. Thus, the natural attitude is already a theoretical position, a frame of reference, an interpretation of experience which the researcher must break out of in order to escape the overpowering effects of its thesis. A phenomenological analysis of educational leadership attempts to get behind the taken-for-granted thesis of the natural attitude. This precritical, presupposed world of the educational leader includes a heavy load of cultural baggage which largely determines the meaning of educational leadership. The unexamined language of educational leadership is imported from business, politics, religion, and the military. Further, a host of myths and symbols have grown up around the meaning and practice of leadership which color what educational leadership is. The Western mind-set, which is a particular bias, has a profound influence on how educational leadership is interpreted. Bracketing the natural attitude of educational leadership is imperative if the researcher expects to probe the "is-ness," the nature, of what leadership means in the world of education.

INTENTIONALITY OF CONSCIOUSNESS

After the contingent facts, prejudices, and biases have been bracketed, the phenomenological method attends to the ways and modes in which phenomena appear and are constituted into meaning. Phenomenologists refer to this process of meaning-intending as intentionality of consciousness. In his earlier writings Husserl considered intentionality as the main theme of his phenomenology.[11] Intentionality is the distinctive characteristic of the experience of the consciousness *of* something. However, this does not mean simply that all knowledge has an object or content, as is often stated. Rather, intentionality focuses on "how" knowledge is related to an object or to the content of consciousness. The main function of intentionality is an epistemological method of analyzing the intending of meaning which is directed toward the consciousness of phenomena. The object of intentionality is to demonstrate that the meaning of thinghood cannot be established without reference to a wider context of circumstances, casualties, and ultimately to the horizon of the world itself.

The intentionality of all phenomena must be grasped in its correlation to consciousness because each given becomes accessible to a person insofar as it has meaning for that particular person. From this position regional ontologies, or realms of being, develop. The essential moment of each conscious experience is broadened as the genuine synthesis of several experiences are bound into one meaning, yet retaining their individual meanings.[12] Consciousness does not simply record phenomena passively; it is an act of constituting the experiences into meaningful wholes.

The constitution of intended meaning and judgment in the consciousness involves a focal awareness of the object of intention as well as all the subsidiary knowledge accompanying or surrounding the object of intention. For example, a paper on a cluttered desk can be singled out and perceived while the background of books and pencils becomes secondary in perception. Every perception of a thing has a zone of background intuitions, background awarenesses, horizons, or landscapes. Thus, the zone of consciousness is a vital factor in the constitution of meaning for the subject of the consciousness. No meaningful knowledge can be acquired except by an act of comprehension which consists in merging our awareness of a set of particulars into our focal awareness of their joint significance. The subject involves the self in the shaping of all forms of knowledge, even scientific knowledge. Intentionality of consciousness denies the division of subject and object, mind and body, thinking and thought, consciousness and content of consciousness.

Intentionality of the consciousness of educational leadership shows the interrelatedness of the various dimensions of the experience of leadership in education. Further, the mundanity of the human condition of being a leader is the foundation and grounding of the experience of educational leadership and shows the absurdity of idealistic or solipsistic musings. Intentionality also provides a way of interpreting the meaning of consciousness of educational leadership through the technique of hermeneutics.

The Lived-World

The vantage point of constituting the meaning of consciousness in an everyday world of existence is called the "lived-world" (*Lebenswelt*, also translated "life-world") by Husserl. The lived-world is simply the sum of a person's total involvement in everyday affairs: including one's knowledge, interpretation, response, and organization of his or her experience. [13] The goal is to recover the lived-world as a constitution of meaning and to ground the ego in its mundanity. In other words, how can the phenomenological method make use of the natural sciences without buying into the positivistic exclusion of all non-empirical evidence? The empirical sciences operate within the natural attitude, but are organized and interpreted according to perspectives and meanings which are intuitively based. All sciences are based ultimately on personal knowledge.

Merleau-Ponty, a disciple of Husserl, holds that perception is not incipient science, but that science is a form of perception. He wants to return to the world of actual experience which is prior to the objective world, to restore to things their concrete physiognomy, to permit organisms to adopt their own individual ways of dealing with the world, and to base subjectivity firmly in history. This insistence on the primacy of lived existence is a defense against the charge of fabricating a world out of one's own imagination. "Because we are in the world, we are *condemned to meaning*, and we cannot do or say anything without its acquiring a name in history." [14] The "world" emerges at the state of reflection and implies organization of knowledge by the scientist or the philosopher. Therefore, "world" is a personal, intuitive constitution and not the presupposition of human existence. Science is not merely a method to explain and predict, but rather is an attitude of wonder, openness to dialogue with the world so that the world will disclose itself in all its mystery, complexity, and meaning. Since the body is the medium of experiencing the world, the body-organism is a mode of being-in-the-world, i.e. belonging in the world through the openness of the world to the givenness of the world. The body is also the mode of experiencing others. In fact, the intersubjective experience is the way back to the reduced world.

Heidegger criticizes Husserl's attempt to describe everything as correlates of consciousness because such dimensions of existence as dread, anxiety, alienation, and death are overlooked. Heidegger correctly sees that access to these aspects of existence is not through reduction but through finding the basic modalities of being-in-the-world. Human reality is *Dasein* ("to be there," an infinitive in the German language which Heidegger uses as a noun), in contrast to *Sein* ("being," which Heidegger capitalized to refer to Being of beings). Dasein emphasizes the situatedness of human reality in the world, which is always existence *in* the world. The basic mode of Dasein is "care" (*Sorge*, care about Being, others, and other entities). The two possibilities of Dasein are "authentic," when Being is freely chosen, and "inauthentic," when being-in-the-world is determined by external forces. Thus, analysis of Dasein leads to ontology, or the Being of beings.

Heidegger's phenomenology is a methodological concept built on an etymological study of the Greek words *phainomenon* and *logos*. *Phainomenon* is that which "shows itself," the "manifest;" and *logos* is "discourse" or "letting something be seen," "letting entities be perceived." Therefore, "phenomeno-logy" means "to let something which shows itself to be seen from out of itself in the very way it shows itself from its own true being."[15] Heidegger's phenomenology is existential in that he tries to use the phenomenological method to open up the way back to the completely unfamiliar, to analyze the Being of beings.

Sartre also adopts the phenomenological method to describe essences in the lived-world, but he contends that there is no ego in or behind consciousness, although he agrees with Husserl's contention that consciousness does not have contents. Consciousness is a sheer activity transcending toward objects, present to objects as a great emptiness, a wind blowing toward objects. Intentionality is a *feature* of consciousness for Husserl, but *is* consciousness for Sartre. However, consciousness can never be separated from Sartre's world, even as a fiction for analytical purposes. Being-in-the-world for humans means that one is free to choose being or to choose non-being, but one creates essence (essence is not pre-given) by accepting responsibility for being in the world.[16]

Intentionality of the consciousness of educational leadership focuses on the lived-world of a leader situated in the world of education. The lived-world of an educational leader is the vantage point of constituting meaning in the everyday world of an educational leader. All of the knowledge, experiences, and interpretations of the educational leader comprise the lived-world and are the sum of the leader's involvement in the everyday affairs of education. Thus, a phenomenology of educational leadership will explore the horizons, landscapes, and background awarenesses of the educational leader as the meanings of educational leadership are constituted in the consciousness of each particular leader. The researcher looks for tendencies, patterns, exceptions, beliefs, values, attitudes, feelings, illusions, or any other frame of reference as they are constituted into meaningful wholes in the everyday life of the educational leader.

The Social Reality

Alfred Schutz has applied the phenomenological method to a sociological analysis of the reality of everyday life to uncover, describe, and analyze the essential features of the world of daily living. This organized knowledge of social reality is the totality of objects, consciousness, and actions within the socio–cultural world as experienced by the common sense thinking of persons who are living their daily lives among their fellow–beings, connected, involved, and bound up with them in all of the relationships and interactions of human existence. [17] If the reality of everyday life is to be understood, the investigator must recognize that the intrinsic character of everyday life is such that it presents itself as a reality which is interpreted by persons and is subjectively meaningful to them as a coherent, whole world. Thus, the beginning point of a phenomenological analysis of a social reality is the description and clarification of that reality as it is available to the common sense perspective of the ordinary members of society.

Obviously, Schutz's position is rooted in the notion of the intentionality of consciousness and the lived–world. In fact, he refers to his work as a "phenomenology of the natural attitude." In ordinary social life he is no longer concerned with the constituting phenomena as they are presented within the sphere of the phenomenological reduction, but is concerned only with the phenomena corresponding to everyday situations from within the natural attitude. [18] Whereas the phenomenological reduction sets aside the natural attitude to focus on the essence of phenomena, a phenomenology *of* the natural attitude is a clarification of everyday life and does not raise the question of the transcendental subjectivity. Schutz finds the materials from which social reality comes to be constructed as meaningful for ordinary persons as well as philosophers and social scientists in what he labels the "taken–for–granted" and "typifications" of daily life. This analysis of the world of daily life takes place within the natural attitude, holding fast to the natural attitude in the act of reflecting on it. [19]

Access to the "truth" of the natural world is one's interpretation of nature within the limits of one's own life. The phenomenological method sets those limits in relief and reveals how meaning is constituted by the interpreter. Taken to its most basic foundations, the natural attitude becomes the guide to the whole realm of one's immediate experience as a being in the midst of everydayness.[20] Recovery of the full meaning of the natural attitude opens the world of everydayness to the exploration and analysis of the unity of the relationship between worldliness and consciousness.

Schutz seems so determined to avoid Husserl's use of the phenomenological reduction to expose the transcendental ego that he cannot use reduction to examine the natural attitude. He attempts to elucidate the structures of the consciousness of the everyday world in terms of the phenomenological attitude, but he does not attempt to bracket the natural world.

However, Merleau-Ponty can bracket the natural attitude in order to become conscious of man's indestructible relationship to the world. By reducing the natural attitude, Merleau-Ponty does not mean to withdraw from the world toward pure consciousness as does Sartre. Merleau-Ponty insists that one must break with our familiar acceptance of the world in order to see and grasp the world as paradoxical.[21] Herein, reduction is employed as a means rather than an end in order to reveal a protogenesis of the world and reflection within the facticity of existence.

Merleau-Ponty correctly recognizes the need to question even that stock of knowledge which derives from everyday life in the world. Schutz seems to acknowledge this need when he comments on the stock of knowledge which a person inherits from another. He says that all interpretations of this world are based on a stock of previous experiences of the world; the natural attitude is based on the interpretations of the world, as well as those handed down to us by parents, teachers, or significant others. These experiences in the form of `knowledge at hand' function as a frame of reference, or the natural attitude.[22] Schutz fails to see that his "scheme of reference" is also a bias which needs to be acknowledged in order to open up more of the essence of human existence which is occurring in the world.

Nevertheless, the analysis of the lived-world within the natural attitude by Schutz is a valuable exercise, as far as it goes. He finds that the world of everyday life originates in the thoughts and actions of ordinary members of society and is maintained as real and meaningful by a subjective process. Following Max Weber's doctrine of *Verstehen* ("understanding") as interpretative sociology, Schutz contends that all interpretations of the social world are intuitive constructions of the interpreter. Thus, the foundation of the knowledge of the social world is constructed out of one's perceptions of the phenomena which present themselves to the interpreter's consciousness.

All typifications of common sense thinking are themselves integral elements of the concrete historical socio-cultural *Lebenswelt* ("lived-world") within which they prevail as taken for granted and as socially approved. Their structure determines among other things the social distribution of knowledge and social environment of a concrete group in a concrete, historical situation.[23]

The social world is fundamentally intersubjective, and the individual has a stock of knowledge at hand which has been acquired and structured by past experiences and prior knowledge. This stock of knowledge (horizon, halo, tacit knowledge, or background awareness) allows one to live in the common sense world without performing an experiment each time a new object or experience is encountered. For instance, one may never have seen a bedouin teacher, but someone could provide enough typical features and actions of a bedouin teacher for anyone to recognize one on a trip to the Arabian desert.

Schutz makes a distinction between knowledge of a person in a face-to-face relationship ("con-sociates") in which the person is known immediately ("we" relationship) and knowledge of predecessors, contemporaries, and successors in which the other is known by means of typifications ("they" relationship). If the other person is encountered in terms of an immediate lived-experience and can be identified at the pre-theoretical, common sense level, the other person is said to be in a "thou" relationship.

To explain the structural relationships existing among all of these aspects of social order, Schutz defines social action as "purposive conduct projected by the actor," while an act is defined as "accomplished action." The meaning of social action is determined by the meaning which the actor bestows upon his or her action. The goal of the action is viewed by the actor as if that action had already been accomplished (in pluperfect tense). Furthermore, typical acts have two kinds of motives: "in-order-to" motives which are explained in terms of the actor's goals and ends and which are grammatically structured in the future tense as purpose clauses; and "because" motives which are structured as results of past dispositions and experiences.

Seeing a qualitative difference between natural and social science, Schutz objects to using a natural science model in social science. Natural science investigates objects that are constructs in the mind of the observer; social science is concerned with constructs that are *in* a world and that *have* a world. The people who are the main concern of social scientists are the interpreters of their own lives and actions. In other words, social science interprets the interpreters. Schutz's distinctive achievement was to focus on the paradigm of action instead of the traditional theme of perception and to approach both the social actor and action by way of the typifications of common sense life.

Thus, a phenomenology of educational leadership investigates the construction of the meaning of the concept of leadership in the everyday life of leaders and followers. Knowledge about educational leadership cannot be separated from those who have constructed the meaning of educational leadership out of their own consciousness and experiences. The doctrine of *Verstehen*, or interpretative sociology, is a valuable tool for investigating the intersubjective world of the educational leader. The stock of knowledge at hand which becomes the horizon or landscape of educational leadership is of prime concern to the interpretative sociologist. Further, the typifications of an educational leader must be identified, described, and interpreted within the everyday world of leaders and followers within the educational world.

HERMENEUTICS

Since hermeneutics is not exclusive to phenomenology nor properly classified under phenomenological reduction or intentionality of consciousness, it is treated here as a separate exercise within the phenomenological method. Hermeneutics as a "science" of revealing or interpretation of subject matter is an extension of the phenomenological method. The phenomenological exercises of reduction, description, intentionality, and analysis are used in an attempt to show the pre-philosophical understanding of human beings in the world. Hermeneutics is a method of phenomenology which provides an analysis of the basic assumptions, presuppositions, prejudices, and precritical understandings of any body of knowledge or any concept. The goal of Heidegger's brand of hermeneutics is to bring to light a basic interpretation of Being, but Gadamer is more concerned with the hermeneutics of language. Ricoeur's hermeneutics focuses on religious symbols, will, and psychoanalysis, and Schutz uses hermeneutics to interpret social knowledge.

The English term "hermeneutics" is borrowed from the classical Greek term, *hermeneia*, which meant "interpretation" in a very broad sense; it referred to any activity of clarifying the unclear, hidden, mysterious, or obscure. Prior to Friedrich Schleiermacher (1768–1834) books on hermeneutics dealt with the clarification and interpretation of legal and biblical texts. However, Schleiermacher conceived of hermeneutical theory in universal terms without specific reference to any particular type of texts. Hermeneutics is the capacity to journey into the past, to migrate into distant, foreign lands and languages, and to enter the minds and passions of strange people whose discourse is being interpreted. [24]

Wilhelm Dilthey, following Schleiermacher, reinterprets the hermeneutical method to obtain a humanistic methodology for the study of the cultural sciences. Focusing on historical and literary texts, Dilthey's method requires the interpreter to engage in a deeply felt experience with the text to recreate the original situation and those experiences which produced the text. In a real sense then, texts, documents, and manuscripts are expressions of the life which have become fixed through writing. Language itself is interpretation, not just the object of interpretation, as an interpretation of a musical composition is not simply a factual treatment of the composition. What is inside an individual can find its complete and objectively intelligible expression only in patterns and structures of language. Thus, hermeneutics has its center in the interpretation of the residue of human existence contained in writing, and language is the objectification of a person's interpretation of the existence which expresses itself in the texts and artifacts of human existence.

Heidegger regards interpretation as a basic existential experience whose articulation in interpretation *may* lead to expression in language, art, poetry, and myth. However, the central question for Heidegger is not what is there, what can be known, or what is the fundamental reality; rather, his question is: What is the meaning of being? But being is opaque, covered over, hidden, ambiguous, obscure; even the nature of the question is unclear. By isolating and analyzing the fundamental "structures of being" which are "conditions of possibility" of being in the world, Heidegger endeavors to make the meaning of being explicit by bringing out little by little the structures and modes of being, by bringing into view that which remains hidden and illusive. This method of "showing" (*Aufweisung*), of "laying bare" (*Freilegung*), of "making explicit" (*Auslegung*), of bringing to light or rediscovering the forgotten being, Heidegger calls hermeneutics.

Not only is Heidegger's hermeneutics concerned with how the meaning of Being is signified, he (along with Ricoeur) is confronted by the opacity and ambiguity between appearances and personal meaning, between existence and the meaning of existence. Trying to overcome *all* misunderstanding of human existence, Heidegger turns toward a foundation of meaning which would be so primordinal that it could not be named; he calls this foundation of the foundation the "Being of being," which is beyond the transcendental. Paul Tillich refers to this founding of being as the "Ground of Being," by which he means God. Heidegger wants to go beyond any being, even beyond God to the radical foundation below transcendental consciousness. [25]

Husserl also recognizes the need to deal with "unconscious intentionalities," "repressed emotions," "unknown intentionalities," "hidden intentionalities," and areas of consciousness which the process of reduction seems unable to expose. [26] Depth psychologists give major attention to the need to get these hidden, repressed meanings out in the open through analysis, catharsis, sensitivity training, etc. These hermeneutical exercises seek to identify the "real" meaning of the motives, feelings, and behavior which is eclipsed or hidden in the consciousness of the subject. One need not be a professional psychotherapist to utilize these hermeneutical practices to explore the domain of human consciousness.

Jurgen Habermas uses the hermeneutics of Dilthey to overcome the positivistic ossification of sociological logic. Habermas sees in the analysis of historicity a way of access into the realm of sociology. The historian is so closely related to the ongoing traditions being examined that he or she contributes to the growth and development of those traditions. [27] To understand history or any other social phenomenon is a kind of happening. In fact, the hermeneutics of Habermas would insist that the interpreter of educational leadership cannot consider leadership as an object which is separate from the leadership environment or lived-world.

Language is not only an object in the hands of the sociologist, according to Habermas; it is also the reservoir of culture and the medium in and through which the world is experienced and interpreted. Hermeneutics becomes a way to experience the world as well as a way to analyze grammatically the world of experience. Analysis of linguistic structures, modes, and styles opens up all sorts of sociological data for deeper understanding.

The concrete whole of societal relationships is obviously animated not only by language but also by action. Thus hermeneutical reflection must pass into a criticism of ideology. Habermas points out that understanding can also take the form of action; psychologists have noted that nonverbal communication of meaning can occur in a way similar to that of language.

Hans–Georg Gadamer embraces the hermeneutical principle that one should try to understand everything that can be understood. This is what he means by the sentence: "Being that can be understood is language." [28] Ultimately the question is not what is real or true, but what is the *meaning* of what is real and what is true.

The task of philosophical hermeneutics, therefore is ontological rather than methodological. Hermeneutics seeks to throw light on the fundamental conditions: that underlie the phenomenon of understanding in all its modes, scientific and nonscientific alike; and that constitute understanding as an event over which the interpreting subject does not ultimately preside. [29]

Other perspectives of hermeneutics are offered by Paul Ricoeur. He describes the elements and modalities of willing (motive, consent, decision, action), insisting that willing is no less meaning–giving than is perception. Through an ontological reflection on evil Ricoeur develops a hermeneutics of symbolism in which he shows that the criteria of interpretation of symbols is relative to the theoretical structure of the hermeneutical system being considered. For example, the interpretation of myths, rites, and religious symbols is dependent on the theoretical structure of the lived–world in which the symbols are used. Further, Ricoeur uses insights from psychoanalysis to show the need for interpretation of the delicate balance between the position of the self and the world. Since all hermeneutics is explicitly or implicitly self understanding by means of understanding others, all interpretation must attempt to overcome this distance and remoteness between self understanding and understanding of the world. [30]

In a study of the nature and meaning of educational leadership hermeneutics is an important method of probing the pre–theoretical interpretations of educational leadership. All theories of educational leadership assume a host of precritical understandings of the world, humanity, education, and leadership. Thus, hermeneutics is not a specific tool separate from the phenomenological method, but is the name given to the process of interpretation of the most basic viewpoints of the body of knowledge about educational leadership. In educational leadership theory hermeneutical principles bring to light and reveal that understanding of leadership which is basic to the situation of education in which a person is a leader. Hermeneutics is an inquiry about the nature and interpretation of that knowledge which is accepted as "theory" of educational leadership.

CONCLUSION

The purpose of this presentation of the phenomenological method is to show the reader how sharply this method contrasts with the logico-empirical method which is assumed in almost all contemporary studies of educational leadership. However, the reader is cautioned about despairing over not understanding the foregoing chapter without prior serious reading of Husserl and other continental philosophers. An experienced phenomenologist will insist that one must actually practice phenomenology before one understands it. Further, I do not claim to be an expert in phenomenology although I have read in this area for years and have taught university courses on phenomenology. The point is that the value of this book does not hinge on thoroughly comprehending the phenomenological method. My obvious reluctance to include so much "philosophical" material is outweighed by my conviction that readers have a right to the frame of reference of any writer; also, colleagues strongly encouraged inclusion of the above material.

NOTES

1. Wayne K. Hoy and Cecil G. Miskel, *Educational Administration: Theory, Research, and Practice* (New York: Random House, Inc., 1978), 20.

2. Edmund Husserl, "Husserl's Inaugural Lecture at Freiburg in Breisgau (1917)," trans. Robert Welch Jordan, in *Life–World and Consciousness: Essays for Aron Gurwitsch*, ed. Lester E. Embree (Evanston: Northwestern University Press, 1972), 18.

3. Husserl, *Ideas: General Introduction to Pure Phenomenology*, trans. W.R. Boyce Gibson (New York: Macmillan Publishing Co., Inc., 1931; Collier Books, 1962), 101.

4. Richard M. Zaner, "On the Sense of Method in Phenomenology," in *Phenomenology and Philosophical Understanding*, ed. Edo Pivcvic (London: Cambridge University Press, 1975), 125.

5. Eugen Fink, "The Phenomenological Philosophy of Edmund Husserl and Contemporary Criticism," in *The Phenomenology of Husserl: Selected Critical Readings*, ed. and trans. with an intro. R. O. Elveton (Chicago: Quadrangle, 1970), 74–75.

6. Harry Stack Sullivan, *The Psychiatric Interview*, ed. Helen Swick Perry and Mary Gawel, with intro. by Otto Allen Will (New York: W.W. Norton and Company, Inc., 1954).

7. Husserl, *Ideas*, 75–76. The English word "dator" in Husserl's text is in German a participle, *gebendes*, which means "giving, presenting, conferring."

8. Husserl, *Ideas*, 39.

9. Maurice Natanson, *Edmund Husserl: Philosopher of Infinite Tasks* (Evanston: Northwestern University Press, 1973), 12.

10. Husserl, *Ideas*, 91.

11. Ibid., 222.

12. Husserl, *The Crisis of European Sciences and Transcendental Phenomenology*, trans. David Carr (Evanston: Northwestern University Press, 1970), 234.

13. Natanson, *Husserl*, 127.

14. Maurice Merleau-Ponty, *Phenomenology of Perception*, trans. Colin Smith (New York: The Humanities Press, 1962), xix.

15. Martin Heidegger, *Being and Time*, trans. John Macquarrie and Edward Robinson (New York: Harper and Row, Publishers, 1962), 58.

16. Jean-Paul Sartre, *The Transcendence of the Ego*, trans. Forrest Williams and Robert Kirkpatrick (New York: The Noonday Press, Inc., 1957), 22, 25.

17. Alfred Schutz, *Collected Papers I*, ed. Maurice Natanson (The Hague: Martinus Nijhoff, 1962), 53.

18. Schutz, *The Phenomenology of the Social World*, trans. George Walsh and Frederick Lehnert, with intro. by George Walsh (Evanston: Northwestern University Press, 1967), 44.

19. Ibid., 76.

20. Ibid., 124.

21. Merleau-Ponty, *Phenomenology of Perception*, xiv.

22. Schutz, *Collected Papers I*, 7

23. Ibid., 149.

24. Wilhelm Dilthey, *Pattern and Meaning in History: Thoughts on History and Society* (London: Allen and Unwin, Ltd., 1961; New York: Harper and Row, Publishers; Harper Torchbook, 1962), 43.

25. Heidegger, *Basic Writings*, ed. David Farrell Krell (New York: Harper and Row, Publishers, 1977), 86.

26. Husserl, *The Crisis of European Sciences*, 235-36.

27. Jurgen Habermas, *Knowledge and Human Interests*, trans. Jeremy J. Shapiro (Boston: Beacon Press, 1971), 179ff.

28. Hans–Georg Gadamer, *Philosophical Hermeneutics*, trans. David E. Linge (Berkeley: University of California Press, 1976), 31.

29. Ibid., xi.

30. Charles E. Reagan and David Steward, eds., *The Philosophy of Paul Ricoeur: An Anthology of His Work* (Boston: Beacon Press, 1978), 97–108.

Bibliography

Aristotle. *Politics*, 1254a, 12.

Achinstein, P., and Barker, S.F., eds. *The Legacy of Logical Positivism*. Baltimore: The John Hopkins Press, 1969.

Bachelard, Suzanne. *A Study of Husserl's "Formal and Transcendental Logic."* Evanston: Northwestern University Press, 1968.

Bales, Robert F. *Interaction Process Analysis*. Cambridge: Addison-Wesley Press, 1950.

Bales, R.F., and Strodtbeck, F.L. "Phases in Group Problem-Solving." *Journal of Abnormal and Social Psychology* 46 (October 1951):485-95.

Ballard, Edward G. "On the Method of Phenomenological Reduction, Its Presuppositions, and Its Future." In *Life–World and Consciousness: Essays for Aron Gurwitsch*, 101-23. Edited by Lester E. Embree. Evanston: Northwestern University Press, 1972.

Barbe, Walter B. *Educator's Guide to Personalized Reading Instruction*. Englewood Cliffs: Prentice-Hall, Inc., 1961.

Barnard, Chester I. *The Functions of the Executive*. Cambridge: Harvard University Press, 1938, 1972.

Bass, Bernard M. *Stogdill's Handbook of Leadership*. Revised and expanded edition. New York: The Free Press, A Division of Macmillan Publishing Co., Inc., 1981.

Becker, Oskar. "The Philosophy of Edmund Husserl." In *The Phenomenology of Husserl: Selected Critical Readings*, 40–72. Edited, translated, and with an introduction by R. O. Elveton. Chicago: Quadrangle Books, 1970.

Bennett, William J. "The Humanities Pay Off." *Across the Board* 22 (April 1985):61–63.

Bennis, Warren. *Leaders: The Strategies for Taking Charge*. New York: Harper & Row, Publishers, 1985.

Berger, Peter L., and Luckmann, Thomas. *The Social Construction of Reality*. Garden City, N.Y.: Doubleday and Company, Inc., 1966.

Bergmann, Frithjof. *On Being Free*. Notre Dame: University of Notre Dame Press, 1977.

Bettis, Joseph Dabney, ed. *Phenomenology of Religion: Eight Modern Descriptions of the Essence of Religion*. New York: Harper and Row, Publishers, 1969.

Bidwell, Charles E. "The School as a Formal Organization." In *Handbook of Organizations*. Edited by J.G. March. Chicago: Rand McNally, 1965.

Blackman, H.J. *Six Existentialist Thinkers*. New York: Harper and Row, Publishers; Harper Torchbooks, 1952, 1959.

Blau, Peter M. *Exchange and Power in Social Life*. New York; John Wiley and Sons, 1964.

Blitz, Mark. *Heidegger's "Being and Time" and the Possibility of Political Philosophy*. Ithaca, N.Y.: Cornell University Press, 1981.

Block, E.M. A speech to the Texas Independent College Fund, 1983 Annual Meeting and Symposium, Lakeway Conference Center, Austin, Texas, April 11, 1983.

Boettinger, Henry M. "Is Management Really an Art?" *Harvard Business Review* 53 (January–February 1975):54–64.

Bothwell, Lin. *The Art of Leadership*. New York: Prentice–Hall, Inc., 1983.

Bronowski, Jacob. *The Visionary Eye: Essays in the Arts, Literature, and Science*. Edited by Piero E. Ariotti. Cambridge: The MIT Press, 1978.

Brown, Richard Harvey. "Bureaucracy as Praxis: Toward a Political Phenomenology of Formal Organizations." *Administrative Science Quarterly* 23, no. 3 (September 1978):365–82.

Bruzina, Ronald, And Wilshire, Bruce, eds. *Crosscurrents in Phenomenology*. The Hague: Martinus Nijhoff, 1978.

Buber, Martin. *I and Thou*. Second edition. Translated by R.G. Smith. New York: Charles Scribner's Sons, 1958.

——. "The Training and Education of a Child." In *The World of the Child*, 428–47. Edited by Toby Talbot. Garden City: Doubleday and Company, Inc., 1967; Anchor Books, 1968.

Burns, James MacGregor. *Leadership*. New York: Harper and Row, Publishers, 1978; Harper Colophon Books, 1979.

——. *The Power to Lead: The Crisis of the American Presidency*. New York: Simon and Schuster, Inc., 1984.

Burrell, Gibson, and Morgan, Gareth. *Sociological Paradigms and Organizational Analysis: Elements of the Sociology of Corporate Life*. London: Heinemann Educational Books, Inc., 1979.

Buscaglia, Leo. *Love*. New York: Ballentine Books, a Division of Random House, Inc., 1972.

Buytendijk, Frederik J.J. "Husserl's Phenomenology and Its Significance for Contemporary Psychology." In *Readings in Existential Phenomenology*, 352–64. Edited by Nathaniel Lawrence and Daniel O'Conner. Englewood Cliffs: Prentice–Hall, Inc., 1967.

Byrne, John A. "Let's Hear It for Liberal Arts." *Forbes* 136 (July 1, 1985):111–15.

Camus, Albert. *The Fall*. Translated by Justin O'Brian. New York: Alfred A. Knopf, Inc., 1956.

Cantril, Hadley. *The Psychology of Social Movements*. New York: John Wiley and Sons, Inc., 1941.

Capra, Fritjof. *The Tao of Physics*. New York: Bantam Books, 1977.

Chamberlin, J. Gordon. *The Educating Act: A Phenomenological View*. Washington, D.C.: University Press of America, 1981.

Chapman, Harmon M. "Realism and Phenomenology." In *Essays in Phenomenology*, 79–115. Edited by Maurice Natanson. The Hague: Martinus Nijhoff, 1966.

Cherryholmes, Cleo H. *Power and Criticism: Poststructural Investigations in Education*. New York: Teachers College Press, 1988.

Cochran, Clarke E. "Authority and Community: The Contributions of Carl Friedrich, Yves R. Simon, and Michael Polanyi." *The American Political Science Review* 71 (June 1977):546–58.

Combs, Arthur W. "The Perceptual Approach to the Helping Professions." *Journal of the Association for the Study of Perception* 5, no. 11 (Fall 1970):1–7.

Combs, Arthur W., Richards, Anne Cohen, and Richards, Fred. *Perceptual Psychology: A Humanistic Approach to the Study of Persons*. New York: Harper and Row, Publishers, 1976.

Combs, Arthur W., et. al. *The Professional Education of Teachers: A Humanistic Approach to Teacher Preparation*. 2nd edn. Boston: Allyn and Bacon, Inc., 1974.

Conger, Jay; Kanungo, Rabindra N.; and Associates. *Charismatic Leadership: The Elusive Factor in Organizational Effectiveness*. San Francisco: Jossey-Bass Publishers, 1988.

Culbertson, Jack. "Antecedents of the Theory Movement." *Educational Administration Quarterly* 17, no. 1 (Winter 1981):25–47.

Culbertson, Jack. "Three Epistemologies and the Study of Educational Administration." *UCEA Review* 22, no. 1 (Winter 1981):1–6.

Curtis, Bernard, and Mays, Wolfe, eds. *Phenomenology and Education.* London: Methuen and Co., Ltd., 1978.

Dahl, Robert A. *International Encyclopedia of Social Science* (1968). Vol. 12:406.

Dallmayr, Fred R. "Phenomenology and Social Science." In *Exploration in Phenomenology*, 133–66. Edited by David Carr and Edward S. Casey. The Hague: Martinus Nijhoff, 1973.

Davies, A.F. *Skills, Outlooks and Passions.* Cambridge: Cambridge University Press, 1980.

Deeken, Alfons. *Process and Permanence in Ethics: Max Scheler's Moral Philosophy.* New York: Paulist Press, 1974.

DeNicola, Daniel R. "Liberal Arts and Business." *Nation's Business* 74 (December 1986):4.

Denton, David E., ed. *Existentialism and Phenomenology in Education: Collected Essays.* New York: Teachers College Press, 1974.

——. *The Language of Ordinary Experience.* New York: Philosophical Library, 1970.

Dewey, John. *Democracy and Education.* New York: The Free Press, 1916, 1966.

——. *Experience and Education.* New York: Macmillan Publishing Company, "Collier Books," 1938.

Dilthey, Wilhelm. "Die Entstehung der Hermeneutik." *Gesammelte Schriften*, vol. 5, 317–38. Edited by B. Groethuysen. Gottingen: Vandenhoeck and Ruprecht, 1924.

——. *Pattern and Meaning in History: Thoughts on History and Society.* Edited and introduced by H.P. Rickman. London: George Allen and Unwin Ltd., 1961; New York: Harper and Row, Publishers, Harper Torchbook, 1962.

Drucker, Peter F. *Innovation and Entrepreneurship: Practice and Principles*. New York: Harper and Row, Publishers, 1985.

——. *Management: Tasks, Responsibilities, Practices*. New York: Harper and Row, Publishers, 1973, 1974.

Ecker, David W. and Kaelin, Eugene F. "The Limits of Aesthetic Inquiry: a Guide to Educational Research." In *Philosophical Redirection of Educational Research: The Seventy–First Yearbook of the National Society for the Study of Education*, vol. 71, pt. 1, 258–86. Edited by Lawrence G. Thomas. Chicago: University of Chicago Press, 1972.

Edelman, Murray. *Political Language: Words That Succeed and Policies That Fail*. New York: Academic Press, Inc., 1977.

"Editorial: How to Make People Smaller Than They Are." *The Saturday Review* (December 1978):15.

Embree, Lester E. "Toward a Phenomenology of Theoria." In *Life–World and Consciousness: Essays for Aron Gurwitsch*, 191–207. Edited by Lester E. Embree. Evanston: Northwestern University Press, 1972.

Encyclopaedia Britannica, 1966 ed. S.V. "Crown, Regalia"; and "Phenomenology," by J.N. Findlay.

Encyclopaedia Britannica, 1974 ed. S.v. "Phenomenology," by Walter Biemel.

Encyclopedia of Philosophy, 1967 ed. S.v. "Alfred Schutz," by Maurice Natanson; "Phenomenology," by Richard Schmitt.

Farber, Marvin. *The Foundation of Phenomenology: Edmund Husserl and the Quest for a Rigorous Science of Philosophy*. 3rd ed. Albany: The Research Foundation of the State University of New York, 1943; First paperbound printing, 1968.

Farish, Phil. "HRM Update." *Personnel Administrator* 29 (August 1984):21–22.

Fast, Julius. *Body Language*. New York: Simon and Schuster, Inc.; Pocket Books, 1971.

Fetterman, David M. *Ethnography Step by Step*. Applied Social Research Methods Series, Vol. 17 (Newbury Park, California: Sage Publications, Inc., 1989.

——, ed. *Qualitative Approaches to Evaluation in Education: The Silent Revolution*. New York: Praeger, 1988.

Fink, Eugen. "The Phenomenological Philosophy of Edmund Husserl and Contemporary Criticism." In *The Phenomenology of Husserl: Selected Critical Readings*, 73–147. Edited, translated, and introduced by R.O. Elveton. Chicago: Quadrangle, 1970.

Fischer, Frank. *Politics, Values, and Public Policy: The Problem of Methodology*. Boulder: Westview Press, 1980.

Fosnot, Catherine Twomey. *Enquiring Teachers, Enquiring Learners: A Constructivist Approach for Teaching*. New York: Teachers College Press, 1989.

Foster, William. *Paradigms and Promises: New Approaches to Educational Administration*. Buffalo: Prometheus Books, 1986.

Foucault, Michel. *Power and Knowledge: Selected Interviews and Other Writings 1972–1977*. Edited by Colin Gordon. Translated by Colin Gordon, Leo Marshall, John Mepham, and Kate Soper. New York: The Harvester Press; Pantheon Press, 1980.

Frankfort, H.A., et al. *Before Philosophy*. Baltimore: Penguin Books, 1949.

Freire, Paulo. *Cultural Action for Freedom*. Cambridge: Center for the Study of Development and Social Change, *Harvard Educational Review*, 1970.

——. *Education for Critical Consciousness*. New York: The Seabury Press, 1973.

——. *Pedagogy of the Oppressed*. Translated by Myra Bergman Ramos. New York: The Seabury Press; A Continuum Book, 1968.

Freire, Paulo. *The Politics of Education: Culture, Power, and Liberation.* Translated by Donaldo Macedo. South Hadley, MA: Bergin & Garvey Publishers, Inc., 1985.

French, J.R.P. and Raven, Bertram. "The Bases of Social Power." In *Group Dynamics.* 3rd ed. Edited by Dorwin Cartwright and Alvin Zander. New York: Harper and Row, Publishers, 1968.

Freud, Sigmund. *Group Psychology and the Analysis of the Ego.* London: Hogarth, 1922; New York: W.W. Norton and Co., 1959.

Friedrich, Carl J. "Phenomenology and Political Science." In *Phenomenology and the Social Sciences,* v. 2, 175–95. Edited by Maurice Natanson. Evanston: Northwestern University Press, 1973.

Fromm, Erich. *Escape from Freedom.* New York: Avon Books, 1941.

Gadamer, Hans–Georg. *Philosophical Hermeneutics.* Translated, edited, and introduced by David E. Linge. Berkeley: University of California Press, 1976.

Gardner, John W. *The Tasks of Leadership.* Leadership Papers/2. Washington, D.C.: Independent Sector, 1986.

Garfinkel, Harold. "Studies in the Routine Grounds of Everyday Activities." *Social Problems* 11 (1967):225–50.

Garfinkel, Harold, and Sacks, Harvey. "On Formal Structures of Practical Actions." In *Theoretical Sociology,* 337–66. Edited by J.D. McKinney and Edward A. Tiryakian. New York: Appleton Century Crofts, 1970.

Giddens, Anthony. *New Rules of Sociological Method.* New York: Basic Books, 1976.

Giroux, Henry A. "Ideology and Agency in the Process of Schooling." *Journal of Education* 165, no. 1 (Winter 1983):12–34.

Gray, Hanna Holborn. "Education as a Way of Reflecting on the Future." Working Paper/1 of the Corporate Council on the Liberal Arts. Norton's Woods, 136 Irving Street, Cambridge, MA 02138, 1987.

A Greek–English Lexicon, 7th ed., 1883. Compiled by Henry George Liddell and Robert Scott. S.v. *"dunamis"* and *"theoria."*

Green, Madeleine F., ed. *Leaders for a New Era: Strategies for Higher Education*. New York: Macmillan Publishing Company, 1988.

Greene, Maxine. *The Dialectic of Freedom*. New York: Teachers College Press, 1988.

——. *Landscapes of Learning*. New York: Teachers College Press, 1978.

Greenfield, Thomas Barr. "Ideas Versus Data: How Can the Data Speak for Themselves?" In *Problem–Finding in Educational Administration: Trends in Research and Theory*, 167–90. Edited by G.L. Immegart and W.L. Boyd. Lexington: D.C. Heath, 1979.

——. "The Man Who Comes Back through the Door in the Wall: Discovering Truth, Discovering Self, Discovering Organizations." *Educational Administration Quarterly* 16, no. 3 (Fall 1980):26–59.

——. "Organizations as Social Inventions: Rethinking Assumptions about Change." *The Journal of Applied Behavioral Science* 9, no. 5 (1973):551–73.

——. "Organization Theory as Ideology." *Curriculum Inquiry* 9, no. 2 (1979):97–112.

——. "Reflections on Organization Theory and the Truths of Irreconcilable Realities." *Educational Administration Quarterly* 14, no. 2 (Spring 1978):1–23.

——. "Research in Educational Administration in the United States and Canada." *Educational Administration* 8 (Winter 1979/1980):207–45.

——. "Research on the Behavior of Leaders: Critique of a Tradition." *Alberta Journal of Educational Research* 14, no. 1 (March 1968):55–76.

Greenfield, Thomas Barr. "Theory about Organizations: A New Perspective and Its Implications for Schools." In *Administering Education: International Challenge*, 71–99. Edited by M. Hughes. London: Athlone Press, 1973.

Griffiths, Daniel E. "Evolution in Research and Theory: A Study of Prominent Researchers." *Educational Administration Quarterly* 19, no. 3 (Summer 1983):201–21.

———. "The Individual in Organization: A Theoretical Perspective." *Educational Administration Quarterly* 13 (Spring 1977):1–18.

———. "Intellectual Turmoil in Educational Administration." *Educational Administration Quarterly* 15, no. 3 (Fall 1979):43–65.

Gurwitsch, Aron. "The Life-World and the Phenomenological Theory of Science." In *Phenomenology and the Theory of Science*, 3–32. Edited by Lester Embree. Evanston: Northwestern University Press, 1974.

———. "On the Intentionality of Consciousness." In *Philosophical Essays in Memory of Edmund Husserl*, 65–83. Edited by Marvin Farber. New York: Greenwood Press, Publishers, 1968.

Gyllenhammar, Pehr. *People at Work*. Reading, Mass.: Addison-Wesley Publishing Co., 1977.

Habermas, Jurgen. *Knowledge and Human Interests*. Translated by Jeremy J. Shapiro. Boston: Beacon Press, 1971.

———. *Zur Logik der Sozialwissenschaften*. Frankfurt am Main: Suhrkamp Verlag, 1970.

Halberstam, David. *The Powers That Be*. New York: Dell Publishing Company, Inc., 1970.

Hall, Edward T. *Beyond Culture*. Garden City: Doubleday and Company, Inc., 1976; Anchor Books, 1977.

———. *The Silent Language*. Garden City: Doubleday-Anchor Press, 1959, 1973.

Halpin, Andrew W., ed. *Administrative Theory in Education*. New York: Macmillan Company, 1958.

Hanson, D.A., and Johnson, V.A. *The Social Contexts of Learning in Bilingual Classrooms: An Interpretive Review of the Literature on Language Attitudes*. Rosslyn, VA: National Clearinghouse for Bilingual Education, 1981.

Harrison, E. Frank. *The Managerial Decision-Making Process*. 2nd edition. Boston: Houghton Mifflin Co., 1981.

Heidegger, Martin. *Basic Writings*. Edited by David Farrell Krell. New York: Harper and Row, Publishers, 1977.

Heidegger, Martin. *Being and Time*. Translated by John Macquarrie and Edward Robinson. New York: Harper and Row, Publishers, 1962.

——. *Existence and Being*. Introduction and analysis by Werner Brock. South Bend: Regnery/Gateway, Inc., 1979.

Hersey, Paul, and Blanchard, Kenneth H. *Management of Organizational Behavior: Utilizing Human Resources*. 4th ed. Englewood Cliffs: Prentice-Hall, Inc., 1982.

Hills, Jean. "A Critique of Greenfield's `New Perspective.'" *Educational Administration Quarterly* 16, no. 1 (Winter 1980):20–44.

Hodgkinson, Christopher. *The Philosophy of Leadership*. New York: St. Martin's Press, 1983.

——. *Towards a Philosophy of Administration*. New York: St. Martin's Press, 1978.

Homans, George. *The Human Group*. New York: Harcourt, Brace, and World, Inc., 1950.

Hook, Sidney. *The Hero in History*. Boston: Beacon Press, 1943.

Horney, Karen. *Self Analysis*. New York: W.W. Norton and Company, Inc., 1942.

Howe, Reuel L. *The Miracle of Dialogue*. New York: The Seabury Press, 1963.

Hoy, Wayne K., and Miskel, Cecil G. *Educational Administration: Theory, Research, and Practice*. New York: Random House, Inc., 1978.

Hunt, J.G., and Larson, L.L., eds. *Crosscurrents in Leadership*. Carbondale: Southern Illinois University Press, 1979.

——. *Leadership: The Cutting Edge*. Carbondale: Southern Illinois University Press, 1977.

Huseman, Richard C., et. al. eds. *Interpersonal & Organizational Communication*. 2nd ed. Boston: Holbrook Press, Inc., 1969, 1973.

Husserl, Edmund. *Cartesian Meditations: An Introduction to Phenomenology*. Translated by Dorion Cairns. The Hague: Martinus Nijhoff, 1977.

——. *The Crisis of European Sciences and Transcendental Phenomenology*. Translated by David Carr. Evanston: Northwestern University Press, 1970.

——. *Experience and Judgment*. Translated by James S. Churchill and Karl Ameriks. Evanston: Northwestern University Press, 1973.

——. *Formal and Transcendental Logic*. Translated by Dorion Cairns. The Hague: Martinus Nijhoff, 1969.

——. "Husserl's Inaugural Lecture at Freiberg in Breisgau (1917)." Translated by Robert Welsh Jordan. In *Life-World and Consciousness: Essays for Aron Gurwitsch*, 3-18. Edited by Lester E. Embree. Evanston: Northwestern University Press, 1972.

——. *The Idea of Phenomenology*. Translated by William P. Alston and George Nakhnikian. The Hague: Martinus Nijhoff, 1964.

——. *Ideas: General Introduction to Pure Phenomenology*. Translated by W.R. Boyce Gibson. New York: Macmillan Publishing Co., Inc., 1931; Collier Books, 1962.

Husserl, Edmund. *Logical Investigations*. 2 vols. Translated by J.N. Findlay. New York: Humanities Press, 1970.

———. *Phenomenology and the Crisis of Philosophy*. Translated with an introduction by Quentin Lauer. New York: Harper and Row, Publishers, Inc.; Harper Torchbook, 1965.

———. "'Phenomenology' Edmund Husserl's Article for the 'Encyclopaedia Britannica' (1927): New Complete Translation by Richard E. Palmer." *The Journal of the British Society for Phenomenology* 2, no. 2 (May 1971):77–90.

———. "Syllabus of a Course of Four Lectures on 'Phenomenological Method and Phenomenological Philosophy.'" Translated by G. Dawes Hicks. In *Husserl: Shorter Works*, 67–74. Edited by Peter McCormick and Frederick A. Elliston. Notre Dame: University of Notre Dame Press, 1981.

International Encyclopedia of Social Science, 1978 ed. S.v. "Power," by Robert A. Dahl.

Jacobs, T.O. *Leadership and Exchange in Formal Organizations*. Alexandria, Virginia: Human Resources Organization, 1971.

Jehenson, Roger. "A Phenomenological Approach to the Study of the Formal Organization." In *Phenomenological Sociology: Issues and Applications*, 219–47, edited by George Psathas. New York: John Wiley and Sons, 1973.

Jewell, Fredrick S. *School Government*. New York: A.S. Barnes & Co., 1866.

Jones, R.L., Jr. "Phenomenological Balance and Aesthetic Response." *Journal of Aesthetic Education* 13, no. 1 (January 1979):93–106.

Kaelin, Eugene F. "Method and Methodology in Literary Criticism." *School Review* 72 (1964):289–308.

Kaplan, Gary M. "How Exposure to Arts Leads to Better Management." *Business Marketing* 70 (Fall 1985):160.

Katz, Daniel, and Kahn, Robert L. *The Social Psychology of Organizations*. 2nd edn. New York: John Wiley and Sons, Inc., 1977, 1978.

Katz, Elihu, and Paul F. Lazarsfeld. *Personal Influence*. Glencoe, Illinois: Free Press, 1955.

Kellner, Hansfried. "On the Cognitive Significance of the System of Language in Communication." In *Phenomenology and Sociology*, 324–42. Edited by Thomas Luckmann. New York: Penguin Books, Inc., 1978.

Kenny, Shirley Strum. "Humanities and Business: Educational Reform for Corporate Success." *Business Society Review* 48 (Winter 1984):23–26.

Kiechel, Walter III. "The Case against Leaders" *Fortune* (November 21, 1988):217–20.

Knickerbocker, Irving. "Leadership: A Conception and Some Implications." *Journal of Social Issues* 4 (1968):23–40.

Kohak, Erazim. *Idea and Experience: Edmund Husserl's Project of Phenomenology in "Ideas I."* Chicago: The University of Chicago Press, 1978.

Kouzes, James M., and Posner, Barry E. *The Leadership Challenge*. San Francisco: Jossey–Bass Publishers, 1987.

Kreitner, Robert. *Management*. 2nd ed. Boston: Houghton Mifflin Company, 1983.

Labich, Kenneth. "The Seven Keys to Business Leadership." *Fortune* (October 24, 1988):58–66.

Landgrebe, Ludwig. "The Problem of a Transcendental Science of the A Priori of the Life–World." Translated by Donn Welton. In *The Phenomenology of Edmund Husserl*, essays by Landgrebe, 176–200. Edited by Donn Welton. Translated by Welton, et al. Ithaca, New York: Cornell University Press, 1981.

Laing, R.D. *The Divided Self.* Baltimore: Penguin Books, Inc., 1959, 1969.

Lauer, J. Quentin, S.J. *The Triumph of Subjectivity: An Introduction to Transcendental Phenomenology.* New York: Fordham University Press, 1958.

Levin, David Michael. *Reason and Evidence in Husserl's Phenomenology.* Evanston: Northwestern University Press, 1970.

Levison, Arnold B. *Knowledge and Society.* New York: The Bobbs-Merrill Co., Inc., Publishers, 1974.

Lewin, Kurt. *Field Theory in Social Science: Selected Theoretical Papers.* Ed. Dorwin Cartwright. Chicago: The University of Chicago Press, 1951; Midway Reprint, 1976.

Leys, Wayne A.R. *Ethics for Policy Decisions: The Art of Asking Deliberating Questions.* New York: Prentice-Hall, Inc., 1952.

Liles, Bruce L. *An Introduction to Linguistics.* Englewood Cliffs: Prentice-Hall, Inc., 1975.

Lincourt, John M., and Olezak, Paul V. "C.S. Peirce and H.S. Sullivan on the Human Self." *Psychiatry* 37, no. 1 (1974):78-87.

Louis, Kenneth R.R. Gros. "Why Humanities Are More Important Than Ever." *Business Horizons* 24 (January/February 1981):19-24.

Lukes, Steven. "On the Relativity of Power." In *Philosophical Disputes in the Social Sciences*, 26-74. Edited by S.C. Brown. Atlantic Highlands, New Jersey: Humanities Press, Inc., 1979.

Lyons, Joseph. "A Bibliographic Introduction to Phenomenology and Existentialism." *Existential Psychology*, 101-26. Edited by Rollo May. New York: Random House, Inc., 1961.

McCall, Morgan W., Jr., and Lombardo, Michael M., eds. *Leadership: Where Else Can We Go?* Durham: Duke University Press, 1978.

Maccoby, Michael. *The Leader: A New Face for American Management.* New York: Simon and Schuster, 1981.

McGregor, Douglas. *The Professional Manager.* Edited by Caroline McGregor and Warren G. Bennis. New York: McGraw Hill Book Company, 1967.

McHale, John. *The Future of the Future.* New York: Ballantine Books, Inc., 1971.

Macleod, Robert B. "The Phenomenological Approach to Social Psychology." In *The Phenomenological Problem*, 149–81. Edited by Alfred E. Kuenzli. New York: Harper and Brothers, Publishers, 1959.

McLuhan, Marshall. *Understanding Media: The Extensions of Man.* New York: the New American Library, Inc.; a Signet Book, 1964.

Macquarrie, John. *Existentialism.* New York: Penguin Books, 1973.

McWhinney, Will. "Phenomenarchy: A Suggestion for Social Redesign." *The Journal of Applied Behavioral Science* 9, no. 2/3 (1973):163–80.

Magoon, A.J. "Constructivist Approaches in Educational Research." *Review of Educational Research* 47 (Fall 1977):651–93.

Maslow, Abraham H. *Eupsychian Management: A Journal.* Homewood, Illinois: Richard D. Irwin, Inc. and The Dorsey Press, 1965.

———. "Liberal Leadership and Personality." *Freedom* 2 (1942):27–30.

Massarik, Fred. "'Mental Systems': Towards a Practical Agenda for a Phenomenology of Systems." In *Systems Theory for Organization Development*, 61–68. edited by Thomas G. Cummings. New York: John Wiley and Sons, 1980.

Mayntz, Renate. "The Study of Organizations." *Current Sociology* 13, no. 3 (1964): 95–155.

Merleau-Ponty, Maurice. *Adventures of the Dialectic.* Translated by Joseph Bien. Evanston: Northwestern University Press, 1973.

———. *Phenomenology of Perception.* Translated by Colin Smith. New York: The Humanities Press, 1962.

Merleau-Ponty, Maurice. *The Primacy of Perception*. Translated and edited by James M. Edie. Evanston: Northwestern University Press, 1964.

———. *Sense and Non-Sense*. Translated by Hubert L. Dreyfus and Patricia Allen Dreyfus. Evanston: Northwestern University Press, 1964.

———. *Signs*. Translated with and introduction by Richard C. McLeary. Evanston: Northwestern University Press, 1964.

———. *The Structure of Behavior*. Translated by Alden L. Fisher. Boston: Beacon Press, 1963.

———. *The Visible and the Invisible*. Translated by Alphonso Lingis. Evanston: Northwestern University Press, 1968.

Milgram, Stanley. "Behavioral Study of Obedience." In *Contemporary Issues in Social Psychology*, 241–47. Edited by Lawrence S. Wrightsman, Jr. Belmont, California: Wadsworth Publishing Co., 1968.

Mintzberg, Henry. *The Nature of Managerial Work*. Englewood Cliffs,New Jersey: Prentice-Hall, Inc., 1973.

Montagu, Ashley. *On Being Human*. 2nd ed. New York: Hawthorn Books, 1966.

Mulligan, Thomas M. "The Two Cultures in Business Education." *Academy of Management Review* 12, no. 4 (October 1987):593–99.

Natanson, Maurice. "Alfred Schutz on Social Reality and Social Science." In *Phenomenology and Social Reality: Essays in Memory of Alfred Schutz*, 101–121. Edited by Maurice Natanson. The Hague: Martinus Nijhoff, 1970.

———. *Edmund Husserl: Philosopher of Infinite Tasks*. Evanston: Northwestern University Press, 1973.

Nietzsche, Friedrich. *The Will to Power*. Translated by Walter Kaufmann. New York: Random House, Inc., 1967; Vintage Books, 1968.

O'Neill, John. *Perception, Expression, and History: The Social Phenomenology of Maurice Merleau–Ponty*. Evanston: Northwestern University Press, 1970.

Ouchi, William G. *Theory Z*. New York: Avon Books, 1982.

Ozmon, Howard A. and Craver, Samuel M. *Philosophical Foundations of Education*. 4th ed. Columbus: Merrill Publishing Company, 1990.

Palazzalo, Charles S. *Small Groups: An Introduction*. New York: D. Von Nostrand Co., 1981.

Parsons, Talcott. *Social Structure and Personality*. New York: Free Press, 1964.

——. *The Social System*. New York: Free Press, 1951.

Pascale, Richard Tanner, and Athos, Anthony G. *The Art of Japanese Management*. New York: Warner Books, Inc., 1981.

Paths Toward Personal Progress: Leaders Are Made Not Born. Compilation of Reprints from *Harvard Business Review*. Boston: President and Fellows of Harvard College, 1980.

People: Managing Your Most Important Asset. Compilation of Reprints from *Harvard Business Review*. Boston: President and Fellows of Harvard College, 1987.

Peters, Thomas J., and Waterman, Robert H., Jr. *In Search of Excellence*. New York: Harper and Row, Publishers, 1982.

Pettit, Philip. "The LIfe–World and Role–Theory." In *Phenomenology and Philosophical Understanding*, 251–70. Edited by Edo Pivcevic. Cambridge: Cambridge University Press, 1975.

Peursen, Cornelis A. van. *Phenomenology and Analytical Philosophy*. Pittsburgh: Duquesue University Press, 1972.

Pfeffer, Jeffrey. *Power in Organizations*. Boston: Pitman Publishing, Inc., 1981.

Piaget, Jean. *Structuralism*. Translated and edited by Chaninah Maschler. New York: Harper and Row, Publishers; Harper Colophon Books, reprinted by arrangements with Basic Books, Inc., 1970.

Pivcevic, Edo., ed. "Editor's Introduction." In *Phenomenology and Philosophical Understanding*. London: Cambridge University Press, 1975.

Polanyi, Michael. *Knowing and Being*. Essays edited with an introduction by Majorie Grene. Chicago: University of Chicago Press, 1969.

———. *Personal Knowledge: Towards a Post-Critical Philosophy*. New York: Harper and Row, Publishers, Inc., 1958, 1962; Harper Torchbook, 1964.

———. *The Study of Man*. Chicago: University of Chicago Press, 1958.

Psathas, George. "Ethnomethodology as a Phenomenological Approach in the Social Sciences." In *Interdisciplinary Phenomenology*, 73–98. Edited by Don Ihde and Richard M. Zaner. The Hague: Martinus Nijhoff, 1977.

———, ed. *Phenomenological Sociology: Issues and Applications*. New York: John Wiley and Sons, 1973.

Purkey, William Watson, and Novak, John M. *Inviting School Success: A Self-Concept Approach to Teaching and Learning*. 2nd edn. Belmont, California: Wadsworth Publishing Company, 1984.

Ranson, Steward; Hinings, Bob; and Greenwood, Royston. "The Structuring of Organizational Structures." *Administrative Science Quarterly* 25 (March 1980):1–17.

Reagan, Charles E., and Steward, David, eds. *The Philosophy of Paul Ricoeur: An Anthology of His Work*. Boston: Beacon Press, 1978.

Reddin, William J. *Managerial Effectiveness*. New York: Mcgraw-Hill Book Company, 1970.

Redl, Fritz. "Group Emotion and Leadership." *Psychiatry* 5, no. 4 (1942):573-96.

"Refresher Course on Life." *Nation's Business* 69 (November 1981):61-62.

Rice. Albert K. *Learning for Leadership: Interpersonal and Intergroup Methods*. London: Tavistock, 1965.

Richards, Max D., and Nielander, William A., eds. *Readings in Management*. 2nd ed. Cincinnati: South-Western Publishing Company, 1963.

Ricoeur, Paul. *Husserl: An Analysis of His Phenomenology*. Translated by Edward G. Ballard and Lester E. Embree. Evanston: Northwestern University Press, 1967.

Riffel, J.A. "The Theory Problem in Educational Administration." *Journal of Educational Administration* 16, no. 2 (October 1978):139-49.

Robinson, James M. "Hermeneutics Since Barth." In *The New Hermeneutics*, 1-77. Edited by James M. Robinson and John B. Cobb, Jr. New York: Harper and Row, Publishers, 1964.

Rogers, Carl. *On Becoming a Person*. Boston: Houghton Mifflin Company; Sentry Edition, 1961.

——. *A Way of Being*. Boston: Houghton Mifflin Company, 1980.

Rokeach, Milton. *Beliefs, Attitudes, and Values*. San Francisco: Jossey-Bass, 1969.

——. *Understanding Human Values: Individual and Societal*. Edited by Milton Rokeach. New York: Free Press, 1979.

Rosenbach, William E., and Taylor, Robert L., eds. *Contemporary Issues in Leadership*. Boulder: Westview Press, 1984.

Rustow, Dankwart A., ed. *Philosophers and Kings: Studies in Leadership.* New York: George Braziller, Inc., 1970.

Sartre, Jean-Paul. *Being and Nothingness: A Phenomenological Essay on Ontology.* Translated with an introduction by Hazel E. Barnes. New York: Pocket Books, 1966; Quokka Book 1978; Published by arrangement with Philosophical-Library, Inc., 1956.

———. "Faces, Preceded by Official Portraits." Translated by Anne P. Jones. In *Essays on Phenomenology*, 157–63. Edited by Maurice Natanson. The Hague: Martinus Nijhoff, 1970.

———. *The Philosophy of Jean-Paul Sartre.* Edited and introduced by Robert Denoon Cumming. New York: Random House, Inc., 1965; Vintage Book Edition, 1972.

———. *The Transcendence of the Ego: An Existentialist Theory of Consciousness.* Translated by Forrest Williams and Robert Kirkpatrick. New York: the Noonday Press, Inc., 1957.

Satir, Virginia. *Peoplemaking.* Palo Alto: Science and Behavior Books, Inc., 1972.

Schein, Edgar H. *Organizational Culture and Leadership.* San Francisco: Jossey-Bass Publishers, 1985.

Schlick, Moritz. "The Origin and Spirit of Logical Positivism." In *Logical Positivism.* Edited by A.J. Ayer. Glencoe, Illinois: The Free Press, 1959.

Schmidt, Warren H., and Posner, Barry Z. *Managerial Values and Expectations.* New York: AMACOM; An AMA Survey Report, 1982.

Schutz, Alfred. *Collected Papers I.* Edited by Maurice Natanson. The Hague: Martinus Nijhoff, 1962.

———. *Collected Papers III.* Edited by I. Schutz. The Hague: Martinus Nijhoff, 1966.

Schutz, Alfred. *The Phenomenology of the Social World*. Translated by George Walsh and Frederick Lehnert with an introduction by George Walsh. Evanston: Northwestern University Press, 1967.

Schutz, Alfred, and Luckmann, Thomas. *The Structures of the Life-World*. Translated by Richard M. Zaner and J. Tristram Englehardt, Jr. Evanston: Northwestern University Press, 1973.

Searle, John R. *Intentionality: An Essay in the Philosophy of Mind*. New York: Cambridge University Press, 1983.

Selznick, Philip. *Leadership in Administration*. New York: Harper and Row, Publishers, 1957.

Sergiovanni, Thomas J., and Corbally, John E., eds. *Leadership and Organizational Culture*. Chicago: University of Illinois Press, 1984.

Sherif, Muzafer, and Sherif, Carolyn W. *An Outline of Social Psychology*. Revised ed. New York: Harper and Row, Publishers, 1948, 1956.

Silvert, K.H. "National Values, Development, and Leaders and Followers." *International Social Science Journal* 15, no. 4 (1963):560-70.

Simmel, Georg. *On Individuality and Social Forms*. Edited with an introduction by Donald N. Levine. Chicago: University of Chicago Press, 1971.

———. *The Sociology of Georg Simmel*. Translated and edited with an introduction by Kurt H. Wolff. Glencoe, Illinois: The Free Press, 1950.

Simon, Herbert A. *Administrative Behavior: A Study of Decision Making Processes in Administrative Organizations*. 3rd ed. New York: The Free Press, 1945, 1947, 1957, 1976.

———. *The New Science of Management Decision*. New York: Harper and Row, 1960.

Smith, Huston. *Condemned to Meaning*. New York: Harper and Row, Publishers, 1965.

Smith, Roger. "Humanities & Business: The Twain Shall Meet—But How?" *Management Review* (April 1985):36–39.

_____. "What's Good for General Motors: Liberal Arts." *Across the Board* 23 (May 1986):7–9.

Smuts, Jan Christiaan. *Holism and Evolution*. New York: Viking Press, 1961.

Snygz, Donald. "The Need for a Phenomenological System of Psychology." In *The Phenomenological Problem*, 3–27. Edited by Alfred E. Kuenzli. New York: Harper and Brothers, Publishers, 1959.

Spiegelberg, Herbert. *Doing Phenomenology*. The Hague: Martinus Nijhoff, 1975.

——. *The Phenomenological Movement: A Historical Introduction*. 2nd ed. 2 vols. The Hague: Martinus Nijhoff, 1969.

Spurling Laurie. *Phenomenology and the Social World: The Philosophy of Merleau-Ponty and Its Relation to the Social Sciences*. London: Routledge and Kegan Paul, 1977.

Stevens, Richard. *James and Husserl: The Foundations of Meaning*. The Hague: Martinus Nijhoff, 1974.

Stewart, David, and Mickunas, Algis. *Exploring Phenomenology: A Guide to the Field and Its Literature*. Chicago: American Library Association, 1974.

Stogdill, Ralph M. *Handbook of Leadership: A Survey of Theory and Research*. New York: Free Press, 1974.

Sturman, Emanuel (Skip). "Do Corporations Really Want Liberal Arts Grads?" *Management Review* 75 (September 1987):

Sullivan, Harry Stack. *The Interpersonal Theory of Psychiatry*. New York: W.W. Norton and Company, Inc., 1953.

Sullivan, Harry Stack. *The Psychiatric Interview*. Edited by Helen Swick Perry and Mary Ladd Gawel with an introduction by Otto Allen Will. New York: W.W. Norton and Company, Inc., 1954.

——. "Psychiatric Training as a Prerequisite to Psychoanalytic Practice." In *Schizophrenia as a Human Process*, 309–18. New York: W.W. Norton and Company, Inc., 1962.

Szent–Györgi, Albert. *The Crazy Ape*. New York: The Philosophical Library, 1970.

Tanner, Richard Pascale, and Athos, Anthony G. *The Art of Japanese Management*. New York: Warner Books, Inc., 1981.

Taylor, Frederick W. *The Principles of Scientific Management*. New York: W.W. Norton and Co, Inc., 1911, 1967.

Tead, Ordway. *The Art of Administration*. New York: McGraw–Hill Book Company, Inc., 1951.

——. *The Art of Leadership*. New York: McGraw–Hill Book Company, Inc., 1935.

Theologisches Wörterbuch zum Neuen Testament. 1964 ed. S.v. "dunamai/dunamis."

Thevenaz, Pierre. *What Is Phenomenology? And Other Essays*. Edited with an introduction by James M. Edie. Translated by James M. Edie, Charles Courtney, and Paul Brockelman. Chicago: Quadrangle Books, Inc., 1962.

Tillich, Paul. *Love, Power, and Justice*. London: Oxford University Press, 1954.

——. *Systematic Theology*. Vol. I. Chicago: University of Chicago Press, 1951.

Toffler, Alvin. "The Third Wave." In *Technology and the Future*. 4th ed. Edited by Albert H. Teich. New York: St. Martin's Press, 1968.

Vaill, Peter. *Managing as a Performing Art*. San Francisco: Jossey–Bass Publishers, 1989.

Vivian, C.T. *Black Power and the American Myth*. Philadelphia: Fortress Press, 1970.

Waldenfels, Bernhard. "Perception and Structure in Merleau-Ponty." Translated by J. Claude Evans. *Research in Phenomenology* 10 (1980):21-38.

Watkins, W.N. "Historical Explanation in the Social Sciences." In *Theories of History*. Edited by P. Gardiner. Glencoe, Illinois: The Free Press, 1959.

Watzlawick, Paul; Beavin, J.H.; and Jackson, D.D. *Pragmatics of Human Communication*. New York: W.W. Norton and Company, Inc., 1967.

Weber, Max. *The Theory of Social and Economic Organization*. Translated and edited by Talcott Parsons. New York: The Free Press, a Division of Macmillan Publishing Company, Inc., 1957.

Webster's Third New International Dictionary of the English Language: Unabridged. 1967 ed. S.v. "Leadership."

Weick, Karl E. *The Social Psychology of Organizing*. Reading, Mass.: Addison-Wesley Publishing Company, Inc., 1969.

Whitehead, Alfred North. *The Aims of Education*. New York: The Free Press, a Division of Macmillan Publishing Company, Inc., 1929, 1967.

——. *Process and Reality*. Corrected ed. New York: The Free Press, a Division of Macmillan Publishing Company, Inc., 1929, 1978.

Wild, John. "Husserl's Life-World and the Lived-Body." In *Phenomenology: Pure and Applied*, 10-28. Edited by Erwin W. Straus. Pittsburgh: Duquesne University Press, 1964.

——. "Man and His Life-World." In *For Roman Ingarden: Nine Essays in Phenomenology*, 90-109. Edited by Anna-Teresa Tymieniecka. The Hague: Martinus Nijhoff, 1959.

Williams, Daniel Day. *The Minister and the Cure of Souls*. New York: Harper and Brothers, Publishers, 1961.

Williams, Forrest, and Kirkpatrick, Robert. "Translator's Preface." In *The Transcendence of the Ego* by Jean–Paul Sartre. New York: The Noonday Press, Inc., 1957.

Willower, Donald J. "Contemporary Issues in Theory in Educational Administration." *Educational Administration Quarterly* 16, no. 3 (Fall 1980):1–25.

——. "Ideology and Science in Organization Theory." *Educational Administration Quarterly* 15, no. 3 (Fall 1979):20–42.

Wingo, G. Max. *Philosophies of Education: An Introduction.* Toronto: D.C. Heath and Company, 1974.

Winter, David G. "Framework for the Analysis of Liberal Arts Education and Corporate Leadership." A paper prepared for the Corporate Council on the Liberal Arts Symposium, "Corporations at Risk: Liberal Learning and Private Enterprise," Cambridge, MA, September 3, 1986.

Wittgenstein, Ludwig. *On Certainty.* Edited by G.E.M. Anscombe and G.H. von Wright. Translated by Denis Paul and G.E.M. Anscombe. New York: Harper and Row, Publishers, 1969; Harper Torchbooks, 1972.

Yukl, Gary A. *Leadership in Organizations.* Englewood Cliffs: Prentice–Hall, Inc., 1981.

Zaner, Richard M. "On the Sense of Method in Phenomenology." In *Phenomenology and Philosophical Understanding,* 25–41. Edited by Edo Pivcevic. Cambridge: Cambridge University Press, 1975.

——. "Solitude and Sociality: The Critical Foundations of the Social Sciences." In *Phenomenological Sociology: Issues and Applications,* 25–43. Edited by George Psathas. New York: John Wiley and Sons, 1973.

Index